T0212728

Lecture Notes in Computer Science   **8907**

Commenced Publication in 1973
Founding and Former Series Editors:
Gerhard Goos, Juris Hartmanis, and Jan van Leeuwen

More information about this series at http://www.springer.com/series/7407

Florin Pop · Maria Potop-Butucaru (Eds.)

Adaptive Resource Management and Scheduling for Cloud Computing

First International Workshop, ARMS-CC 2014
held in Conjunction with ACM Symposium
on Principles of Distributed Computing,
PODC 2014
Paris, France, July 15, 2014
Revised Selected Papers

 Springer

Editors
Florin Pop
Computer Science Department
University Politehnica of Bucharest
Bucharest
Romania

Maria Potop-Butucaru
Sorbonne Universités
Université Pierre et Marie CURIE, LIP6
Paris
France

ISSN 0302-9743   ISSN 1611-3349 (electronic)
Lecture Notes in Computer Science
ISBN 978-3-319-13463-5   ISBN 978-3-319-13464-2 (eBook)
DOI 10.1007/978-3-319-13464-2

Library of Congress Control Number: 2014956238

Springer Cham Heidelberg New York Dordrecht London

Printed on acid-free paper

Springer International Publishing AG Switzerland is part of Springer Science+Business Media (www.springer.com)

Preface

Cloud Computing concerns large-scale interconnected systems and it has the main purpose to aggregate and to effcient exploit the power of widely distributed resources. Resource Management and Task Scheduling play an essential role, in cases where one is concerned with optimized use of resources. The ubiquitous networks are highly dynamic distributed systems so the changes in overlay are frequent. On the other hand, the Cloud systems are highly dynamic in its structure because the user requests must be respected as an agreement rule. When ubiquitous networks become clients for Cloud systems new algorithm for events and tasks scheduling and new methods for resource management should be designed in order to increase the performance of such systems. The adaptive methods used in context are oriented on: self-stabilizing, self-organizing, and autonomic systems; dynamic, adaptive, and machine learning-based distributed algorithms; fault tolerance, reliability, availability of distributed systems.

This volume contains the papers presented at ARMS-CC-2014: Workshop on Adaptive Resource Management and Scheduling for Cloud Computing held in conjunction with PODC 2014 (ACM Symposium on Principles of Distributed Computing) in Paris, France, on July 15, 2014. The papers of this volume have identified several important aspects of the problem addressed by ARMS-CC: foundational models for resource management in Cloud, scheduling algorithms, and services and applications. We strongly believe that the papers included in this volume will serve as reference for the researchers and scientists in the field of Cloud Computing. The selected papers for this volume comprise a variety of successful approaches including: Distributed Scheduling Algorithms; Load-Balancing and Co-Allocation; Dynamic, Adaptive, and Machine Learning-based Distributed Algorithm; Many-Task Computing in the Cloud; Self-* and Autonomic Cloud Systems; Cloud Resource Virtualization and Composition; Fault Tolerance, Reliability, Availability of Cloud Systems; Cloud Workload Profiling and Deployment Control; Cloud Quality Management and Service Level Agreement (SLA); High-Performance Cloud Computing, Mobile Cloud Computing; and Green Cloud Computing.

There were 29 initial submissions. Each submission was peer-reviewed by Program Committee members or invited external reviewers. Each submission was reviewed by three Program Committee members. Finally, 14 high-quality papers were selected (about 48 % acceptance ratio) for publishing in the LNCS Post-Proceedings and presented during the workshop. This volume consists of 15 papers (14 papers from ARMS-CC and 1 short invited paper) and two invited talks, which are organized as follows.

The two invited talks were given by Thilo Kielmann (VU Amsterdam, Netherlands) and Marc Shapiro (INRIA & LIP6, Université Pierre et Marie Curie, Paris, France).

The invited paper, "In-Memory Runtime File Systems for Many-Task Computing" by Alexandru Uta, Andreea Sandu, Ion Morozan, and Thilo Kielmann, presents a distributed, in-memory runtime file system called MemFS that replaces data locality by uniformly spreading file stripes across all storage nodes. Due to its striping mechanism, MemFS leverages full network bisection bandwidth, maximizing I/O performance while avoiding storage imbalance problems.

The 14 papers presented in ARMS-CC workshop are organized as follows.

In the first paper, titled "A Multi-Capacity Queuing Mechanism in Multi-Dimensional Resource Scheduling," Mehdi Sheikhalishahi et al. present a queuing mechanism based on a multi-resource scheduling technique by modeling multi-resource scheduling as a multi-capacity bin-packing scheduling algorithm at the queue level to reorder the queue in order to improve the packing and as a result improve scheduling metrics. The proposed solution demonstrates performance improvements in terms of wait-time and slowdown metrics.

The second paper, "A Green Scheduling Policy for Cloud Computing," presented by Jordi Vilaplana et al., introduced a power-aware scheduling policy algorithm called Green Preserving SLA (GPSLA) for Cloud Computing systems with high workload variability. GPSLA aims to guarantee the SLA (Service-Level Agreement) by minimizing the system response time and, at the same time, tries to reduce the energy consumption. The authors present a formal solution, based on linear programming, to assign the system load to the most powerful Virtual Machines, while respecting the SLA and lowering the power consumption as far as possible.

Ansuman Banerjee et al. describes in the third paper, "A Framework for Speculative Scheduling and Device Selection for Task Execution on a Mobile Cloud," the problem of opportunistic task scheduling and workload management in a mobile cloud setting considering computation power variation. The authors gathered mobile usage data for a number of persons and applied supervised clustering to show that a pattern of usage exists and that follows a state-based model. The proposed solution is used as a strategy to choose and offoad work on a mobile device.

The fourth paper, named "An Interaction Balance Based Approach for Autonomic Performance Management in a Cloud Computing Environment," was presented by Rajat Mehrotra et al. In this paper, a performance management approach is introduced that provides dynamic resource allocation for deploying a general class of services over a federated Cloud Computing infrastructure. This performance management approach is based on distributed control, and is developed by using an interaction balance methodology, which has previously been successfully used in developing management solutions for traditional large-scale industrial systems.

Jordi Arjona Aroca et al. present the problem Virtual Machine Assignment (VMA) in the fifth paper, "Power-Efficient Assignment of Virtual Machines to Physical Machines." The optimization criterion is to minimize the power consumed by all the physical machines. The authors present in this paper four VMA problems depending on whether the capacity or the number of physical machines is bounded or not.

Alexandru-Florian Antonescu and Torsten Braun in the sixth paper, named "Simulation of Multi-Tenant Scalable Cloud-Distributed Enterprise Information Systems," present a simulation approach for validating and comparing SLA-aware scaling policies using the CloudSim simulator, using data from an actual Distributed Enterprise Information System (dEIS). This work extends CloudSim with concurrent and multi-tenant task simulation capabilities.

Vlad Serbanescu et al. present in the seventh paper, "Towards Type-Based Optimizations in Distributed Applications using ABS and JAVA 8," an API to support modeling applications with Actors based on the paradigm of the Abstract Behavioral Specification (ABS) language. The authors validate this solution through a case study where we obtain significant performance improvements as well as illustrating the ease with which simple high- and low-level optimizations can be obtained by examining topologies and communication within an application.

The eighth paper, "A Parallel Genetic Algorithm Framework for Cloud Computing Applications," presented by Elena Apostol et al. describes the use of subpopulations for the GA MapReduce implementations. Second, the paper proposes new models for two well-known genetic algorithm implementations, namely island and neighborhood model.

Raphael Gomes et al. discuss in the ninth paper the scalability strategies to enact service choreographies using cloud resources. The authors present efforts at the state-of-the-art technology and an analysis of the outcomes in adopting different strategies of resource scaling. The paper is titled "Analysing Scalability Strategies for Service Choreographies on Cloud Environments."

Shadi Ibrahim et al., on behalf ok KerData team from Inria Rennes, presents in the 10th paper, "Towards Efficient Power Management in MapReduce: Investigation of CPU-Frequencies Scaling on Power Effciency in Hadoop," the impact of dynamically scaling the frequency of compute nodes on the performance and energy consumption of a Hadoop cluster. Taking into account the nature of a MapReduce application (CPU-intensive, I/O-intensive, or both) and the fact that its subtasks execute different workloads (disk read, computation, network access), there is significant potential for reducing power consumption by scaling down the CPU frequency when peak CPU performance is not needed. To this end, a series of experiments are conducted to explore the implications of Dynamic Voltage Frequency scaling (DVFS) settings on power consumption in Hadoop-clusters: benefiting from the current maturity in DVFS research and the introduction of governors (e.g., performance, power-save, on-demand, conservative, and user-space).

The 11th paper, "Self-management of Live Streaming Application in Distributed Cloud Infrastructure," presented by Patricia Endo et al., describes an autonomic strategy that manages the dynamic creation of reectors for reducing redundant traffic in live streaming applications. Under this strategy, nodes continually assess the utilization level by live streaming ows. When necessary, the network nodes communicate and self-appoint a new reector node, which switches to multicasting video ows hence alleviating network links.

Cristina Marinescu et al., in the 12th paper, "Towards the Impact of Design Flows on the Resources Used by an Application," make the assumption that the presence of design aws in the implementation of a software system may lead to a suboptimal resource usage. The investigations on the impact of several design aws on the amount of resources used by an application indicate that the presence of design aws has an inuence on memory consumption and CPU time, and that proper refactoring can have a beneficial inuence on resource usage.

"Policy-Based Cloud Management Through Resource Usage Prediction" is the 13th paper, presented by Catalin Leordeanu et al. The paper proposes a novel solution, which offers an efficient resource management mechanism for Clouds. The solution is based on monitoring hosts belonging to the Cloud in order to obtain load data. A policy-based system uses the monitoring information to make decisions about deployment of new virtual machines and migration of already running machines from overloaded hosts.

In the last paper, "An Inter-Cloud Architecture for OpenStack Infrastructures," Stelios Sotiriadis et al. explore an inter-cloud model by creating a new cloud platform service to act as a mediator among OpenStack, FI-WARE datacenter resource management, and Amazon Web Service cloud architectures, therefore to orchestrate communication of various cloud environments.

Florin Pop and Maria Potop-Butucaru acknowledge support by PHC Bilateral Research Project: SideSTEP – Scheduling Methods for Dynamic Distributed Systems: a self-* approach, ID: PN-II-CT-RO-FR-2012-1-0084.

We also express our gratitude and thank to all of the members of the Program Committee, to all of the reviewers, for their hard work in finalizing the reviews on time, as well as the authors for submitting their papers to ARMS-CC-2014. We address our personal warm regards to PODC-2014 organizers, especially to Workshop chairs, Sebastien Tixeuil and Dariusz Kowalski for their support and advices offered during the workshop organization. The editors would like to thank Alfred Hofmann, Peter Steasser, and Anna Kramer for the editorial assistance and excellent cooperative collaboration to produce this valuable scientific work. We appreciate the support offered by EasyChair system team to handle the paper submission, review process, and communications with authors and reviewers. We thank them for this important support.

July 2014   Florin Pop
                                                                                    Maria Potop-Butucaru

Organization

Program Committee

Ajith Abraham	Machine Intelligence Research Labs (MIR Labs), USA
Marcos Aguilera	Microsoft Research Silicon Valley, USA
Silvia Bonomi	Università degli Studi di Roma "La Sapienza", Italy
Alexandru Costan	Inria/INSA Rennes, France
Valentin Cristea	University Politehnica of Bucharest, Romania
Ciprian Dobre	University Politehnica of Bucharest, Romania
Pascal Felber	Université de Neuchâtel, Switzerland
Pierre Guillome	IRISA/Université de Rennes 1, France
Adriana Iamnitchi	University of South Florida, USA
Thilo Kielmann	VU University Amsterdam, TheNetherlands
Joanna Kolodziej	Institute of Computer Science, Cracow University of Technology, Poland
Young Lee	University of Sydney, Australia
Iosif Legrand	California Institute of Technology, USA/CERN, Switzerland
Florin Pop	University Politehnica of Bucharest, Romania
Maria Potop-Butucaru	UPMC Sorbonne Universités, LIP6, France
Vivien Quéma	Grenoble INP/ENSIMAG, France
Ioan Raicu	Illinois Institute of Technology/Argonne National Laboratory, USA
Marc Shapiro	UPMC Sorbonne Universités, LIP6, France
Nicolae Tapus	University Politehnica of Bucharest, Romania
Albert Zomaya	University of Sydney, Australia

Additional Reviewers

Ene, Stefan	Pintilie, Andreea	Tudoran, Radu
Millet, Laure	Sadooghi, Iman	Wang, Ke
Pathak, Animesh		

Contents

Invited Paper

In-Memory Runtime File Systems for Many-Task Computing. 3
   Alexandru Uta, Andreea Sandu, Ion Morozan, and Thilo Kielmann

Scheduling Methods and Algorithms

A Multi-capacity Queuing Mechanism in Multi-dimensional
Resource Scheduling 9
   *Mehdi Sheikhalishahi, Richard M. Wallace, Lucio Grandinetti,
   José Luis Vazquez-Poletti, and Francesca Guerriero*

A Green Scheduling Policy for Cloud Computing. 26
   *Jordi Vilaplana, Francesc Solsona, Ivan Teixido, Jordi Mateo,
   Josep Rius, and Francesc Abella*

A Framework for Speculative Scheduling and Device Selection
for Task Execution on a Mobile Cloud 36
   *Ansuman Banerjee, Himadri Sekhar Paul, Arijit Mukherjee,
   Swarnava Dey, and Pubali Datta*

An Interaction Balance Based Approach for Autonomic Performance
Management in a Cloud Computing Environment 52
   Rajat Mehrotra, Srishti Srivastava, Ioana Banicescu, and Sherif Abdelwahed

Power-Efficient Assignment of Virtual Machines to Physical Machines 71
   *Jordi Arjona Aroca, Antonio Fernández Anta, Miguel A. Mosteiro,
   Christopher Thraves, and Lin Wang*

Services and Applications

SLA-Driven Simulation of Multi-Tenant Scalable Cloud-Distributed
Enterprise Information Systems. 91
   Alexandru-Florian Antonescu and Torsten Braun

Towards Type-Based Optimizations in Distributed Applications
Using ABS and JAVA 8 103
   *Vlad Serbanescu, Chetan Nagarajagowda, Keyvan Azadbakht,
   Frank de Boer, and Behrooz Nobakht*

A Parallel Genetic Algorithm Framework for Cloud Computing Applications . . . 113
   Elena Apostol, Iulia Băluţă, Alexandru Gorgoi, and Valentin Cristea

Analysing Scalability Strategies for Service Choreographies
on Cloud Environments.................................... 128
   Raphael Gomes, Fabio Costa, and Ricardo Rocha

Foundational Models for Resource Management in Cloud

Towards Efficient Power Management in MapReduce: *Investigation
of CPU-Frequencies Scaling on Power Efficiency in Hadoop*............ 147
   *Shadi Ibrahim, Diana Moise, Houssem-Eddine Chihoub,
   Alexandra Carpen-Amarie, Luc Bougé, and Gabriel Antoniu*

Self-management of Live Streaming Application in Distributed
Cloud Infrastructure...................................... 165
   *Patricia Endo, Marcelo Santos, Jônatas Vitalino, Glauco Gonçalves,
   Moisés Rodrigues, Djamel F.H. Sadok, Judith Kelner, and Azimeh Sefidcon*

Towards the Impact of Design Flaws on the Resources
Used by an Application.................................... 180
   Cristina Marinescu, Şerban Stoenescu, and Teodor-Florin Fortiş

Policy-Based Cloud Management Through Resource Usage Prediction....... 193
   Cătălin Leordeanu, Silviu Grigore, Octavian Moraru, and Valentin Cristea

An Inter-Cloud Architecture for Future Internet Infrastructures........... 206
   Stelios Sotiriadis, Nik Bessis, and Euripides G.M. Petrakis

Author Index 217

Invited Paper

In-Memory Runtime File Systems
for Many-Task Computing

Alexandru Uta, Andreea Sandu, Ion Morozan, and Thilo Kielmann[✉]

Department of Computer Science, Vrije Universiteit, Amsterdam, The Netherlands
Thilo.kielmann@vu.nl

1   Introduction

Many scientific computations can be expressed as Many-Task Computing (MTC) applications. In such scenarios, application processes communicate by means of intermediate files, in particular input, temporary data generated during job execution (stored in a runtime file system), and output. In data-intensive scenarios, the temporary data is generally much larger than input and output. In a 6×6 degree Montage mosaic [3], for example, the input, output and intermediate data sizes are 3.2 GB, 10.9 GB and 45.5 GB, respectively [6]. Thus, speeding up I/O access to temporary data is key to achieving good overall performance.

General-purpose, distributed or parallel file systems such as NFS, GPFS, or PVFS provide less than desirable performance for temporary data for two reasons. First, they are typically backed by physical disks or SSDs, limiting the achievable bandwidth and latency of the file system. Second, they provide POSIX semantics which are both too costly and unnecessarily strict for temporary data of MTC applications that are written once and read several times. Tailoring a runtime file system to this pattern can lead to significant performance improvements.

Memory-based runtime file systems promise better performance. For MTC applications, such file systems are co-designed with task schedulers, aiming at data locality [6]. Here, tasks are placed onto nodes that contain the required input files, while write operations go to the node's own memory. Analyzing the communication patterns of workflows like Montage [3], however, shows that, initially, files are created by a single task. In subsequent steps, tasks combine several files, and final results are based on global data aggregation. Aiming at data locality hence leads to two significant drawbacks: (1) Local-only write operations can lead to significant storage imbalance across nodes, while local-only read operations cause file replication onto all nodes that need them, which in worst case might exceed the memory capacity of nodes performing global data reductions. (2) Because tasks typically read more than a single input file, locality-aware task placement is difficult to achieve in the first place.

To overcome these drawbacks, we designed a distributed, in-memory runtime file system called MemFS that replaces data locality by uniformly spreading file stripes across all storage nodes. Due to its striping mechanism, MemFS leverages full network bisection bandwidth, maximizing I/O performance while avoiding storage imbalance problems.

F. Pop and M. Potop-Butucaru (Eds.): ARMS-CC 2014, LNCS 8907, pp. 3–5, 2014.
DOI: 10.1007/978-3-319-13464-2_1

2   MemFS

The MemFS distributed file system [5] consists of three key components: a *storage* layer, a *data distribution* component, and a *file system client*. Typically, all three components run on all application nodes. In general, however, it would also be possible to use a (partially) disjoint set of storage servers, for example when the application itself has large memory requirements.

The storage layer exposes a node's main memory for storing the data in a distributed fashion. We use the Memcached [2] key-value store. MemFS equally distributes the files across the available Memcached servers, based on file striping. For mapping file stripes to servers, we use a hashing function provided by Libmemcached [1], a Memcached client library. We use the file names and stripe numbers as hash keys for selecting the storage servers. We expose our storage system using a FUSE [4] layer, exposing a regular file system interface to the MTC applications. At startup, the FUSE clients are configured with a list of storage servers. Through the Libmemcached API, the FUSE file system communicates with the Memcached storage servers.

Figure 1 shows the overall system design of MemFS, using the example of a write operation, issuing Memcached *set* commands; for read operations, *get* commands would be used instead.

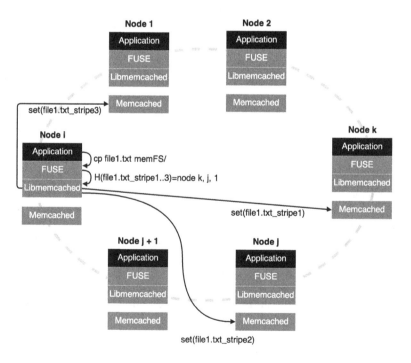

Fig. 1. MemFS system design

MemFS had originally been designed for tightly-coupled compute clusters where premium networks like Infiniband provide intersection bandwidth of several tens of Gb per second. Experimentation has shown that MemFS works very well with these networks. But also with slower interconnects, like Gb Ethernet, MemFS shows its superiority, compared to locality-based approaches.

Currently, a limiting factor for MemFS performance is the user-space implementation based on FUSE, that causes significant CPU load for processing file-system operations on the client side. An alternative MemFS implementation is providing a kernel-based file system that reduces the amount of context switches between user space and kernel space to the absolute minimum. Our kernel-based version of MemFS shows significant reduction in CPU loads on the client side.

The drawback of a kernel-space file system is that it requires superuser privileges, which can be a limiting factor for deployment on cluster machines. When using MemFS in virtualized cloud environments, however, the kernel-space implementation can be used easily and efficiently.

3   Conclusions

MemFS is a fully-symmetrical, in-memory distributed runtime file system. Its design is based on uniformly distributing file stripes across the storage nodes belonging to an application by means of a distributed hash function, purposefully sacrificing data locality for balancing both network traffic and memory consumption. This way, reading and writing files can benefit from full network bisection bandwidth, while data distribution is balanced across the storage servers.

Acknowledgments. This work is partially funded by the Dutch public-private research community COMMIT/.

References

1. Aker, B.: Libmemcached (2014). http://libmemcached.org/libMemcached.html
2. Fitzpatrick, B.: Distributed caching with memcached. Linux J. **2004**(124), 5 (2004)
3. Jacob, J.C., Katz, D.S., Berriman, G.B., Good, J.C., Laity, A., Deelman, E., Kesselman, C., Singh, G., Su, M.-H., Prince, T., et al.: Montage: a grid portal and software toolkit for science-grade astronomical image mosaicking. Int. J. Comput. Sci. Eng. **4**(2), 73–87 (2009)
4. Szeredi, M., et al.: FUSE: Filesystem in userspace (2014). http://fuse.sourceforge.net/
5. Uta, A., Sandu, A., Kielmann, T.: MemFS: An In-memory runtime file system with symmetrical data distribution. In: IEEE Cluster 2014, Madrid, Spain, September 2014 (poster paper)
6. Zhang, Z., Katz, D.S., Armstrong, T.G., Wozniak, J.M., Foster, I.: Parallelizing the execution of sequential scripts. In: 2013 International Conference for IEEE High Performance Computing, Networking, Storage and Analysis (SC) (2013)

Scheduling Methods and Algorithms

A Multi-capacity Queuing Mechanism in Multi-dimensional Resource Scheduling

Mehdi Sheikhalishahi[1]([⊠]), Richard M. Wallace[2], Lucio Grandinetti[1], José Luis Vazquez-Poletti[2], and Francesca Guerriero[1]

[1] Department of Electronics, Computer Sciences and Systems, University of Calabria, Rende, CS, Italy
mehdi.alishahi@gmail.com
[2] Department of Computer Architecture and Automation, Complutense University, Madrid, Spain

Abstract. With the advent of new computing technologies, such as cloud computing and contemporary parallel processing systems, the building blocks of computing systems have become multi-dimensional. Traditional scheduling algorithms based on a single-resource optimization like processor fail to provide near optimal solutions. The efficient use of new computing systems depends on the efficient use of all resource dimensions. Thus, the scheduling algorithms have to fully use all resources. In this paper, we propose a queuing mechanism based on a multi-resource scheduling technique. For that, we model multi-resource scheduling as a multi-capacity bin-packing scheduling algorithm at the queue level to reorder the queue in order to improve the packing and as a result improve scheduling metrics. The experimental results demonstrate performance improvements in terms of waittime and slowdown metrics.

Keywords: Multi-resource · Queuing mechanism · Resource management · Scheduling · Bin-packing · Performance

1 Introduction

From a scheduling and resource view for computing, there can be a few major issues and problems to consider: low utilization, overloaded systems, poor performance, and resource contention. Solving these issues and problems requires answering complex questions that start with, *"When...,"* *"Which...,"* and *"Where...."* For instance, "Which types of applications should be consolidated together in a server?", "When should some workloads be migrated to other servers?", and "Where should a workload be placed?" These examples are the type of resource management questions to consider and this list has many more resource management questions of this type.

Scheduling algorithms based on *First-Come First-Served* schemes (FCFS) pack jobs from the job queue into the system in order of their arrival until a resource is exhausted. If there is a large job at the head of the queue which

© Springer International Publishing Switzerland 2014
F. Pop and M. Potop-Butucaru (Eds.): ARMS-CC 2014, LNCS 8907, pp. 9–25, 2014.
DOI: 10.1007/978-3-319-13464-2_2

requires more resources than those left available in the system, the job allocation scheme is blocked from scheduling further jobs until sufficient resources become available for this large job. This results in potentially large resource fragments being *under-utilized*. *Back-filling* mechanisms overcome this issue by skipping over jobs that cannot be allocated and by finding smaller jobs that can make use of remaining resources.

With the advent of new computing technologies such as cloud computing as a recent development in the field of computing and massively parallel processing systems such as the most recent *Cray JK7* system (Titan), the *Chinese Tianhe-1A* system (NUDT YH MPP)[1], and the quite old *SUN E10000* and *SGI O2K* systems, the building blocks of computing systems have become multi-dimensional. The *Titan* system is installed at Oak Ridge, achieving 17.59 Petaflop/s on the Linpack benchmark with 560,640 processors, including 261,632 *NVIDIA K20x* accelerator cores[2].

Scheduling in older computer systems, such as the massively parallel processing systems *TMC CM-5* and the *CRAY T3E*, were focused on a single resource dimension allocation (processing nodes) where single capacity bin-packing algorithms were used to solve this problem[3].

From the processing point of view, according to the *Top500* list, a total of 62 systems on the *Top500* list are using accelerator/co-processor technology including *Titan* and the *Chinese Tianhe-1A* system which uses *NVIDIA GPUs* to accelerate its computation. Moreover, *Stampede* and six other supercomputers are accelerated by the new *Intel Xeon Phi* processors (Intel MIC architecture)[4]. As a result there are multiple computing elements to be taken into account in scheduling at the processor level.

In multi-dimensional resource environment a single resource still becomes exhausted while others remain under-used even with the *back-filling* strategy as the scheduling algorithm. This is due to the design of *FCFS* algorithms which are restricted in job selection based on their arrival order and not addressing capacity imbalance between resources in a multi-resource environment. *Back-filling* strategy is an instance of FCFS mechanism. Thus, single capacity bin-packing algorithms are inadequate as they are unable to provide optimal scheduling for multi-dimensional resources of *CPU, GPU, memory, shared memory, large disk farms, I/O channels, bandwidth, network input, network output,* and even *software licenses* of current computing system architectures.

The scheduling scheme must be free to select any job based on matching all of the jobs' resource requirements with the available system resources in order to address the efficient use of resources in a multi-resource environment. Therefore, the target of efficient use of new computing architectures depends on efficient usage of all resource dimensions with the scheduling algorithm fully using all resources.

---

[1] http://top500.org/lists/2012/11/

[2] https://www.olcf.ornl.gov/titan/

[3] http://www.top500.org/system/166997

[4] https://www.tacc.utexas.edu/stampede/

In this paper, we investigate research on *multi-resource scheduling* by modeling this problem as a *multi-capacity bin-packing* problem. We propose a queuing mechanism based on multi-resource scheduling technique. We model multi-resource scheduling as a multi-capacity bin-packing scheduling algorithm at the queue level to reorder the queue in order to improve the packing and as a result to improve scheduling metrics.

In summary, our paper makes the following contributions:

- A proposal for multi-capacity bin-packing algorithms for scheduling problem.
- A proposal for queuing mechanism based on multi-capacity bin-packing scheduling algorithm.
- We show experimentally that our multi-capacity bin-packing queuing policy performs more efficiently than the back-filling policy as measured by waittime and slowdown metrics.

The remainder of this paper is organized as follows. Section 2 reviews related work. Section 3 presents our multi-resource scheduling approach that is modeled based on a multi-capacity bin-packing algorithm. Then, it details a queuing mechanism based on multi-capacity bin-packing algorithm. Section 4 explains detailed design and implementation issues such as workload traces, and resource model for experiments of this paper. After that, it discusses simulation experimentations and experimental results. Finally, Sect. 5 presents our conclusions and future work.

2   Related Work

Single-and multi-capacity bin-packing problems and their connection to the generalized scheduling problem have been studied in [5,6,10,11,25].

The two-dimensional vector packing problem [25] consists in orthogonally packing a subset of a set of rectangular-shaped boxes, without overlapping, into a single bounding rectangular area, maximizing the ratio between the area occupied by the boxes and the total available area.

The d-capacity bin-packing solution approaches extend the single capacity bin-packing solutions, i.e., *First-Fit* (FF), *Next-Fit* (NF), and *Best-Fit* (BF), to deal with the d-capacity jobs (items) and nodes (bins). FF, NF, and BF are considered as *Job-To-Node* placement rules. Those d-capacity bin-packing algorithms that are extensions of the single capacity bin-packing do not scale well with increasing d since they do not take advantage of the information in the additional capacities. [2] presents a first-fit approximation algorithm for the bin packing problem. The algorithm was devised for the single resource problem, but tips are given about the extension to multiple resources. Orthogonal to the *Job-To-Node* placement rules is the job queue preprocessing method used before the packing operation. For the single capacity bin-packing algorithm sorting the list based on a scalar value in a non-increasing order with respect to the job resource requirement improves the performance of the packing. The *First-Fit Decreasing* (FFD) algorithm first sorts the list in a non-increasing order and then applies the FF packing algorithm. The NF and BF algorithms can be extended in a similar manner.

Leinberger et al. [15] proposed a d-capacity bin-packing algorithm named *Multi-Capacity Bin Packing* (MCBP). It is a particular vector packing algorithm that uses the additional capacity information to provide better packing by addressing the capacity imbalance. Authors show how their algorithms lead to better multi-resource allocation and scheduling solutions.

In addition, the problem of optimally mapping virtual machines (VMs) to servers can be reduced to the *bin packing problem* [1,20,24]. This problem is known to be NP-hard, therefore heuristic approaches can only lead to suboptimal solutions. With regard to recent work finding a FFD algorithm that has better execution time [19] provides an algorithm that maximizes the dot product between the vector of remaining capacities and the vector of remaining or residual capacities of the current open bin, i.e. subtract from the bin's capacity the total demand of all the items currently assigned to it. It places the item that maximizes the weighted dot product with the vector of remaining capacities without violating the capacity constraint vector of demands for the item. This bin-centric method did show better performance. This method is an alternative to our method and is intended for allocation of VM images rather than scientific job placement. The argument can be made that a VM image can have the same processing footprint as a long-lived scientific application.

Moreover, novel job scheduling mechanisms use d-capacity bin-packing algorithms. For instance, [22,23] employ an algorithm based on MCBP proposed by Leinberger et al. in [15]. In [23], a novel job scheduling approach for homogeneous cluster computing platforms is proposed. Its key feature is the use of VM technology to share fractional node resources in a precise and controlled manner. Other VM-based scheduling approaches have focused primarily on technical issues or extensions to existing batch scheduling systems, while in [23] authors take a more aggressive approach and seek to find heuristics that maximize an objective metric correlated with job performance. They derive absolute performance bounds and develop algorithms for the online, non-clairvoyant version of scheduling problem. Their results demonstrate that virtualization technology coupled with lightweight online scheduling strategies can afford dramatic improvements in performance for executing high performance computing (HPC) workloads.

Eco4cloud [16] adaptively consolidates the workload using VM migration and balances the assignment of *CPU*- and *RAM*-intensive applications on each server, which helps to optimize the use of resources. Live migration of VMs between servers is adopted by the VMware Distributed Power Management system, using lower and upper utilization thresholds to enact migration procedures [13]. The heuristic approaches presented in [1] and in [20] use techniques derived from the Best Fit Decreasing and the First Fit Decreasing algorithms, respectively. In both cases, the goal is to place each migrating VM on the server that minimizes the overall power consumption of the data center. On the other hand, consolidation is a powerful means to improve IT efficiency and reduce power consumption [3,12,21]. Some approaches - e.g., [4,17] - try to forecast the processing load and aim at determining the minimum number of servers that should be switched on to satisfy the demand, so as to reduce energy consumption and maximize data center revenues. However, even a correct setting of this number is only a part of the problem: algorithms are needed to decide how the VMs should be mapped to servers in a dynamic environment, and how live migration of VMs can be exploited to unload servers and switch them off when possible, or to avoid SLA violations. In [9] the multi-resource scheduling problem is tackled by using an linear programming (LP) formulation that gives higher priority to VMs with more stable workload. *ReCon* [18] is a tool that analyzes the resource consumption of various applications, discovers applications which can be consolidated, and subsequently generates static or dynamic consolidation recommendations. In *ReCon*, only CPU utilization is considered, the complete extension to the multi-resource problem is left to future research.

In comparison, these works are coupled with advanced technologies, like virtualization, to improve scheduling metrics. Our approach is based on optimization techniques to improve pure scheduling metrics with simple heuristics. The framework presented in [7] tackles the consolidation problem by exploiting constraint programming paradigm. Rule-based constraints concerning SLA negotiation are managed by an optimizer that adopts a branching approach: the variables are considered in a priority descending order, and at each step one of the variables is set to the value that is supposed to guide the solver to a good solution. The Entropy resource manager presented in [14] performs dynamic consolidation based on constraint programming, where constraints are defined on CPU and on RAM utilization. All these approaches represent important steps ahead for the deployment of green-aware data centers, but they do not model multi-resource aspects of scheduling in their problem completely.

Our multi-resource scheduling approach is in line with consolidation approaches in such a way to increase the number of allocated workloads to a node. With that we increase the consolidation degree of nodes leading to improvement of resources utilization, and consequently improving energy efficiency.

3   Multi-resource Scheduling

In this section, first we review bin-packing algorithms. We then devise the basics of a multi-capacity bin-packing algorithm to address the problem of multi-resource scheduling. After that, we develop this algorithm as part of the queuing mechanism of the scheduler.

3.1   The Multi-capacity Bin-Packing Problem

Due to multiple resource dimensions in computing systems, resource allocation problem is related to the *multi-dimensional bin-packing*, or vector packing. Vector packing is bin-packing with multi-dimensional items and bins. In order to model the parallel job scheduling problem as a multi-capacity bin-packing problem the parallel system node is represented by a bin with d capacities, e.g. $\overrightarrow{B_k}$, corresponding to the multiple resources in the system. And a job (item) is represented by a d-capacity, e.g. $\overrightarrow{J_i}$, resource requirements vector. Jobs are obtained from a list L, and the total number of jobs to be packed is denoted by n.

In a homogeneous computing system, the capacity of each node is represented by a d-capacity vector, $\overrightarrow{C} = (C_1, ..., C_j, ..., C_d)$, where $C_j, C_j \geq 0$, represents the jth component capacity, so that $\sum_{j=1}^{d} C_j > 0$. A job is also represented by a d-capacity vector, $\overrightarrow{J_i} = (J_{i1}, ..., J_{ij}, ..., J_{id})$, where $J_{ij}, 0 \leq J_{ij} \leq C_j$, denotes the j-th component requirement of the ith job, and $\forall i \mid 1 \leq i \leq n$ and $\sum_{j=1}^{d} J_{ij} > 0$.

$\overrightarrow{B_k}$ represents node k. A job $\overrightarrow{J_i}$ can be packed into a node (bin) $\overrightarrow{B_k}$, if $\overrightarrow{B_k} + \overrightarrow{J_i} \leq \overrightarrow{C}$, or $\forall j \mid 1 \leq j \leq d$ and $B_{kj} + J_{ij} \leq C_j$, i.e., there is enough free capacity for all resources in node $\overrightarrow{B_k}$ for job $\overrightarrow{J_i}$ placement.

The FF algorithm tries to fit the next job to be placed into any of the currently non-empty nodes. If the next job cannot fit into any of the current nodes, then the next node is considered. Or, if it does not fit into any of the nodes, it will return to queue and it will be considered at the next scheduling cycle. The BF algorithm adds a further node selection heuristic to the FF algorithm by scheduling the best-fit job from the queue on a node which minimizes unused resources.

The NF algorithm takes the next d-capacity job $\overrightarrow{J_i}$ and attempts to place it in the current node $\overrightarrow{B_k}$. If it does not fit: If $B_{kj} + J_{ij} > C_j$ for some j, then the next node $\overrightarrow{B_{k+1}}$ is considered. The point being that no node that does not meet the condition $\overrightarrow{B_l}$, $1 \leq l < k$ is considered as a candidate for job $\overrightarrow{J_i}$.

In d-capacity formulation the jobs are sorted based on a scalar representation of the d components; that is the summation of d components. Other extensions include the maximum component, sum of squares of components, etc. The goal is to somehow capture the relative size of each d-capacity item.

3.2 A Heuristic to the Multi-capacity Bin-Packing Problem

Bin-packing in the computing system scheduling domain is basically an abstraction of a restricted batch processing scenario in which all jobs arrive before processing begins and all jobs have the same execution time. The goal is to process the jobs as fast as possible. Basically, each bin corresponds to a scheduling cycle on the system resources, and the scheduling algorithm must pack jobs onto the system in an order such that all jobs are scheduled using the fewest cycles. Thus, the scheduling goal is to partition the list L into as few nodes (bins) as possible.

At the start of a scheduling cycle, a bin is created in which each component is initialized to reflect the amount of the corresponding machine resource which is currently available. Jobs are selected from the job queue (list L) and packed into the machine until there are not sufficient quantities of resources to fill the needs of any of the remaining jobs.

The prior *Job-To-Node* placement rules described in Sect. 2 fails to provide a near optimal scheduling solution. For example, in the FF algorithm the node selection mechanism for job placement ignores the resources' requirement (weights) for the job and the current component capacities of the nodes and its only criteria for job placement is that the job fits. Hence, a single capacity of a node may fill up sooner than the other capacities, which leads to lower overall utilization. Based on this analysis, a *Job-To-Node* placement would provide more optimized packing if the current relative weights or rankings of d-capacities are considered; that is, if B_{kj} has the lowest available capacity, then search for a job $\overrightarrow{J}_i$ which fits into $\overrightarrow{B}_k$ and has J_{ij} as its smallest component weight. This reduces pressure on B_{kj}, which may allow additional jobs to be added to the node $\overrightarrow{B}_k$. This heuristic attempts to correct a *capacity imbalance* in the node. Thus, the capacities are all kept balanced, so that more jobs will likely fit into the node which gives a multi-capacity aware approach and is the basis of this paper.

Our proposed heuristic attempts to find jobs in which the largest components are exactly ordered with respect to the ordering of the corresponding smallest elements in the current node. For instance, in the case of $d = 5$ with the capacities of the current node $\overrightarrow{B}_k$ ordered as follows:

$$B_{k1} \leq B_{k3} \leq B_{k4} \leq B_{k2} \leq B_{k5}$$

In this instance, the algorithm would first search the list L for a job in which the resource requirements were ranked as follows:

$$J_{i1} \geq J_{i3} \geq J_{i4} \geq J_{i2} \geq J_{i5}$$

which is exactly opposite of the current node state. Adding $\overrightarrow{J}_i$ to $\overrightarrow{B}_k$ has the effect of increasing the capacity levels of the smaller components more than it increases the capacity levels of the larger components. If no jobs were found with this relative ranking between their components, then the algorithm searches the list again, relaxing the ordering of the smallest components first, working up to the largest components. For example, the next two job rankings that would be searched for are:

$J_{i1} \geq J_{i3} \geq J_{i4} \geq J_{i5} \geq J_{i2}$
and
$J_{i1} \geq J_{i3} \geq J_{i2} \geq J_{i4} \geq J_{i5}$
... and finally,
$J_{i5} \geq J_{i2} \geq J_{i4} \geq J_{i3} \geq J_{i1}$

The algorithm searches each logical sublist in an attempt to find a job which fits into the current node. If no job is found in the current logical sublist, then the sublist with the next best ranking match is searched, and so on, until all lists have been searched.

In summary, these heuristics match jobs to hosts, based on sorting the host resources according to their capacity, and the jobs requirements in the opposite order, such that the largest requirement would correspond to the highest capacity.

3.3   Multi-capacity Queuing Mechanism

In this paper, we focus on queuing mechanism of scheduling system. We extend the proposed packing technique of the multi-capacity bin-packing algorithm developing a multi-capacity bin-packing queuing mechanism.

Our multi-capacity bin-packing queuing mechanism heuristic orders jobs based on the free capacity ordering of nodes. Free capacities at the next scheduling cycle are considered by sorting the resources of the nodes based on their free capacity; that is, from highest to lowest free capacity. The mechanism then transits the resource ordering for the nodes evaluating the best match of job resource requirements to a node by summing the differences between job resource requirements. This summation reflects the degree to which it is feasible to use a node based on the capacity imbalance for a job. This step attempts to correct a capacity imbalance.

The pseudo code of multi-capacity aware queuing mechanism is represented in the algorithm 1. t as an input parameter is the next scheduling cycle. Some description about the data structures used in the algorithm 1 are as the following:

- A *slot table* is essentially just a collection of resource reservations. It tracks the capacity of the physical nodes on which jobs can be scheduled, contains the *resource reservations* of all the jobs, and allows efficient access to them.
- A particularly important operation with the slot table is determining the *"availability window"* of resources starting at a given time. Availability window provides easier access to the contents of a slot table by determining the availability in each node starting at a given time.
- *getAvailabilityWindow* function creates an availability window starting at a given time.

In brief, an availability window provides a convenient abstraction over the slot table, with methods to answer questions such as:

- "If I want to start at least at time T, are there enough resources available to start the job?"
- "Will those resources be available until time $T+t$?"
- "If not, what is the longest period of time those resources will be available?"

and so on.

4   Experiments

In this section, we present simulation experiments to evaluate the multi-capacity bin-packing queuing policy in terms of scheduling metrics. For that, we first describe resource model and workload characteristics, then we present workload traces explored. In closing we give specific and precise configuration used.

Algorithm 1. MultiCapacityQueuingMechanism(t: the next scheduling cycle)

$multi\_capacity\_queue = []$

$job\_res\_req = \{\}$

$job\_res\_req[RES\_CPU] = 0$

$job\_res\_req[RES\_MEM] = 0$

$job\_res\_req[RES\_IO] = 0$

$job\_res\_req[RES\_NETIN] = 0$

$job\_res\_req[RES\_NETOUT] = 0$

$node\_free\_capacity\_norm = \{\}$

$node\_free\_capacity\_res\_ordering = \{\}$

for $res \in job\_res\_req.keys()$ **do**

   $node\_res\_capacity[res] = slottable.nodes[1].capacity.get\_by\_type(res)$

end for

$aw = slottable.get\_availability\_window(t)$

for $node\_id \in slottable.nodes.keys()$ **do**

   $node\_free\_capacity\_norm[node\_id] = \{\}$

   for $res \in job\_res\_req.keys()$ **do**

      $node\_free\_capacity\_norm[node\_id][res] =$

      $aw.get\_availability(t, node\_id).get\_by\_type(res)/node\_res\_capacity[res]$

   end for

   $node\_free\_capacity\_norm\_items[node\_id] = node\_free\_capacity\_norm[node\_id].items()$

   <**Sorting resources for a** node_id **based on the free resource capacity, in descending order.**>

   $node\_free\_capacity\_norm\_items[node\_id].sort()$

   $node\_free\_capacity\_res\_ordering[node\_id]$ =   [res for res, capacity in

      $node\_free\_capacity\_norm\_items[node\_id]]$

end for

while Queue is not empty **do**

   <**Get the job at the head of the queue.**>

   $job = queue.dequeue()$

   $score = 0$

   <**Traversing all nodes and evaluating the job score.**>

   for $node\_id \in slottable.nodes.keys()$ **do**

      for $r1 \in node\_free\_capacity\_res\_ordering[node\_id]$ **do**

         del $node\_free\_capacity\_res\_ordering[node\_id][0]$

         for $r2 \in node\_free\_capacity\_res\_ordering[node\_id]$ **do**

            if $node\_free\_capacity\_norm[node\_id][r1]$ >

            $node\_free\_capacity\_norm[node\_id][r2]$ **then**

            $score+ = job\_res\_req[r1] - job\_res\_req[r2]$

         end if

         end for

      end for

   end for

   $multi\_capacity\_queue.append((job, score))$

end while

<**Sorting the multi-capacity queue based on the job score in descending order and moving the best matched jobs to the head of the queue.**>

$multi\_capacity\_queue.sort()$

$multi\_capacity\_queue = [l \text{ for } (l, s) \text{ in } multi\_capacity\_queue]$

<**Copying the multi-capacity queue into the wait queue.**>

for $l \in multi\_capacity\_queue$ **do**

   $queue.enqueue(l)$

end for

4.1   Resource Model and Workload Characteristics

We consider commodity cluster infrastructure as resource model in this study each physical node has *CPU, Memory, IO, Network input*, and *Network output* as resource types and conventional interconnection between them. Furthermore, the simulated cluster of a configuration is modeled after the corresponding workload trace's cluster.

4.2   Workload Traces

For this paper, we construct workloads by adapting the *SDSC Blue Horizon* cluster job submission trace[5] from the *Parallel Workloads Archive*. We alter these derived traces to incorporate all resource dimensions requirements. For that, we simply add *Net-in, Net-out*, and *IO* resource types to jobs resource requirements that were missing, and set their resource requirements based on a random uniform distribution to present a random use of resources for jobs. This is to present multi-dimensional resource requirements for jobs. We treat all resource types the same. That is a job can be allocated to a node if all its resources requirements will be satisfied by the node.

4.3   Configurations

We conduct a number of experiments over a wide range of derived traces. We extract all *30*-day traces from *SDSC Blue Horizon* to build derived traces for our experiments. Specifically, the extract is from the beginning of day *300* until day *330*. This would be trace one. From day *330* to day *360* would be trace two, and so on. In sum, we build 21 derived traces from day 300 until day 960 in increments of 30 days. For each trace, we carry out two experiments: one for the multi-capacity queuing policy(MCBP), and the other for back-filling queuing policy(BKFL).

In addition to the variable parameters, we have fixed parameters such as an *intermediate back-filling* strategy as the packing mechanism. Thus, the scheduling function periodically evaluates the *queue*, using an *intermediate back-filling* algorithm to determine whether any job can be scheduled. In sum, we compare a multi-capacity-enabled back-filling queuing policy against a pure back-filling queuing policy.

4.4   Results

In simulation experiments, we explore the impact of the multi-capacity bin-packing queuing mechanism on the waittime, and slowdown metrics. We performed experiments on the 21 derived workload traces of *SDSC Blue Horizon* according to configurations above.

---

[5] http://www.cs.huji.ac.il/labs/parallel/workload/l_sdsc_blue/index.html

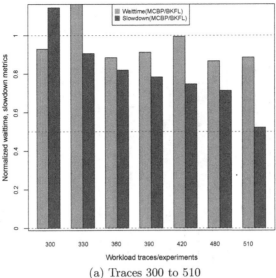

(a) Traces 300 to 510

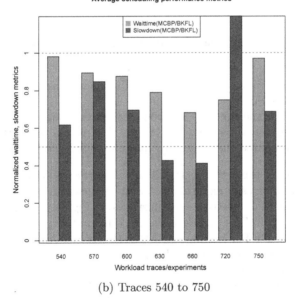

(b) Traces 540 to 750

Fig. 1. Average of simulation results for experiments 300 to 750

For each experiment, for each job, we collected time values: t_a, the arrival time, or time when the job request is submitted; t_s, the start time of the job; and t_e, the time the job ends. At the end of an experiment, we compute the following metrics:

Average scheduling performance metrics

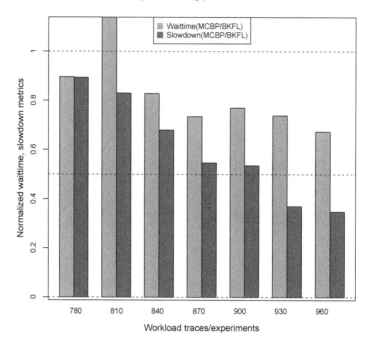

Fig. 2. Average of simulation results for experiments 780 to 960

– *Waittime*: This is time $t_s - t_a$, the time a job request must wait before it starts running. The time units are in *minute*.
– *Slowdown*: If t_u is the time the job would take to run on a dedicated physical system, the job's slowdown is $(t_e - t_a)/t_u$. If t_u is less than 10 seconds, the slowdown is computed the same way, but assuming t_u to be 10 seconds [8].

The optimization of these two metrics is a *minimization* problem. We analyze simulation results for each experiment based on mean and standard deviation statistics measure. Mean statistics are illustrated in Figs. 1, 2, and standard deviation are illustrated in Figs. 3, 4. In order to compare two policies, we normalize **MCBP** results to **BKFL** results, i.e., $MCBP/BKFL$. All values presented in the graphs are based on this normalized value. This is to better present and compare two policies with a value.

In general, we have got better results for both metrics in terms of mean statistic measure. However, in terms of standard deviation waittime metric gets higher values for MCBP policy, while slowdown gets lower values. While on average we have got better results for waittime and slowdown metrics, we have more discrepancy of waittime values for MCBP policy respect to BKFL policy. Nonetheless, we have got more concentrated values for slowdown metric for MCBP policy. This observation implies that in total we have better scheduling with MCBP policy respect to BKFL policy. This means that with MCBP total

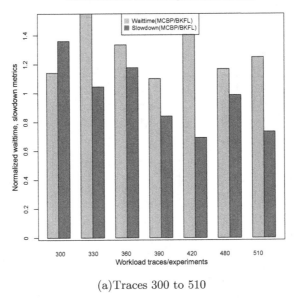

(a)Traces 300 to 510

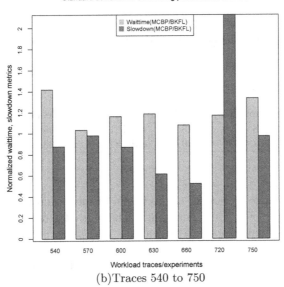

(b)Traces 540 to 750

Fig. 3. Standard deviation of simulation results for experiments 300 to 750

jobs get allocated to the system faster (as it is also demonstrated with statistics measure over all experiments in Table 1). In sum, MCBP outperforms BKFL policy in terms of both scheduling metrics.

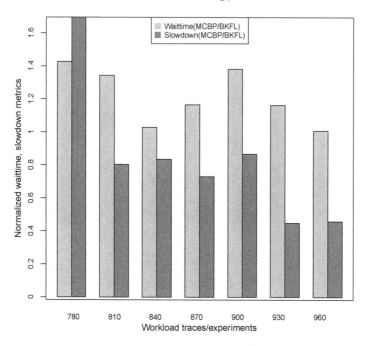

Fig. 4. Standard deviation of simulation results for experiments 780 to 960

Table 1. Statistics measures of simulation results over all experiments

	(a) Mean			(b) Standard deviation	
Config	Waittime (minute)	Slowdown	Config	Waittime (minute)	Slowdown
BKFL	324.58	48.03	BKFL	606.40	149.24
MCBP	270.31	30.02	MCBP	723.23	133.29

In addition, Table 1 presents the outcome of mean and standard deviation statistics measures over all experiments. These results demonstrate that the multi-capacity queuing approach provides a consistent performance improvement over the back-filling one. More specifically, in total we have **54** minutes improvement for the **waittime** metric, and **18** unit improvement of the **slowdown** metric.

5   Conclusions and Future Work

The building blocks of contemporary computing systems are multi-dimensional. Therefore, architecture of these systems and algorithms which deal with these systems have to take into account this shift from single-dimension resource model. In this paper, we considered scheduling aspects of such a systems. Traditional scheduling algorithms based on single-resource optimization cannot provide optimal solutions. As a result, the efficient utilization of new computing systems depends on the efficient use of all resource dimensions. The scheduling algorithms have to fully utilize all resources. To address this problem, we have proposed a multi-resource scheduling mechanism at the queuing mechanism. For that, we studied multi-capacity bin-packing queuing policy.

Through exhaustive simulation experimentation on 21 derived workload traces of SDSC Blue Horizon, we have demonstrated that the multi-capacity bin-packing queuing policy addresses multi-dimensional scheduling aspects of computing system resources to achieve improved waittime, slowdown. In addition, this approach provides better consolidation degree, that is, it increases the number of allocated workloads to a node leading to an improvement of resources utilization, and energy efficiency.

In this paper we conducted experiments with homogeneous systems based on realistic simulation while our multi-capacity bin-packing queuing policy can support more general instances. In addition, our solution can be integrated with real frameworks, like Nimbus Toolkit, and OpenNebula resource managers.

In this paper, we studied multi-capacity bin-packing queuing policy for each single job. We can apply this heuristic at a group of jobs to address capacity imbalance. For example, as a future work we plan to study how to schedule a group of jobs at the queue based on the multi-capacity heuristic.

Acknowledgement. We gratefully acknowledge Carlo Mastroianni from the Italian National Research Council, and Tapasya Patki from University of Arizona for reviewing this paper. This work was partially performed under the auspices of the Spanish National Plan for Research, Development and Innovation under Contract TIN2012-31518 (ServiceCloud).

References

1. Beloglazov, A., Abawajy, J., Buyya, R.: Energy-aware resource allocation heuristics for efficient management of data centers for cloud computing. Future Gener. Comput. Syst. **28**(5), 755–768 (2012)
2. Bobroff, N., Kochut, A., Beaty, K.: Dynamic placement of virtual machines for managing SLA violations. In: 10th IFIP/IEEE International Symposium on Integrated Network Management, (IM 2007), pp. 119–128 (2007)
3. Cardosa, M., Korupolu, M.R., Singh, A.: Shares and utilities based power consolidation in virtualized server environments. In: Proceedings of the 11th IFIP/IEEE Integrated Network Management (IM 2009), Long Island, NY, USA, June 2009
4. Chen, Y., Das, A., Qin, W., Sivasubramaniam, A., Wang, Q., Gautam, N.: Managing server energy and operational costs in hosting centers. SIGMETRICS Perform. Eval. Rev. **33**(1), 303–314 (2005)
5. Coffman, E.G., Garey, M.R., Johnson, D.S.: An application of bin-packing to multiprocessor scheduling. SIAM J. Comput. **7**(1), 1–17 (1978)
6. Coffman, E.G., Garey, M.R., Johnson, D.S.: Dynamic bin packing. SIAM J. Comput. **12**(2), 227–258 (1983)

7. Dhyani, K., Gualandi, S., Cremonesi, P.: A constraint programming approach for the service consolidation problem. In: Lodi, A., Milano, M., Toth, P. (eds.) CPAIOR 2010. LNCS, vol. 6140, pp. 97–101. Springer, Heidelberg (2010)

8. Feitelson, D.G., Rudolph, L.: Metrics and benchmarking for parallel job scheduling. In: Feitelson, D.G., Rudolph, L. (eds.) IPPS-WS 1998, SPDP-WS 1998, and JSSPP 1998. LNCS, vol. 1459, p. 1. Springer, Heidelberg (1998)

9. Ferreto, T., Netto, M., Calheiros, R., De Rose, C.: Server consolidation with migration control for virtualized data centers. Future Gener. Comp. Syst. **27**(8), 1027–1034 (2011)

10. Garey, M.R., Graham, R.L.: Bounds for multiprocessor scheduling with resource constraints. SIAM J. Comput. **4**(2), 187–200 (1975)

11. Garey, M.R., Graham, R.L., Johnson, D.S.: Resource constrained scheduling as generalized bin packing. J. Comb. Theory Ser. A **21**(3), 257–298 (1976)

12. Graubner, P., Schmidt, M., Freisleben, B.: Energy-efficient virtual machine consolidation. IT Prof. **15**(2), 28–34 (2013)

13. Gulati, A., Holler, A., Ji, M., Shanmuganathan, G., Waldspurger, C., Zhu, X.: VMware distributed resource management: design, implementation, and lessons learned. VMware Techn. J. (2012). https://labs.vmware.com/vmtj/vmware-distributed-resource-management-design-implementation-and-lessons-learned

14. Hermenier, F., Lorca, X., Menaud, J.-M., Muller, G., Lawall, J.: Entropy: a consolidation manager for clusters. In: Proceedings of the 2009 ACM SIGPLAN/SIGOPS International Conference on Virtual Execution Environments (VEE 2009), pp. 41–50. ACM, New York (2009)

15. Leinberger, W., Karypis, G., Kumar, V.: Multi-capacity bin packing algorithms with applications to job scheduling under multiple constraints. In: Proceedings of the International Conference on Parallel Processing 1999, pp. 404–412 (1999)

16. Mastroianni, C., Meo, M., Papuzzo, G.: Probabilistic consolidation of virtual machines in self-organizing cloud data centers. IEEE Trans. Cloud Comput. **1**(2), 215–228 (2013)

17. Mazzucco, M., Dyachuk, D., Deters, R.: Maximizing cloud providers' revenues via energy aware allocation policies. In: 10th IEEE/ACM International Symposium on Cluster Computing and the Grid (CCGrid 2010), Melbourne, Australia, pp. 131–138, May 2010

18. Mehta, S., Neogi, A.: ReCon: a tool to recommend dynamic server consolidation in multi-cluster data centers. In: Proceedings of the Network Operations and Management Symposium, IEEE NOMS 2008, pp. 363–370 (2008)

19. Panigrahy, R., Talwar, K., Uyeda, L., Wieder, U.: Heuristics for vector bin packing (2011). http://research.microsoft.com

20. Quan, D.M., Basmadjian, R., de Meer, H., Lent, R., Mahmoodi, T., Sannelli, D., Mezza, F., Telesca, L., Dupont, C.: Energy efficient resource allocation strategy for cloud data centres. In: 26th International Symposium on Computer and Information Sciences (ISCIS 2011), London, UK, pp. 133–141, September 2011

21. Schröder, K., Nebel, W.: Behavioral model for cloud aware load and power management. In: Proceedings of HotTopiCS '13, 2013 International Workshop on Hot Topics in Cloud Services (HotTopiCS '13), pp. 19–26. ACM, New York, May 2013.

22. Stillwell, M., Schanzenbach, D., Vivien, F., Casanova, H.: Resource allocation algorithms for virtualized service hosting platforms. J. Parallel Distrib. Comput. **70**, 962–974 (2010)

23. Stillwell, M., Vivien, F., Casanova, H.: Dynamic fractional resource scheduling vs. batch scheduling. IEEE Trans. Parallel Distrib. Syst. **23**(3), 521–529 (2012). doi:10.1109/TPDS.2011.183

24. Verma, A., Ahuja, P., Neogi, A.: pMapper: power and migration cost aware application placement in virtualized systems. In: Issarny, V., Schantz, R. (eds.) Middleware 2008. LNCS, vol. 5346, pp. 243–264. Springer, Heidelberg (2008)
25. Wu, Y.-L., Wenqi, H., Lau, S.-C., Wong, C.K., Young, G.H.: An effective quasi-human based heuristic for solving the rectangle packing problem. Eur. J. Oper. Res. **141**(2), 341–358 (2002)

A Green Scheduling Policy
for Cloud Computing

Jordi Vilaplana[1]([✉]), Francesc Solsona[1], Ivan Teixido[1], Jordi Mateo[1],
Josep Rius[1], and Francesc Abella[2]

[1] Department of Computer Science and INSPIRES, University of Lleida,
Jaume II 69, 25001 Lleida, Spain
{jordi,francesc,iteixido,jmateo}@diei.udl.cat
jrius@icg.es
http://gcd.udl.cat
[2] Department of Basic Medical Sciences and IRBLleida, University of Lleida,
Alcalde Rovira Roure 80, 25198 Lleida, Spain
abella@gss.scs.es

Abstract. This paper presents a power-aware scheduling policy algorithm called Green Preserving SLA (GPSLA) for cloud computing systems with high workload variability. GPSLA aims to guarantee the SLA
(Service-Level Agreement) by minimizing the system response time and,
at the same time, tries to reduce the energy consumption. We present a
formal solution, based on linear programming, to assign the system load
to the most powerful Virtual Machines, while respecting the SLA and
lowering the power consumption as far as possible. GPSLA is thought
for one node load-aware and jobs formed by embarrassingly parallel heterogeneous tasks.

The results obtained by implementing the model with the IBM CPLEX
prove the applicability of our proposal for guaranteeing SLA and saving
energy. This also encourages its applicability in High Performance Computing due to its good behavior when scaling the model and the workload.
The results are also highly encouraging for further research into this model
in real federated clouds or cloud simulation environments, while adding
more complexity.

Keywords: Green cloud computing · SLA · Power-aware scheduling ·
Linear programming

1 Introduction

In cloud computing, hardware and software services can be added and released
dynamically in order to guarantee an SLA (Service-Level Agreement) to clients [1].

This work was supported by the MEyC under contract TIN2011-28689-C02-02. The
authors are members of the research group 2009-SGR145 and 2014-SGR163, funded
by the Generalitat of Catalunya.

© Springer International Publishing Switzerland 2014
F. Pop and M. Potop-Butucaru (Eds.): ARMS-CC 2014, LNCS 8907, pp. 26–35, 2014.
DOI: 10.1007/978-3-319-13464-2_3

An SLA is an agreement between a service provider and a consumer where the provider agrees to deliver a service to the consumer under specific terms, such as time or performance. In order to comply with the SLA, the service provider must monitor the QoS (Quality of Service) closely through such performance metrics as response or waiting time, throughput or makespan [2].

We focus our attention on the response time as the QoS metric. In this scenario, the SLA contract usually states that the consumer only pays for the resources and services used according to the agreed QoS requirements at a given price [3]. Studying and determining SLA-related issues is a big challenge, mainly due to the complex nature of cloud computing and especially its high variability [5].

Our proposal, Green Preserving SLA (GPSLA), is designed to lower power consumption [6] as much as possible. At the same time, GPSLA is aimed at guaranteeing a negotiated SLA and power-aware [4] solutions, leaving aside such other cloud-computing issues as variability [5], system security [6] and availability [7]. Job response time is perhaps the most important QoS metric in a cloud-computing context [3]. For this reason, it is also the QoS parameter chosen in this work. In addition, despite good solutions having been presented by some researchers in the literature dealing with QoS [8,9] and power consumption [10,11], the model presented aims to obtain the best scheduling taking both criteria into account.

There is a great deal of work in the literature on linear programming (LP) solutions and algorithms applied to scheduling, as the one presented in [14,15]. Other remarkable work was performed in [12], where authors designed a Green Scheduling Algorithm that integrated a neural network predictor in order to optimize server power consumption in Cloud Computing. Also, in [13] authors proposed a genetic algorithm that takes into account both makespan and energy consumption. Our main objective is the designing of an LP scheduling algorithm to minimize power consumption and maximizing SLA guaranties (based on the response time as the QoS performance metric) at the same time.

An important contribution of this paper is the way we model the power of the virtual machines in function of its workload. We rely on the work done in [16], where the authors formulate the problem of assignment of persons from various groups to different jobs who may complete them in minimum time as an stochastic programming problem. The job completion times were assumed to follow a Gamma distribution. To model the influence of the workload we weighted the powerful of the Virtual Machine by a load factor determined by an Erlang distribution (equivalent to a Gamma). Finally, we obtained an stochastic programming problem and transformed to an equivalent deterministic problem with linear objective function.

The remainder of the paper is organized as follows. In the Green Preserving SLA Schedulers section we present our main contributions, a sort of scheduling policies. These proposals are arranged in order of increasing complexity. The experimentation showing the good behavior of our cloud model is presented in the Results section. Our proposal was tested with the http://www-01.ibm.com/software/commerce/optimization/cplex-optimizer/CPLEX mathematical optimizer, which provides tools to implement the mathematical models presented in the Green Preserving SLA Schedulers section. Finally, the Conclusions section outlines the main conclusions and possible research lines to explore in the near future.

2   Green Preserving SLA Schedulers

Our scheduling proposals are based on linear programming (LP). LP consists of trying to find an objective function (OF) representing one, or if possible more than one, performance criteria. Multiple performance criteria can be taken into account in order to choose the optimal scheduler. The most widely used are the minimization of the power consumption of the cloud and the mean response time of tasks. These are also the ones chosen in this article.

LP applied to scheduling deals with finding one assignment that maximizes or minimizes the OF. This will give the assignment of tasks to VMs or the consolidation of VMs to nodes that maximizes the gains in the chosen performance metric. The formulated solution, the OF and the constraints, can be resolved by any solver, such as IBM CPLEX, or the open-source http://lpsolve.sourceforge.net/5.5/lp_solve.

Cloud scheduling can be split into two more specific phases, the scheduling itself and the consolidation phase. The scheduling phase is the one that assigns tasks to virtual machines (VMs). As an example of this, simple requests/tasks entering a cloud system will be scheduled for execution in one of the VMs that make it up. Then the consolidation phase ensures the efficient use of resources avoiding under-utilized VMs. However, energy savings are related to these two phases, thus encouraging the use of one-step scheduling.

A two-step scheduler can give very distinct results to the ones given by a one-step scheduler. For example, a two-step task scheduler can assign tasks to 2 VMs residing on two different nodes. However, a single-stage task scheduler can only assign these to one VM, thus enabling the idle node to be stopped, and so saving power. The cause of this failure is to consider the return time in the first step and power saving in the second. Incorporating energy savings is the main reason behind that design decision.

We next present our scheduling proposals, called Green Preserving SLA (GPSLA). To better understand the most complete proposal better, we present 3 different scheduler models, arranged according to their increasing complexity.

2.1   GPSLA. One Node

This policy assigns as many requests (tasks) as possible to the most powerful Virtual Machines (VMs), leaving aside the remaining ones. The unused VMs could be then turned off to save energy. The method is based on the computing capacity of the VMs, making assignments in descendent order to their computing power, processing as many requests as possible per unit of time, thus prioritizing the preservation of the SLA contract (for some QoS) with the clients.

We take a cloud made up of a single node, allocating V heterogeneous VMs. Each VM VM_v has a specific amount of Memory M_v. This restricts the workload each VM can host. Given T tasks, all of which are supposed to be homogeneous and, for reasons of simplicity, have the same computing and memory requirements, a single generic unit.

We define the *relative computing power* (Δ_v) of a VM_v as the *normalized score* of such a VM. Formally, given V VMs, $\Delta_v = \frac{\delta_v}{\sum_{k=1}^{V} \delta_k}$, where $\sum_{k=1}^{V} \Delta_v = 1$. δ_v is the score (i.e. the computing power) of VMv. Although δ_v is a theoretical concept, there are many valid benchmarks to obtain it (i.e. Linpack, Lapack or SPEC). Linpack (available in C, Fortran and Java) for example, is used to obtain the number of floating-point operations per second. Note that the closer the relative computing power is to one (in other words, more powerful), the more likely it is that the requests will be mapped into such a VM.

The scheduling is obtained by considering the maximum computing power ($t_v \Delta_v$) of each VM_v. So, we firstly assign tasks to the most powerful VMs. This is a design decision in order to optimize the cloud resources, based on optimizing some QoS performance metrics, such as response or waiting time, throughput or makespan.

As mentioned above, the chosen QoS metric is the response time. Furthermore, by doing it this way, priority is also given to guaranteeing SLA until a certain limit is reached (the one imposed by the cloud capacity) is also prioritized. This objective can be formally defined with the following linear programming model:

$$max(\sum_{v=1}^{V} t_v \Delta_v) \tag{1}$$

$$s.t. : \sum_{v=1}^{V} = T \tag{2}$$

$$t_v \leq M_v, \forall v \leq V \tag{3}$$

Equation 1 is the *Objective Function* (OF) to be maximized. Equality in Eq. 2 and inequality in Eq. 3 are the constraints of the objective function variables. Given the constants T (the total number of requests or tasks), and Δ_v and M_v for each VM_v, the solution that maximizes OF will obtain the values of the variables t_v, representing the number of tasks assigned to VM_v. Thus, the t_v obtained will be the assignment found by this model.

2.2 GPSLA. One Node Load-Aware

Going a step further in the previous model, the loss of power in function of the VM workload is also taken into account. We first consider that VM efficiency rises with the load until some a certain number number of tasks is reached. From then on, the efficiency starts falling asymptotically towards zero. We can model this behaviour with an *Erlang* distribution. Erlang is a continuous probability distribution with two parameters α and λ. The parameter α is called the shape parameter, and the parameter λ is called the rate parameter. These parameters depend on the VM characteristics. When the parameter α equals 1, the distribution simplifies to the exponential distribution. The *Erlang* probability density function is:

$$E(x; \alpha, \lambda) = \lambda e^{-\lambda x} \frac{(\lambda x)^{\alpha-1}}{(\alpha-1)!} \forall x, \lambda \geq 0 \tag{4}$$

We consider that the Erlang modelling parameters of each VM can easily be obtained empirically in an easy way (i.e. by increasing the workload and measuring the mean response times). Figure 1 shows various Erlang plots for some α and λ values by varying the x, designed in this case to represent the workload.

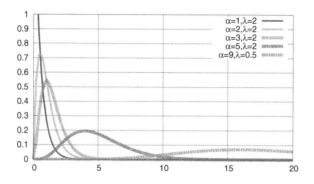

Fig. 1. Erlang plots for different α and λ values.

The Erlang distribution was developed to examine the number of telephone calls which that might be made at the same time to the operators on a switchboard. We use it here to weigh the computing power $(t_v \Delta_v)$ of each VM_v by multiplying it by an Erlang distribution. Here, the x Erlang parameter is replaced by t_v in order to model this distribution in function of each VM workload. Thus giving the new model:

$$max(\sum_{v=1}^{V} t_v \Delta_v E(t_v; \alpha, \lambda)) \tag{5}$$

$$s.t. : \sum_{v=1}^{V} = T \tag{6}$$

$$t_v \leq M_v, \forall v \leq V \tag{7}$$

2.3 GPSLA. One Node Load-Aware and Heterogeneous Tasks

Going even further, we are now also interested in to considering in addition the heterogeneity of task computing requirements. In other words, each task t_i has its *Processing cost* P_{vi}, representing the execution time of task t_i, in VM_v with respect to the execution time of task t_i in the less powerful VM_v (this is, with the lowest Δ_v). M_{vi} is defined as the amount of Memory allocated to task t_i in VM_v. We can suppose that Memory requirements do not change between VMs, so $M_{vi} = M_{v'i} \forall v, v' \leq V$. We define the Boolean variable t_{vi}, representing the assignment of task t_i to VM_v. Then, the new linear model is:

$$max(\sum_{v=1}^{V}(\sum_{i=1}^{T} P_{vi}t_{vi})\Delta_v E(\sum_{j=1}^{T} P_{vj}t_{vj}; \alpha, \lambda)) \tag{8}$$

$$s.t. : \sum_{i=1}^{T} = M_{vi} \leq M_v \forall v \leq V \tag{9}$$

$$\sum_{v=1}^{V} t_{vi} = 1 \forall i \leq T \tag{10}$$

$P_{vi}t_{vi}$ takes into account the computing cost of task t_i in its assigned VM_v. As t_v, representing the number of tasks assigned to VM_v has been changed by the Booleans t_{vi}, which represent the assignment of each task t_i to VM_v, the Erlang function must also be changed in order to compute all the tasks assigned to each VM, so t_v is changed to $\sum_{j=1}^{T} P_{vj}t_{vj}$.

3 Results

Several experiments were performed in order to test the *GPSLA* results in different configurations and for the different stages of complexity of the scheduling policy (Sects. 2.1, 2.2 and 2.3). The experimental results were obtained using the CPLEX mathematical optimizer.

The experimentation case shown here was defined with 3 VMs and 50 tasks. The VM configurations are shown in Table 1.

Table 1. VM configurations.

VM	Relative computing power (Δv)	Memory	Erlang distribution
1	0.45	50	$\alpha = 3, \lambda = 8$
2	0.35	40	$\alpha = 2, \lambda = 8$
3	0.2	10	$\alpha = 2, \lambda = 4$

This simulation was performed by applying the GPSLA policy to the three models described.

3.1 GPSLA. One Node

For the first model (GPSLA. One node), described in Sect. 2.1, the resulting assignation is shown in Table 2.

Table 2. Task distribution obtained with the "GPSLA. One node" model.

VM 1	VM 2	VM 3
50	0	0

As the efficiency drop caused by overloading is not taken into account, all tasks were assigned to VM 1. As VM 2 and VM 3 are not used, they could be turned off to save energy.

In this case, the results obtained are consistent with the model, which tries to consolidate all the tasks in the most powerful virtual machine.

3.2 GPSLA. One Node Load-Aware

For the second model (GPSLA. One node load-aware), described in Sect. 2.2, the Erlang distributions described in Table 1 was applied. The three Erlang charts can be seen in Fig. 2, 3 and 4.

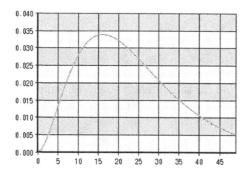

Fig. 2. Erlang distribution chart for VM 1.

These Erlang distributions model the behavior of the VM with different amounts of load. To obtain the best task allocation considering the saturation of virtual machines in the addition of more and more tasks, it is compulsory the Erlang discretization. To realize this discretization, each number or different range of tasks must correspond to a specific discrete value. The set of all these values will be used to calculate the time of the optimization objective function. Thus the parameter relating to the Erlang always have a discrete value.

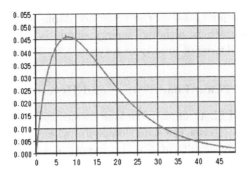

Fig. 3. Erlang distribution chart for VM 2.

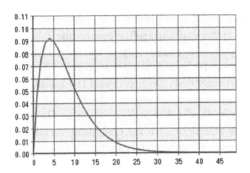

Fig. 4. Erlang distribution chart for VM 3.

This way, the stochastic programming problem is transformed to an equivalent deterministic problem with linear objective function.

It can be seen how, according to its Erlang distribution function, VM 1 reaches its maximum performance between 15 and 25 tasks. VM 2 and VM 3 will have a slightly different behavior and will reach their maximum with fewer tasks. Note that these distributions should be fine-tuned according to each specific system when working with real environments.

Table 3. Task distribution obtained with the "GPSLA. One node load-aware" model.

VM 1	VM 2	VM 3
25	17	8

The resulting assignation is shown in Table 3. It can be seen that when taking into account the system overload the distribution of tasks among virtual machines changes. The scheduler now tries to put all the possible tasks in the most powerful VM, but when the performance starts decreasing significantly, it starts sending further tasks to the other available virtual machines. This behavior is more accurate as, although energy saving is a priority, we still want to preserve a certain degree of quality of service.

3.3 GPSLA. One Node Load-Aware and Heterogeneous Tasks

The third model (GPSLA. One node load-aware and heterogeneous tasks), described in Sect. 2.3, shows the same behavior when tasks are defined with different weights. So the results proved consistent.

4 Conclusions

This paper presents a cloud-based system scheduling mechanism able to respond successfully to a high degree of variability complying with low power consumption and SLA agreements. The complexity of the model developed was increased, thus adding more factors to be taken into account. The model was also tested using the CPLEX mathematical optimizer, and the results obtained proved consistent over a range of scenarios. However, these scenarios have to be tested in such real and simulated cloud environments such as OpenStack and CloudSim. So, the applicability of the algorithm for designing variability- and power-aware cloud systems was proven. To summarize, although more experiments are needed, these preliminary results corroborate the usefulness of our proposal. Future trends are in the direction of exploring different heterogeneous workloads (i.e. jobs/tasks with different computing needs and communication paradigms, and not only the embarrassingly parallel) by expanding the linear programming proposal. The upper and lower SLA boundaries should also be considered. Finally, we want to assess the design of cloud architectures (bearing in mind cloud federation) and VM consolidation. Nevertheless, we believe that this preliminary work is very encouraging and could be further developed and applied in real cloud platforms.

References

1. Armbrust, M., Fox, A., Griffith, R., Joseph, A.D., Katz, R., Konwinski, A., Lee, G., Patterson, D., Rabkin, A., Stoica, I., Zaharia, M.: A view of cloud computing. Commun. ACM **53**(4), 50–58 (2010)
2. Keller, A., Ludwig, H.: The WSLA framework: specifying and monitoring service level agreements for web services. J. Netw. Syst. Manage **11**(1), 57–81 (2003)
3. Aversa, R., Di Martino, B., Rak, M., Venticinque, S., Villano, U.: Performance prediction for HPC on clouds. In: Cloud Computing: Principles and Paradigms (2011)
4. Varia, J.: Architecture for the Cloud: Best Practices. Amazon Web Services (2014)
5. Iosup, A., Yigitbasi, N., Epema, D.: On the performance variability of production cloud services. In: 11th IEEE/ACM International Symposium on Cluster, Cloud and Grid Computing (CCGrid'2011), pp. 104–113 (2011)

6. Vishwanath, K.V., Nagappan, N.: Characterizing cloud computing hardware reliability. In: Proceedings of the 1st ACM Symposium on Cloud Computing (SoCC '10), pp. 193–204 (2010)
7. Martinello, M., Kaâniche, M., Kanoun, K.: Web service availability: impact of error recovery and traffic model. J. Reliab. Eng. Syst. Saf. **89**(1), 6–16 (2005)
8. Vilaplana, J., Solsona, F., Abella, F., Filgueira, R., Rius, J.: The cloud paradigm applied to e-Health. BMC Med. Inform. Decis. Mak. **13**(1), 35 (2013)
9. Vilaplana, J., Solsona, F., Teixidó, I., Abella, F., Rius, J.: A queuing theory model for cloud computing. J. Supercomputing **69**(1), 492–507 (2014)
10. Beloglazov, A., Buyya, R.: Optimal online deterministic algorithms and adaptive heuristics for energy and performance efficient dynamic consolidation of virtual machines in cloud data centers. Concurrency Comput. Pract. Experience **24**, 1397–1420 (2012)
11. Kliazovich, D., Bouvry, P., Khan, S.: GreenCloud: a packet-level simulator of energy-aware cloud computing data centers. J. Supercomputing **62**(3), 1263–1283 (2010)
12. Duy, T.V.T., Sato, Y., Inoguchi, Y.: Performance evaluation of a green scheduling algorithm for energy savings in cloud computing. In: Parallel & Distributed Processing, Workshops and Phd Forum (IPDPSW) 2010, pp. 1–8 (2010)
13. Mezmaz, M., Melab, N., Kessaci, Y., Lee, Y.C., Talbi, E.-G., Zomaya, A.Y., Tuyttens, D.: A parallel bi-objective hybrid metaheuristic for energy-aware scheduling for cloud computing systems. J. Parallel Distrib. Comput. **71**(11), 1497–1508 (2011)
14. Lérida, J.L.I., Solsona, F., Hernández, P., Giné, F., Hanzich, M., Conde, J.: State-based predictions with self-correction on enterprise desktop grid environments. J. Parallel Distrib. Process. **71**(11), 777–789 (2012)
15. Goldman, A., Ngoko, Y.: A MILP approach to schedule parallel independent tasks. In: International Symposium on Parallel and Distributed Computing, ISPDC '08, pp. 115–122 (2008)
16. Khan, M.F., Anwar, Z., Ahmad, Q.S.: Assignment of personnels when job completion time follows gamma distribution using stochastic programming technique. Int. J. Sci. Eng. Res. **3**(3), 274–283 (2012)

A Framework for Speculative Scheduling and Device Selection for Task Execution on a Mobile Cloud

Ansuman Banerjee[1], Himadri Sekhar Paul[2(✉)], Arijit Mukherjee[2],
Swarnava Dey[2], and Pubali Datta[2]

[1] ACMU, Indian Statistical Institute, Kolkata, India
ansuman@isical.ac.in
[2] Innovations Labs, Tata Consultancy Services Ltd., Kolkata, India
{himadriSekhar.paul,arijit.mukherjee,swarnava.dey,
pubali.datta}@tcs.com

Abstract. In this paper, we study the problem of opportunistic task scheduling and workload management in a mobile cloud setting considering computation power variation. We gathered mobile usage data for a number of persons and applied supervised clustering to show that a pattern of usage exists and that follows a state-based model. Based on this model, we present a strategy to choose and offload work on a mobile device. We present a framework and experimental results showing the efficacy of our proposed approach.

1 Introduction

The growing market for smart devices is stimulating the prospect of utilizing them as computing resources [2,13]. Recent studies on the computing capacity of mobile devices claim that their computing power is comparable to that of desktops [17]. This has led to several proposals of Mobile Cloud Computing (MCC) for collaborative execution for executing compute-intensive workflows [3,5,8,10]. The MCC paradigm has attracted considerable attention both in academia and industrial community in recent times.

Several challenges remain to engage a mobile device as part of a computing infrastructure [15]. Some of these challenges are bandwidth, energy constraints, memory capacity, intermittent availability, proper incentive schemes against utilization, security, privacy, etc. In a controlled environment, some of these constraints can be addressed adequately in order to utilize the computation capacity of the mobile devices. For example, many of the reputed commercial organizations distribute smart phones among their senior employees [1]. In such a corporate environment, it is possible to make it a policy that such phones be used for computation for the benefit of the company's infrastructure. Such a device can be used by the infrastructure whenever the device is present in the premises of the organization and is connected to the internal communication network. In such a scenario, the issues of communication reliability and cost, security,

F. Pop and M. Potop-Butucaru (Eds.): ARMS-CC 2014, LNCS 8907, pp. 36–51, 2014.
DOI: 10.1007/978-3-319-13464-2_4

privacy are mitigated. To encourage such an environment, the organization may as well provide incentives in suitable forms. In the company of the authors, points are awarded for additional participation in company tasks (apart from regular assigned duties) and these points can be redeemed against purchases promoted by the organization.

In this paper, we adopt a simple localized mobile grid setting where the devices are accessible through a WiFi connectivity, and examine the problem of computation scheduling and workload management for improved timing performance. We consider a private company infrastructure with a gateway device and a mobile grid, with the gateway device hosting and assimilating an information database on which some computation needs to be executed. The gateway device needs to decide on a computation scheduling and selection mechanism to engage the mobile devices and utilize their donated computation cycles. The primary objective driving this selection is to be able to finish execution of the application in the earliest possible time.

The gateway device is enabled with a task offloader which is the controller of the task selection framework. When the offloader wants to execute a task (in the form of a downloadable application), it invites bids from the owners of all devices connected to the offloader. Additionally, the offloader announces a deadline by which the computation has to finish. Associated with the task is a suitable reward to be earned by the selected bidder and a penalty. Each owner, intending to participate in the bid, executes a pre-installed analysis agent on his device. The agent takes as input the advertised application and the deadline and comes back to the owner with an advice whether to bid or not on the basis of its estimation of the execution time. In this paper, we consider the estimation of execution time of a task with various levels of information available about the device usage pattern. In our architecture, the mobile devices are active agents, who learn and build models of their owner usage patterns. The owner places a bid only if the estimated execution time is less than the advertised deadline of the job. The bid is the promised completion time within which the corresponding device can complete the advertised task. The offloader can possibly select one of the bidding agents for offloading the task based on some criterion. In the simplest case, it may choose the one with earliest promised completion time and offload the task to the selected device. We assume that the owners are rational (aware of penalty) and honest (no false bids). The interesting activity from the device's perspective is to analyze how/when/what to bid for, while designing the selection and scheduling mechanism is the offloader's challenge.

This paper is organized as follows. We present a motivating example in Sect. 2. Section 3 presents a model of the bidding and selection process. Section 4 describes our experiments while the following section presents related work. Finally, Sect. 6 concludes the paper.

2   Motivation for This Work

In this section, we present an example to illustrate the need for modelling a mobile device for its usage. A mobile device has various operational modes in its usage cycle. For example, when a user attends to a call, its communication modules are busy, when he listens to music or radio, its audio system is busy; when he watches a movie, its GPU remains busy. Manufacturers of mobile devices usually specify an operating model of their devices. An operating model is a state transition system where the states represent some high level operation modes (*e.g.* charging, audio on, network on, etc.) with average / maximum / minimum resource usage estimates when the device operates in that particular state, and possible interstate transitions. The operating condition of the device in these states can be attributed to its usage of processor, memory, cache, priority of the running jobs, battery power state, etc. The transitions in such a system are triggered by user interaction of the device and usage of device resources by various applications running in the system. In this paper, we extend this model to an usage-induced operating state model, a transition system based on the operating model and additionally, specialized by the usage pattern of the device owner.

In the context of exploiting a mobile device in our setting, we are interested in the availability of different resources in the device to utilize it for running an external computation. For simplicity, we assume here the states in the usage model of a device are characterized only by the percentage of CPU available. We also assume that the execution time of the advertised application on a given device architecture is known a-priori (or can be computed by dynamic simulation against a given data set or by using established methods like Worst Case Execution Time estimation [19]). Such an estimate typically assumes full (100 %) utilization of the resources in the device. In this work, we assume the execution time of the task is solely and linearly dependent on available CPU cycles in the devices. This essentially implies that if the execution time of a task is estimated as 10 time units, then the task is estimated to be complete in 20 time units when there are competing processes such that the job can avail only 50 % of the CPU.

As an example, we consider here a simple case of two mobile devices and one task to be offloaded to one of the devices. The task has a deadline of 60 time units. Each mobile device needs to estimate its bid based on its operational state model, as depicted in Fig. 1. The events triggering the transitions are not shown in the figure, since they are not required for presentation of these examples. Each state in the state model is annotated with the fraction of CPU available for external computation at that state, which can be used for executing the external task. For the sake of simplicity, we assume here that the device takes one of the out-bound transitions from its current state, including the self loop, after every unit time. In other words, the device stays at each state for one unit of time, executes one of the outgoing transitions from the present state and moves to the next state (may be same as the current one) where it stays for one more unit, and this continues. We assume such transitions are instantaneous.

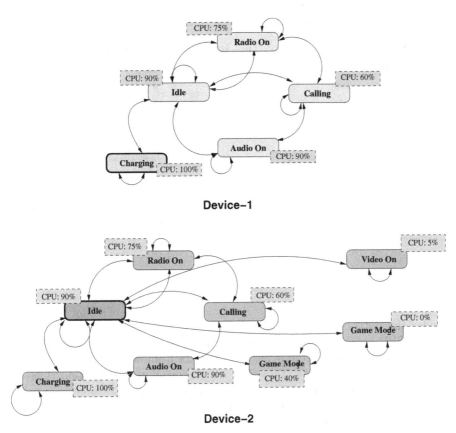

Fig. 1. Usage model with CPU availability

The Simplest Case. Both the devices have an estimate of the execution time of the advertised application on their architecture. Let us assume both of them come up with a value of 40 time units. When bids are invited, Device-1 is in the *charging* state and Device-2 is *idle*. If the devices always remain in the same state, the completion time of the task on Device-1 is 40 time units (100 % CPU availability in *charging* state), while that for Device-2 is $40 \times \frac{100}{90} = 44.44$ time unit. Thus Device-1 bids with a value of 40 and Device-2 bids with 44.44. Assuming the *offloader* awards the job to the one with earlier completion time, Device-1 is selected.

A More Realistic Scenario. In a more realistic setting, each device is expected to transit away from its current state during the job execution and therefore cannot guarantee constant CPU availability. In such a setting, the device can explore all possible paths in its state graph and optimistically choose a path which provides the best estimated completion time. Such a path obviously would go through states with high CPU availabilities. For example, Device-1 would

Table 1. Execution on Device-1

State	CPU availability	Time in the State	Effective execution
charging	100 %	1 s	1 s
idle	90 %	10 s	9 s
calling	60 %	50 s	30 s
Completion time :		61 s	

Table 2. Estimated completion time with best transition

Device-1				Device-2			
State	CPU availability	Time in the State	Effective execution	State	CPU availability	Time in the State	Effective execution
charging	100 %	40 s	40 s	*idle*	90 %	10 s	9 s
				charging	100 %	31 s	31 s
Completion TIme :	40 s			Completion time :		41 s	

consider the path involving only the *charging* state, which always guarantees it 100 % CPU availability for the external job and can bid with value 40. On the other hand, Device-2 would consider the path from *idle* to the highest CPU available state, *i.e. charging*. Table 2 shows the estimated completion times in this case and the offloader may again select Device-1 for offloading.

Typically a state transition is triggered by external events, for example, incoming call, user's operation, etc. The execution paths chosen for bid as depicted above is therefore too optimistic. Consider the following scenario. At the time of execution of the external task, Device-1 remains in *charging state* for 1 time unit, in *idle* state for 10 time units and then moves to the *calling state* and remains there. The execution completion time is shown in Table 1. The device thus completes 40 time units of computation in an effective duration of 61 time units and exceeds the deadline. This shows that only the best timing is not always a good candidate to decide on the bid, since a penalty is involved. A rational owner should ideally take this into account. On the other hand, a pessimistic strategy considering a maximal timing path may yield a completion time

Table 3. Estimated completion time with AP

Device-1				Device-2			
State	CPU availability	Time in the State	Effective execution	State	CPU availability	Time in the State	Effective execution
charging	100 %	30 s	30 s	*idle*	90 %	10 s	9 s
idle	90 %	10.1 s	10 s	*charging*	100 %	31 s	31 s
Completion time :	41.1 s			Completion time :		41 s	

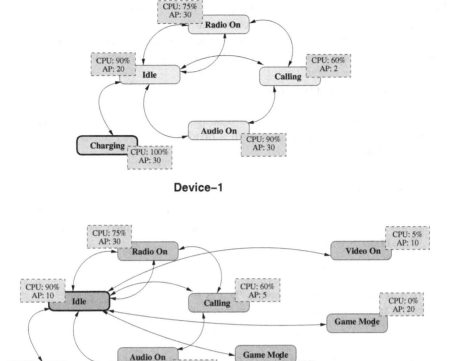

Fig. 2. Usage model with average permanence

beyond the deadline. In either of the strategies, the path chosen for computation of a bid may not be the actual path taken during execution of the external task.

A more realistic estimate can be obtained by considering paths induced by the average usage by the user. To incorporate this, we further associate with each state an *average permanence* (AP) value [11] and a transition probability on each out-going edge. AP implies the average time the device stays at the associated state. The revised model of the devices is depicted in Fig. 2. Now we apply the same optimistic bid selection method based on the AP on states, assuming all transitions are equally likely. Also for each path we compute the probability of taking the path. This probability is a measure of confidence of the device taking that path. Device-1 chooses the path *charging* → *idle* which is associated with confidence value of 1 (since there is a single transition from *charging* state). The best confidence value ($1/8 = 0.125$ considering each of the 8 outgoing transitions are equally likely) for Device-2 occurs for the path *idle* → *charging*. The completion time is computed in Table 3. The offloader may choose

Device-2 based on the better bid proposed by it. The example above assumes the transitions are equally likely. However in reality, they may not be so, as we show in our experiments. We can learn the transition likelihood probabilities from user usage data and utilize them to enrich the bid above with these values.

3   Proposed Methodology

In this section, we present a detailed description of our approach. As discussed earlier, we have an application J with a deadline Δ. Each device has an usage based model as described below.

3.1   Usage Model of Device

We model the mobile device as a Probabilistic Finite State Machine with Average Permanence (PFSM-AP). The PFSM-AP model is defined as a tuple $\mathcal{U} = < \mathbf{S}, \mathcal{I}, \mathbf{T}, \lambda, \mathbf{H}, \mathbf{C} >$ where,

- $\mathbf{S}$ denotes the set of states.
- $\mathcal{I}$ is the set of external events.
- $\mathbf{T}$ denotes the transition function $\mathbf{T} \subseteq \mathbf{S} \times \mathbf{S} \times \mathcal{I}$.
- λ is the transition probability function, defined as

$$\lambda\left(s_i, s_j\right) = p_{ij} \quad \text{where,} \quad s_i, s_j \in \mathbf{T}$$

such that, for each s_i the sum of the transition probabilities on its outgoing edges is 1.
- $\mathbf{H} : \mathbf{S} \rightarrow \Re$ is the average permanence function, defined as,

$$\mathbf{H}\left(s_i\right) = t_i \quad \text{where,} \ s_i \in \mathbf{S}, t_i \in \Re$$

$\Re$ is the set of reals.
- $\mathbf{C} : \mathbf{S} \rightarrow [0,1]$ is the CPU availability fraction (or equivalently availability percentage as used in the example).

3.2   Detailed Methodology

The objective of the PFSM-AP described above is to characterize the device based on its free CPU cycles and duration the device is likely to remain in that state, as depicted in the motivating examples in Sect. 2.

Given a mobile device D_i with a PFSM-AP model $\mathcal{U}_i = < \mathbf{S}_i, \mathcal{I}_i, \mathbf{T}_i, \lambda_i, \mathbf{H}_i, \mathbf{C}_i >$, a task J with its dataset, the device needs to calculate its bid which can be presented to the offloader by the owner. Let us assume the task needs an estimated execution time of w_i on this device. As discussed earlier, this estimate is agnostic to the state model and assumes 100 % CPU utilization. This is where PFSM-AP provides a better estimate. If $w_i > \Delta$, there is no point for the device to participate in the bid (intuitively there is no path in which the task can be completed within deadline even with 100 % utilization all-through). The case is interesting only when $w_i \le \Delta$. The principle behind our bid computation algorithm is as follows.

Algorithm 1. Bid computation on a mobile device

---

    input : J : The task to be executed along with dataset
    input : Δ : Deadline for the tasks
    input : $\mathbf{s}$: Present state of the device D_i
    begin

1   Compute w_i of J;
2   **if** $w_i > \Delta$ **then** No bid and return ;
3       $b_t \leftarrow \varnothing$ // best time
4       $\Pi_i \leftarrow$ paths (π_j^i) on $\mathcal{U}_i$ satisfying C1 and C2;
5   **for** each path $p_j^i \in \Pi_i$ **do**
          if $\rho^i(p_j^i) < \Upsilon$ **then** continue ;
          $t \leftarrow \delta^i(p_j^i)$;
          if $(b_t > t)$ **then** $b_t \leftarrow t$;
6   Bid with b_t;

---

1. Examine all possible paths in the PFSM-AP graph from the state the device is in, at the time when bids are invited
2. Compute expected completion times on each of these paths considering that states in the path have different CPU availability
3. Exclude paths where the expected completion time is greater than the deadline
4. Exclude paths where the corresponding confidence value is less than some pre-determined threshold
5. Determine a path which meets the deadline best and present the expected completion time on that path as the bid.

Execution Path Enumeration. Given the state machine of a device and the current state, there are potentially infinite number of paths from the start state. However, we are interested only in those paths where computation of the task can be completed within the advertised deadline. Since deadline is finite, such paths (excluding cycles involving states which offer 0 % computing capacity) are also finite in number. Let us denote this set of paths as $\Pi_i = \{\pi_1^i, \pi_2^i, \ldots \pi_k^i\}$ for the device D_i where k denotes the number of such deadline-constrained paths. A path π_j^i is a state transition sequence, $< s_1^i, s_2^i, \ldots s_m^i >$, in the underlying PFSM-AP of D_i. We assume transitions to be 0-delay.

For each path $\pi_j^i =< s_1^i, s_2^i, \ldots s_m^i >$, we compute the following attributes which are useful for our algorithm.

– *Path execution time* $(\delta^i(\pi_j^i))$: The execution time of the application on the path π_j^i

$$\delta^i(\pi_j^i) = Z + \frac{w_i - Z}{\mathbf{C}(s_m^i)} \quad \text{where, } Z = \sum_{l=1}^{m-1} \left(\mathbf{H}(s_l^i) \times \mathbf{C}(s_l^i) \right)$$

The value of Z denotes the execution time on the first $m - 1$ states on the path. The other term in $\delta^i(\pi_j^i)$ is the time required to finish the remaining fraction of work in the last state (s_m^i).

- *Confidence Value* $(\rho^i(\pi_j^i))$: The confidence value on the path π_j^i is computed as a product of the likelihood values on the transitions (assuming transition probabilities to be independent for simplicity) as below:

$$\rho^i(\pi_j^i) = \prod_{l=2}^{m} \lambda_i(s_{l-1}, s_l)$$

The following constraints are to be applied on valid paths to bound the search.

- *Task completion constraint*:

$$\mathbf{C1}: \quad \sum_{l=1}^{m} \mathbf{C}(s_l^i) \times \mathbf{H}(s_l) \geq w_i$$

where the term $\mathbf{C}(s_l^i) \times \mathbf{H}(s_l)$ denotes the quantum of computation done at the state s_l^i considering the average permanence and the CPU availability. The summation on the left hand side yields the total computation time on a given path. So the above constraint essentially limits our computation to paths whose time is more than w_i.

- *Deadline constraints*: Paths where the completion time of the task is more than Δ are not useful for bidding. Therefore,

$$\mathbf{C2}: \quad \delta^i(\pi_j^i) < \Delta$$

We modify the standard depth-first traversal [4] algorithm with constraints **C1** and **C2**, and also ignoring self loops involving a state with 0% CPU availability. These conditions bounds the length of the paths (step 4 of Algorithm 1) to finite value since w_i is finite. Therefore the algorithm terminates in finite time. The paths enumerated in the state graph are associated with different confidence values. A path with low confidence of traversing should be excluded to avoid penalties. An example of such a computation was presented in Sect 2. Algorithm 1 uses a threshold Υ to filter out such paths.

4   Experiments and Results

Experiments with our proposed job-offloading technique were carried out in three phases on a set of seven mobile devices which seven of our employees volunteered to donate. The description of the devices are shown in Table 4. Our system had access to two Sony Experia devices, three Samsung Galaxy devices, and one each of Google Nexus and Micromax Canvas devices.

Table 4. Configuration of Mobile devices used in our experiment

		OS	CPU	
Device name	Model	Android Ver	core @ clock speed	Memory
Samsung Galaxy	GT-S6802	2.3.6	Single Core @ 832 MHz	512 MB
Sony Experia L	C2104	4.1.2	Dual Core @ 1 GHz	1 GB
Micromax Canvas 2+	A110Q	4.2 (Jelly Bean)	Quad Core @ 1.2 GHz	1 GB
Google Nexus	Nexus-4	4.2 (Jelly Bean)	Quad Core @ 1.5 GHz	2 GB

4.1 Model Generation

During the first phase of the experiment, we worked towards building the PFSM-AP models of the mobile devices participating in our experiments. We developed and installed a small android application which collects device usage trace data (like free memory and CPU usage) for every second and logs into the devices. The users carried this application, active in their devices, and the application gathered data for a week. We then collected this data and analyzed them offline to discover PFSM-AP models. We extracted the percentage of free CPU cycles only from the data and applied clustering to build the PFSM-AP. The outline of the clustering technique is shown in Algorithm 2.

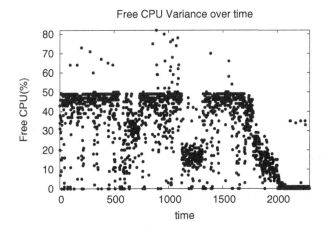

Fig. 3. CPU usage pattern

The first phase of the algorithm creates an initial set of clusters based on the CPU availability (data gathered as % of free CPU cycles). In this part, we create buckets of different sizes and assign data points to these buckets. For example, when bucket size is 2, data points in $[0, 1]$ are put into one bucket, points in $[2, 3]$ are put in another bucket, and so on. Since the CPU availability values are in $[0, 100]$, we will have 50 buckets to be considered in this case. After creation of these buckets, we compute the deviation of the number of points in these buckets. The exact values of a and b are chosen depending on the number of observations. It is intuitively obvious that a very high bucket size will create too few clusters. Then we choose the bucket size where the deviation is the highest. Empirically this captures points which are close in one cluster. This serves as an initial cluster to be refined in the subsequent phase of the algorithm. In the next phase, we identify clusters (formed in the initial stage) where membership count is low. The parameter Δ is used as the threshold of count of data points in a cluster and any cluster having number of data points less than the threshold are removed and data points in this cluster are reassigned to other clusters. The threshold is Δ percent of the average data points in clusters. The Δ value is small and in our experiment $\Delta = 5$. The value indicates cluster removal threshold is 5 % of the average cluster size. We applied this clustering algorithm on the system traces collected from mobile devices by our mobile application and constructed the PFSM-AP models of these devices. Figure 3 shows a part of the CPU usage pattern of one of the users and the PFSM-AP model constructed thereafter is shown in Fig. 4.

Algorithm 2. PFSM-AP Model Determination

---

begin

    // Initial Clustering : Empirical Analysis

1   **for** $i \leftarrow a$ **to** b **do**

        cluster data points in buckets of size i;

        $\delta_i \leftarrow$ deviation of cluster size values;

2   Choose i^* $s.t.$ δ_{i*} is the highest in $\{\delta_i : a \leq i \leq b\}$;

3    $\mathcal{C} \leftarrow$ cluster data points in clusters of size i^*;

    // Reclustering

    while *No change in cluster composition* **do**

4        $\{CC_k\} \leftarrow$ Compute cluster centers of $\mathcal{C}$;

5   Recluster data points around cluster centers $\{CC_k\}$ based on the distance of a point from cluster centers;

6   Remove a cluster if the size of the cluster is less than $\frac{\text{No of data points}}{|\mathcal{C}|} \times \frac{\Delta}{100}$;

7   Each cluster is a state and the mean value is the percentage of the free CPU cycles;

    // Transition and Transition Probabilities

8   Traverse the data and compute average time in a state;

9   Traverse the data and compute number of transitions for all pairs of states;

10   Compute the transition probability of an edge $s \rightarrow d$ as the fraction of transitions from state s to d against all transitions out of state s, $i.e.$, $\frac{\text{No. of transitions from } s \text{ to } d}{\sum_{\forall p} \text{No. of transitions from } s \text{ to } p}$

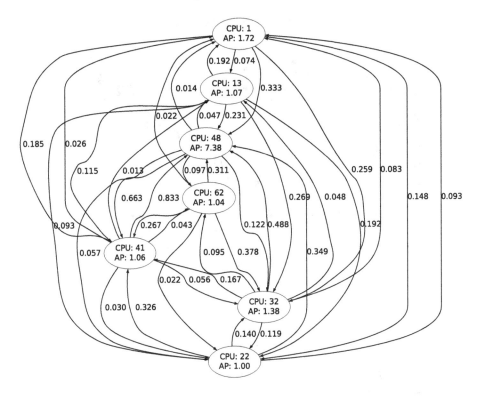

Fig. 4. PFSM-AP model

4.2 Simulation of Offloading System

We developed a simulation system to observe the behavior of our task offloading infrastructure. We simulated the offloader system and also the task execution on device VMs. The VMs simulate the PFSM-AP models generated from the traces on the mobile devices. The simulated offloader generated tasks of various kinds to be offloaded to these devices. When awarded a task, a device simulates task execution while simulating the state transition based on its model. For each task type, 100 similar tasks were generated and offloaded to devices. The number of these tasks successfully completed on the devices (*i.e.* completed within the given deadline) are recorded and used for computing performance of the offloading method. The performance of the system is simply the fraction of the offloaded jobs successfully completed by the bidding device.

In our simulation system, the offloader generates jobs of various durations, assigns various deadlines to these jobs, invites bid and submits the job to the winning device. Figure 5(a) shows the job offloading performance for job execution times ranging from 4 to 29, and deadlines varying from 2× to 10× of the job execution time. The horizontal axis of the figure represents variation in job execution duration, while the vertical axis represents the offloading performance. The offloading performance, as discussed earlier, is the fraction of the number

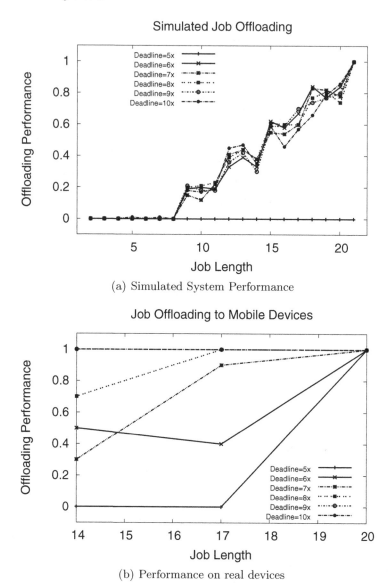

(a) Simulated System Performance

(b) Performance on real devices

Fig. 5. Experiment results

of jobs the infrastructure could complete by offloading them to winning devices and the devices subsequently could complete execution within given deadline. A value of 0 as performance indicates that the infrastructure was unable to effectively utilize any device for computation. On the other hand a value of 1 indicates the infrastructure could execute all jobs using the devices. Please note that in our experiment the infrastructure offloaded one job at a time and concurrent offloading was not considered.

It is evident from the experiment that, when task runtime is low, success rate of task-offloading is low as well. Also when the deadline is very tight in comparison to execution time of the task, task offloading is not beneficial. When deadline is tight, if the device cannot operate with near 100 % CPU availability all the time, the corresponding completion time is more likely to overshoot the task deadline. When the deadline is very relaxed (*e.g.* approximately 7× that of job execution length) offloading works well and is beneficial.

4.3 Working with Real Devices

In this phase, we evaluated the performance of our offloading system with an offloader which has the seven devices, described earlier, for it to exploit. For this experiment, we used an application which estimates the value of π, which is written as a native android application. The application is a compute intensive one. Longer the application runs, the estimation is better. We conducted the experiment for various job durations and the job duration was varied by changing the desired accuracy of π calculation. Figure 5(b) shows the job offloading performance of the system. The result of this experiment shows that jobs with relaxed deadlines are good candidates for offloading.

5   Related Work

In recent times, there has been significant research on the theme of Mobile Cloud Computing (MCC) which propose the use of a collaborative computing infrastructure consisting of mobile devices and a backend cloud. MAUI [5] and CloneCloud [3] are two notable systems which use a backend computing infrastructure for collaborative job execution. Several other articles as well address the problem of workflow partitioning in an MCC setting [16]. The basic intuition behind these partitioning strategies is to decide on the best platform (mobile device or cloud) to execute each sub-task of a given workflow with an objective of optimizing the cost (in terms of energy, time, communication, etc.).

Authors in [14] address the problem of intermittent disconnection and analyzes the problem using Markov-chain model. Markov Decision Process (MDP) has been used to model the behavior of mobile devices to achieve objectives like optimization of power usage [9]. However in our case, we resort to a simpler model since we do not need the full capabilities of an MDP for this problem. A comprehensive survey of Mobile Cloud Computing (MCC) can be found in [6]. Systems like *Misco* [7] and *Hyrax* [12] extend MapReduce so that computation capabilities of mobile devices can be utilized. *Serendipity* is a task dissemination system over a mobile grid [18]. The system relies on collaboration among mobile devices using WiFi connection to share collective computation power. The design of the system accepts that disconnection of devices is a norm and its underlying architecture incorporates the assumption. We consider a more generic usage model driven scenario in this work.

6 Conclusion and Future Work

Proposals of using mobile devices to augment computing infrastructure have been proposed in literature. In this paper we present a basic scheme of job offloading on a mobile grid. Mechanisms for automatic learning of likelihood probabilities, using more advanced models for analysis (*e.g.* MDP), execution time estimation, designing more effective bidding, reward-penalty schemes may be looked into for future explorations. In this paper we also assume the network and the devices are reliable. Issues of fault tolerance in this context are our future research agenda.

References

1. Agarwal, A.: Enterprise smartphone usage trends, June 2011. http://bit.ly/1oIqE1
2. Bonomi, F., Milito, R., Zhu, J., Addepalli, S.: Fog computing and its role in the internet of things. In: Proceedings of the First Edition of the MCC Workshop on Mobile Cloud Computing, pp. 13–16. ACM (2012)
3. Chun, B.-G., Ihm, S., Maniatis, P., Naik, M., Patti, A.: CloneCloud: elastic execution between mobile device and cloud. In: Proceedings of the Sixth Conference on Computer Systems, pp. 301–314. ACM (2011)
4. Cormen, T.H., Stein, C., Rivest, R.L., Leiserson, C.E.: Introduction to Algorithms, 2nd edn. McGraw-Hill Higher Education, Boston (2001)
5. Cuervo, E., Balasubramanian, A., Cho, D.-k., Wolman, A., Saroiu, S., Chandra, R., Bahl, P.: MAUI: making smartphones last longer with code offload. In: Proceedings of the 8th International Conference on Mobile Systems, Applications, and Services, pp. 49–62. ACM (2010)
6. Dinh, H.T., Lee, C., Niyato, D., Wang, P.: A survey of mobile cloud computing: architecture, applications, and approaches. Wireless communications and mobile computing **13**, 1587–1611 (2013)
7. Dou, A., Kalogeraki, V., Gunopulos, D., Mielikainen, T., Tuulos, V.H.: Misco: a mapreduce framework for mobile systems. In: Proceedings of the 3rd International Conference on PErvasive Technologies Related to Assistive Environments, p. 32. ACM (2010)
8. Gordon, M.S., Jamshidi, D.A., Mahlke, S., Mao, Z.M., Chen, X.: Comet: code offload by migrating execution transparently. In: Proceedings of the 10th USENIX Conference on Operating Systems Design and Implementation, OSDI, vol. 12, pp. 93–106 (2012)
9. Jung, E., Maker, F., Cheung, T.L., Liu, X., Akella, V.: Markov decision process (MDP) framework for software power optimization using call profiles on mobile phones. Des. Autom. Embed. Syst. **14**(2), 131–159 (2010)
10. Kosta, S., Aucinas, A., Hui, P., Mortier, R., Zhang, X.: Thinkair: dynamic resource allocation and parallel execution in the cloud for mobile code offloading. In: INFOCOM, 2012 Proceedings IEEE, pp. 945–953. IEEE (2012)
11. Li, X., Gray, A., Jiang, D., Mao, X.: Sufficient and necessary conditions of stochastic permanence and extinction for stochastic logistic populations under regime switching. J. Math. Anal. Appl. **376**(1), 11–28 (2011)
12. Marinelli, E.E.: Hyrax: Cloud Computing on Mobile Devices using MapReduce, September 2009

13. Mukherjee, A., Paul, H.S., Dey, S., Banerjee, A.: Angels for distributed analytics in iot. In: 2014 IEEE World Forum on Internet of Things (WF-IoT), pp. 565–570. IEEE (2014)
14. Park, S.-M., Ko, Y.-B., Kim, J.-H.: Disconnected operation service in mobile grid computing. In: Orlowska, M.E., Weerawarana, S., Papazoglou, M.P., Yang, J. (eds.) ICSOC 2003. LNCS, vol. 2910, pp. 499–513. Springer, Heidelberg (2003)
15. Phan, T., Huang, L., Dulan, C.: Challenge: integrating mobile wireless devices into the computational grid. In: MOBICOM-2002, pp. 271–278 (2002)
16. Rahimi, M.R., Venkatasubramanian, N., Vasilakos, A.V.: MuSIC: mobility-aware optimal service allocation in mobile cloud computing. In: Proceedings of the 2013 IEEE Sixth International Conference on Cloud Computing, CLOUD '13, pp. 75–82. IEEE Computer Society, Washington, DC (2013)
17. Sakr, S.: Nvidia says Tegra-3 is a "PC-class CPU" (2011). http://engt.co/srvibU
18. Shi, C., Lakafosis, V., Ammar, M.H., Zegura, E.W.: Serendipity: enabling remote computing among intermittently connected mobile devices. In: Proceedings of the Thirteenth ACM International Symposium on Mobile Ad Hoc Networking and Computing, pp. 145–154. ACM (2012)
19. Wilhelm, R., Engblom, J., Ermedahl, A., Holsti, N., Thesing, S., Whalley, D., Bernat, G., Ferdinand, C., Heckmann, R., Mitra, T., et al.: The worst-case execution-time problem - Overview of methods and survey of tools. ACM Trans. Embed. Comput. Syst. (TECS) **7**(3), 36 (2008)

An Interaction Balance Based Approach for Autonomic Performance Management in a Cloud Computing Environment

Rajat Mehrotra[1]([⊠]), Srishti Srivastava[2],
Ioana Banicescu[2], and Sherif Abdelwahed[3]

[1] Department of Computer Science, University of Virginia, Charlottesville, VA, USA
rajat@cs.virginia.edu
[2] Department of Computer Science and Engineering,
Mississippi State University, Starkville, MS, USA
srishti@hpc.msstate.edu, ioana@cse.msstate.edu
[3] Department of Electrical and Computer Engineering,
Mississippi State University, Starkville, MS, USA
sherif@ece.msstate.edu

Abstract. In this paper, an autonomic performance management approach is introduced that provides dynamic resource allocation for deploying a set of services over a federated cloud computing infrastructure by considering both, the availability and the demand of the cloud computing resources. This distributed control based approach is developed by using an interaction balance (decomposition-coordination) methodology for interactive bidding of computing resources in cloud computing environment. The primary goals of the proposed approach are to maintain the service level agreements, maximize the profit, and minimize the operating cost for both, the service providers and the cloud brokers. The cloud brokers are considered third party organizations that work as intermediaries between the service providers and the cloud providers to sublet the cloud resources that the cloud brokers rent or lease from a number of cloud providers. The developed approach is novel in applying interaction balance methodology, and giving priority to the profit maximization for both the cloud broker and service providers, while assigning the cloud computing resources.

Keywords: Interaction balance · Autonomic Computing · Cloud broker · Cloud computing

1 Introduction

Recently, research shows an increasing trend towards hosting services in a cloud computing environment in order to eliminate the need for setting up a physical infrastructure, decrease the launching time for a service, provide on demand availability of computing resources, and transfer the management responsibility to the cloud providers, such as Google Apps [7], Amazon Web Services [6],

© Springer International Publishing Switzerland 2014
F. Pop and M. Potop-Butucaru (Eds.): ARMS-CC 2014, LNCS 8907, pp. 52–70, 2014.
DOI: 10.1007/978-3-319-13464-2_5

IBM Cloud [10], and Microsoft Windows Azure [26]. The cloud providers deploy services on multiple computing nodes in accordance with the service level agreements (SLAs) negotiated between the cloud provider and the service provider for a given system resource availability and a specified pay-per-use. According to a survey [9] published in year 2011, only 26 % of the organizations reported improvement in the performance of their applications in a cloud computing environment. The primary reason for this decreased application performance is that these applications (and their various services) require complex configurations of computing, network, and storage resources. Currently, the SLAs between a service provider and a cloud provider cover only resource availability aspects of a cloud computing infrastructure. There is no agreement specifying the application level performance or quality of service (QoS) that the given resources are able to provide to the applications and their underlying services. In general, the designers of service deployment schemes consider multi-dimensional objectives, which are often mutually conflicting in nature. These objectives may include operating costs, SLAs, configuration constraints, resource utilization, availability of the resources, and others. If the deployment scheme is too optimistic (with an underestimation of the resource requirement), it may result in excessive scarcity of resources, leading to the SLA violations. However, in the case of a pessimistic scheme (overestimation of the resource requirement), the deployment may be less efficient with respect to resources, and may result in an increased operating cost for the cloud operation without an increased revenue [22]. Moreover, these deployment schemes are applicable only to the specific application domain and operating conditions. Therefore, the underlying system design process has limited utility, reliability, and scope.

Recently, the use of a third party entity, called a *Cloud Broker*, has become popular for selecting the appropriate cloud provider in the interest of service providers, and deploy their services either in a single or in a federated cloud infrastructure [18,20]. In other words, the cloud brokers work as intermediaries between cloud providers and service providers to select the appropriate cloud provider, negotiate the contract conditions, and facilitate the deployment of a service in the federated cloud infrastructure. In more advanced cases, a cloud broker can rent the resources from multiple cloud providers and host a service in multiple cloud providers; then, a cloud broker can charge the service provider for these cloud resources at higher cost than the actual cost paid to the cloud providers. The business and profit models for the cloud brokers are still evolving and research is ongoing for its development.

This paper considers a federated cloud computing environment, where a cloud broker has the ability to integrate resources from more than one cloud provider to support several service providers [18]. The cloud broker pays the usage (base) cost of the cloud resources to the cloud provider, and charges the service provider for these resources at some premium on the base cost. In this scenario, the cloud broker and service provider(s) try to maximize their respective profits, such that the service provider aims to satisfy the service level agreements (SLAs) of the services that it hosts by using the minimum amount of hardware resources from the cloud broker, whereas the cloud broker improves its profits by leasing maximum percentage of computing resources to the service providers. These objectives are conflicting and contradictory to each other. In addition, due to unpredictable variations in the computing environment, the incoming web request rate towards the services may exceed its expected value, making it necessary for the service providers to request additional resources from the cloud broker. The service providers must negotiate for these resources with the cloud broker using some pricing scheme to maintain its SLAs while minimizing the cost of the utilized cloud resources. Moreover, the cloud broker may be hosting multiple services that may be requesting additional resources at the same time, leading to a competition among the service providers for obtaining these resources, which are limited in number or quantity. This paper introduces a novel negotiation approach between the cloud broker and the various service providers to compute an optimized allocation of cloud resources. The proposed approach is a proof of concept using an interaction-balanced technique for solving the negotiation problem between the cloud broker and the service providers, and represents a step towards a model-based autonomous deployment of robust, adaptive, and reliable services in a cloud computing environment.

This paper is organized as follows. Research efforts made by other groups are presented in Sect. 2, and the proposed performance management approach is introduced in Sect. 3. The application of the proposed approach in a typical cloud infrastructure is demonstrated in Sect. 4, and the benefits of the approach are highlighted in Sect. 5. Finally, conclusions and future work are presented in Sect. 6.

2   Related Work

2.1   Resource Allocation in Cloud Computing Environment

Efficient resource allocation is one of the most challenging problems faced by the cloud infrastructure as a service (IaaS) providers. Academia and research communities have proposed several new technologies for dynamic resource allocation in this domain to maintain the SLAs. A dynamic resource allocation method is developed by considering the SLAs between the user and the Software as a Service (SaaS) provider while allocating resources [27]. The authors ensure that SaaS providers are able to manage the dynamic change in customer's requests, mapping customer requests to infrastructure level parameters, and handling the heterogeneity of the Virtual Machines (VMs). This approach also considers the customers' QoS parameters, such as response time, and the infrastructure level parameters such as service initiation time. However, the burden of evaluating SLAs between the user and the SaaS providers may become a bottleneck for the IaaS cloud provider when the number of SaaS providers is considerably large. Another prominent approach of resource allocation that has been investigated by researchers, is priority driven resource allocation [8,19]. These approaches are classified in two categories: (i) user priority based and (ii) resource priority based. These approaches only consider resource allocation to a single service provider for solving the load balancing problem. A neural network based resource allocation is introduced in [5], where authors focus on maximizing the resource utilization via an efficient resource allocation strategy provided by the genetic algorithms. However, this approach targets a system where the resources are not scarce. There is no competition among the users for obtaining a set of required resources. Another approach uses genetic algorithms to find the optimal resource allocation and assigns resources to the clients or users based on the outcome of the genetic algorithm [2].

Recently, researchers have focused on cloud resource allocation by applying auctioning schemes to the SaaS providers. In these auctioning schemes, the cloud IaaS providers accept requests from SaaS providers and perform an auction of the cloud resources. The highest bidder will be allocated the set of auctioned resources. To deal with such complexities of the resource allocation problem in a dynamic and evolutionary environment, a number of researchers have focused on a study of game theoretical approaches [12]. Game-theory based resource allocation mechanisms have received a considerable amount of attention in cloud computing to solve the optimization problem of resource allocation. However, the recent survey shows that these techniques do not take into consideration essential parameters such as, fairness, resource availability, service deadline and execution efficiency, resource reliability, and others. More often, the game-theoretic approaches focus on solving the cost optimization problems. A combinatorial auction-based mechanism has also been investigated for the allocation and pricing of VM instances in cloud computing platforms [28]. This approach uses three different schemes: fixed-price scheme, linear programming, and a greedy scheme. However, this approach only considers maximizing the user gains as a single constraint that limits the allocation of each type of VM to a pre-determined value.

2.2   Significance of Cloud Brokers

The approaches discussed in the previous subsection present solutions to address the challenges of efficient resource management between a cloud provider and a (or many) service provider(s). However, these approaches do not address the resource management problems in an enterprise framework, which makes use of services provided by various cloud providers to fulfill SLAs. The main advantage of using the cloud brokers in this scenario, is their ability to integrate more than one cloud provider. These capabilities need to be exposed to enable the fulfillment of all orchestration requirements. According to the recent literature, due to the increase in the demand for a federated cloud computing framework, efficient management and operation of cloud computing environment is the most prominent requirement [18, 21]. The cloud brokers are the most promising solution available to deal with the complexities of a federated cloud environment. Therefore, there is a tremendous need for applying efficient resource allocation and management in a cloud broker model.

Recently, researchers in this domain have proposed various solutions to address the problem at different levels, such as, managing the information of a large number of cloud service providers via a unique indexing technique [24], enabling the cloud-computing services broker to use derivative contracts in combination to reliably providing cheaper resources to the consumer and predicting future usage [21], proposing novel algorithms for a secure cloud bursting and aggregation operation, using a secure sharing mechanism such that the cloud resources are shared in a secure manner among different cloud environments [11], and others. However, none of these research directions address the issues of dynamic resource allocation and performance management of hosted services in a cloud broker model. In addition, these resource allocation and performance management issues become more critical in the case of large number of hosted services with limited amount of cloud resources. In these situations, maintaining the SLAs of the service providers' becomes crucial and requires an autonomic performance management approach which can dynamically reallocate the cloud resources among services while maximizing the profitability of the cloud broker.

2.3   Large Scale Control-Based Performance Management Approaches

Large scale control-based methods have recently emerged as promising ways to automate certain system management tasks encountered in distributed computing systems. Algorithms have been developed for optimal control of large scale systems by decomposing the large systems into a number of interconnected subsystems. Thus, the system wide optimization problem is also divided into a number of subsystem optimization problems. These subsystems coordinate with each other through a coordinator using interaction inputs, and thus achieve the system wide performance objectives. These interaction inputs are applied to each subsystem in the form of constraints. These "decomposition and coordination" strategies are primarily implemented in two ways: Interaction Balance (Goal Coordination) and Interaction Prediction (Model Coordination) [25]. Both of these approaches have been applied successfully to a number of large scale systems, where subsystems are "coupled with each other in both system dynamics and system wide performance objectives" [25].

Furthermore, application performance issues in cloud broker environment can be addressed by service providers through developing service specific controllers that can manage the web service requirements for computing, network, and storage resources. These service level controllers can be designed, developed, and deployed by the service providers at each service independent of the cloud level controllers. The cloud level controllers are deployed by the cloud brokers (or providers) to ensure resource availability and minimum downtime for the deployed service as negotiated in SLAs with the service providers. Thus service providers can choose and customize their own control policies inside service level controllers according to the service requirements.

Contribution of this paper: In this paper, a distributed control-based performance management approach is developed for performance management of services hosted in distributed cloud broker environment. The proposed algorithm utilizes the interaction balance based management approach, where each service is *decoupled* from other services with respect to system dynamics, while *coupled* in terms of overall deployment wide operating cost functions by limited amount of system resources in a cloud computing infrastructure. In this performance management approach, we first dynamically allocate the computational resources to all of the service providers through an interaction balance based approach, and then the service level controllers utilize the allocated resources for service deployment to maintain the SLAs their respective services. Important results from prior work on the distributed control of large scale systems [15,16,23,25] are utilized in this paper, where the main idea is of cooperation among multiple independent services to optimize a global cost function under certain constraints (limitation of resources) by independently optimizing the local cost function at each service. Based on our survey, until now, there is no published research or study about applying the interaction balance method for optimal control of service providers and cloud broker (or provider) profit maximization in cloud computing systems. Therefore, our work is a novel contribution to this problem domain.

3   A Distributed Control-Based Performance Management Approach Using the Interaction Balance Principle

In this paper, a single cloud broker interacts with multiple service providers during auctioning of the available cloud computing resources. In this situation, the cloud broker broadcasts the initial unit price β_{ini} of the resource per unit time to the service providers. Service providers solve their control problem by using their own utility function, compute the optimal value of a cloud resource, and request the resource from the cloud broker. If the total amount of resource requested by the service providers is greater than the available resource, the cloud broker increases the unit price of the resource, otherwise the cloud broker reduces the price to encourage the service providers to reserve a higher amount (or number) of resources. The cloud broker sends the updated unit price to the service providers; the service providers again compute the required amount of resource on the updated price. This cycle continues until either the cloud broker sub-lets all of its resources (or very small percentage ϵ left unassigned), or the unit price becomes lower than the minimum (or threshold) price β_{min}, or the service providers refuse to pay the current price considered as β_{max}. Here, $\beta_{min} \leq \beta_{ini} \leq \beta(k) \leq \beta_{max}$, where $\beta(k)$ is the unit price of the cloud resources during time sample k.

In this scenario, N services need to be deployed in the cloud infrastructure through a cloud broker as shown in Fig. 1. The proposed management approach is based on the decomposition of the global profit maximization problem of cloud broker in to N sub-problems, which are further solved by each service provider. These service providers are contesting for total cloud resources $U(k)$ at a particular time instance k. Therefore, in case of limited resources, the resources acquired by the i-th service provider will impact the resource available to all the other service providers j (where $j \neq i$) because they are competing for the same type of cloud resource. The state dynamics at each service provider i can be described by the following set of equations.

$$\hat{q}_i(k+1) = \left[q_i(k) + \hat{\omega}_i(k)) - \frac{u_i(k)T}{\hat{c}_i(k)} \right]^+ \tag{1}$$

$$\hat{r}_i(k+1) = (1 + \hat{q}_i(k+1)) \frac{\hat{c}_i(k)}{u_i(k+1)} \tag{2}$$

$$u_i(k) = \alpha_i(k) U(k) \tag{3}$$

where $[a]^+ = \max(0, a)$, $q_i(k)$ is the local queue size of the service i, and $\hat{\omega}_i(k)$ is the expected arrival rate of web requests at the service. $\hat{q}_i(k+1)$ is the expected queue level of the service i, $\hat{r}_i(k+1)$ is the expected response time, T is sampling interval, and $u_i(k)$ is the amount of computational resources (in frequency) acquired by the i-th service provider as fraction $\alpha_i(k)$ from the total available cloud resource $U(k)$. $\hat{c}_i(k)$ is the predicted average service time per request at one unit of computational resource (1 GHz. frequency).

These Eqs. (1, 2, and 3) represent the aggregate performance behavior of the service providers with respect to available computing resources $u_i(k)$, incoming workload $\omega_i(k)$, and existing queue size $q_i(k)$. The actual i-th service deployment

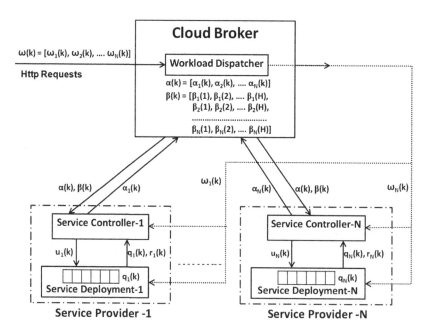

Fig. 1. A Two-level distributed control structure for resource allocation and performance management

problem on multiple computing nodes, and the resource allocation map among these computing nodes is not considered in this paper. However, this problem has already been addressed by the authors previously in a very generic manner [15,16]. Similarly, the problem of allocating the desired resources to each of the service providers by the cloud broker via an appropriate placement map, is also not addressed in this paper. This paper considers the computational resources as a chunk of resources, while solving specific control problems.

The operating cost of the service provider i for a look ahead horizon of H steps, $J_i(k)$ includes SLA violation penalty and renting cost of the cloud resources as expressed in Eq. 4. The renting cost of the cloud resources depends on its computational resource $u_i(k)$ (CPU core frequency) and represented as $E(u_i(k))$. A_i, B_i, and C_i are user defined norm weights. To include the effect of the coordinated goal, the operating cost J_i at the service provider i is indirectly coupled with all the other service providers through limited cloud resources as shown in Eq. 5. Therefore, changes in $u_i(k)$ at service i affects the cost function $J_i(k)$ as well as $J_j(k)$, where $j \neq i$.

$$J_i(k) = \sum_{k=1}^{H} \|q_i(k+1) - q_i^s\|_{A_i} + \|r_i(k+1) - r_i^s\|_{B_i} + \|E(u_i(k))\|_{C_i} \quad (4)$$

$$u_i(k) = \alpha_i(k)\, U(k) \quad (5)$$

$$P(k) = \beta(k) \sum_{i=1}^{N} u_i(k) - \beta_{min}(k)U(k) \quad (6)$$

Here, $k = 1, 2, .., H$ represents the sampling instances in the trajectory of the system operation. According to this quadratic cost function in Eq. 4, the service providers are penalized for the number of the requests remaining in the queue $q_i(k)$ and the average response time $r_i(k)$ observed at the service providers. Therefore, q_i^s is generally set to *zero* for the complete depletion of the queue, and r_i^s is set according to the SLAs. Also, $P(k)$ (in Eq. 6) represents the profitability of the cloud broker for acquiring the cloud resources, and then subletting them out to the service providers. $U(k)$ represents the total resources offered for auction at time instance k.

As described previously, the profitability of the cloud broker will be maximized if it allocates the maximum (close to 100 %) available resources to the service providers. In this process, the cloud broker may have to decrease the unit price $\beta(k)$ (from the initial unit price β_{ini}) of the cloud resources too in order to encourage the service providers for extra resource allocation. Otherwise, the cloud broker can also increase the unit price of a resource (from the initial unit price β_{ini}) when there are not enough resources available to satisfy the requirement of all the service providers. The total revenue of the cloud provider from Eq. 6 can be maximized by having the perfect balance of unit price $\beta(k)$ with total allocated cloud resource $\sum_{i=1}^{N} u_i(k)$.

Therefore, the overall cloud resource optimization problem is : *find the optimal value for unit price $\beta(k)$ of cloud resources and resource fraction $\alpha_i(k)$*

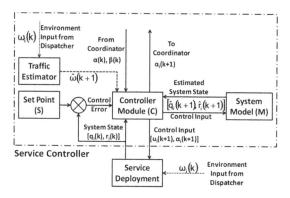

Fig. 2. Service provider level control structure

at each service provider, such that the cloud broker can maximize its profits while service providers maintain their own profitability, SLAs, and operational constraints.

3.1 Problem Decomposition

The cloud broker considered here hosts N service providers, which are coupled only through the cloud resources $u_i(k)$ and cloud level cost function $J(k)$. The cloud level cost function $J(k)$ is the sum of the cost functions related to each service provider i as $J_i(k)$ in Eq. 4. For a proper decomposition, an interaction variable $Z_i(k)$ must be defined at the service provider i to represent the effect of the service provider dynamics on the global cost. $Z_i(k)$ is chosen as the sum of the fractions α_j^* of the cloud resources acquired by other service providers j ($\forall j, j \neq i$) as follows. That is, $Z_i(k) = \sum_{j \neq i}^{N} \alpha_j^*(k)$. The constraint at the service provider i is $\alpha_i(k) = 1 - Z_i(k)$ or $\sum_{j=1, j \neq i}^{N} \alpha_j^*(k) + \alpha_i(k) = 1$. The Lagrangian of each service provider L_i can be represented as follows.

$$L_i(k) = J_i(k) + \sum_{k=1}^{H} \beta_i(k)(1 - \alpha_i(k) - \sum_{j \neq i}^{N} \alpha_j^*(k)) \qquad (7)$$

where $\beta_i \in R^H$ is the price vector corresponding to the service provider i that is extracted from the Lagrange multiplier vector β received from the cloud broker (see Fig. 1), where $\beta \in R^{NH}$. The price vector β is chosen as Lagrange multiplier here because it reflects the change in price with respect to the constraints of total acquired resources ($\sum_{i=1}^{N} \alpha_i^*(k)$) by the service provider. If service providers miss the constraint negatively ($1 < \sum_{i=1}^{N} \alpha_i^*(k)$), the Lagrange multiplier β will increase which is equivalent to increasing the price of the resources if the demand is higher than the availability. Similarly, when constraint is missed positively ($1 > \sum_{i=1}^{N} \alpha_i^*(k)$), the Lagrange multiplier β will decrease, which is the same as decreasing the price of the resources if the demand is lower than the availability to encourage maximum allocation.

The Lagrangian $L(k)$ for the cost function $J(k)$ can be represented as sum of $L_i(k)$: $L(k) = \sum_{i=1}^{N} L_i(k)$. The overall problem of minimizing cost function J can be decomposed in to N first level problems of minimizing L_i, such that Eq. 1 is satisfied with $q_i(1) = 0$. The problem at the cloud broker level can be expressed as updating the value of β, so that the interaction error (see Eq. 9) can become less than a pre-defined small value ϵ, where ϵ can be chosen in percentage of the resource not assigned to any of the service provides (5 %). It indicates that cloud broker will keep running the auction until at least 95 % (or maximum 105 %) of the available resources ($U(k)$) are desired by the service providers. Once the auction is complete, all the service providers will receive resources at the current per unit price $\beta(k)$.

Algorithm 1. Predictive Control Algorithm at the Service Provider-i: $PredictiveControl_i(k)$

Input: Service Provider queue $q_i(k)$, Prediction Horizon H,
Input: Total amount of cloud resource available for auction $U(k)$,
Input: β and $\alpha_j^{*(l)}(k)$ received from the cloud broker,
Input: $\hat{\omega}_i(k)$ estimated by the traffic estimator
Input: Fraction Set at the service provider i, $F_i = [F_{i1}, F_{i2}, ..., F_{iR}]$
Input: Resource share expected at the service provider i, $\alpha_i^l = [\alpha_i^l(1), \alpha_i^l(2), .., \alpha_i^l(H)]$

1: service provider state $x_i(k) = [q_i(k)\ r_i(k)]$
2: $s_k := x(k)$, $Cost(k) = 0$
3: **for all** fraction set $f \in F_i$ **do**
4:    $\alpha_i^l(1) = \alpha_i^l(2) = .. = \alpha_i^l(H) = f$ /* Same resource share at each step */
5:    **for all** k within prediction horizon of depth H **do**
6:       $s_{k+1} := \phi$
7:       **for all** $x \in s_k$ **do**
8:          Compute $\hat{q}_i(k+1)$ /* using Equation 1 */
9:          Compute $\hat{r}_i(k+1)$ /* using Equation 2 */
10:          Compute $L_i(k+1)$ /* using Equation 7 */
11:          $Cost(k+1) := Cost(k) + L_i(k+1)$
12:          $\hat{x} = [\hat{q}_i(k+1)\ \hat{r}_i(k+1)]$
13:          $s_{k+1} := s_{k+1} \cup \{\hat{x}\}$
14:       **end for**
15:       $k := k + 1$
16:    **end for**
17: **end for**
18: Find $x_{min} \in s_N$ having minimum $Cost(k)$
19: Choose f with minimum $L_i(k)$, where $f = \alpha_i^{*(l)} = [\alpha_i^{*(l)}(k), .., \alpha_i^{*(l)}(k+H-1)]$
20: **return** $\alpha_i^{*(l)}$

3.2   Service Provider Level Control

At the service provider level, the Lagrangian L_i is minimized using service dynamics (Eqs. 2 and 3) with the cloud resource as control input $u_i(k)$. We create a uniform discretization for the resource fraction α_i, and with that determine the optimal value of the control inputs $u_i(k)$, which minimizes $L_i(k)$ by using the following steps.

1. Use $\beta_i^l(k)$ and $\alpha_j^{*(l)}(k)$ (where $j \neq i$) as received from the cloud broker to compute the optimal sequence of $(\alpha_i^{*(l)}(k))$ over the horizon $k \in [1, H]$ by using Algorithm 1, which minimizes the Lagrangian $L_i(k)$ in Eq. 7 through a tree search method [1]. Here, l indicates the iteration instance between the service provider and the coordinator within time sample k.
2. Forward the optimal values of $\alpha_i^{*(l)}$ to the cloud broker.

3.3   Cloud Broker Level Control

At the cloud broker level, the goal is to update the values of the Lagrange multipliers β to decrease the interaction error e, defined as:

$$e_i^l(k) = 1 - \sum_{j=1}^{N} \alpha_j^{*(l)}(k) \tag{8}$$

$$e^l = \left(e_1^l \; e_2^l \; \ldots \; e_i^l \; \ldots \; e_N^l\right)^T \tag{9}$$

$$e_i^l = \left(e_i^l(1) \; e_i^l(2) \; \ldots \; e_i^l(k) \; \ldots \; e_i^l(H)\right)^T \tag{10}$$

The interaction error vector e is used as a gradient to modify the Lagrange multipliers $\beta(k)$ using the conjugate gradient method [25] as per following set of equations:

$$\beta^{(l+1)}(k) = \beta^{(l)}(k) + \xi^l \, d^l(k) \tag{11}$$

Where, ξ^l represents the step length, and d^l the represents search direction. $d^l(k)$ is calculated using following set of equations with $d^0 = e^0$.

$$d^{l+1}(k) = -e^{l+1}(k) + \sigma^{l+1} \, d^l(k) \tag{12}$$

$$\sigma^{l+1} = \frac{\|e^{l+1}\|}{\|e^l\|} \tag{13}$$

$\|\cdot\|$ denotes the (Cartesian) ℓ_2-norm. The main steps of the algorithm at the cloud broker level are as follows:

1. Set initial values of the Lagrange multipliers vector β as the initial unit price of a resource (β_{ini}), and forward it to the service provider level controllers.

2. The cloud broker uses the values of α_i^* received from the service provider to calculate the interaction error e using Eq. 9.
3. If $\|e^l\|_2 \leq \epsilon$, stop and assign the cloud resource to service providers in requested ratio, else go to next step.
4. Calculate the values of the Lagrange multipliers β for the next iteration by using Eqs. 11, 12, and 13. If calculated value of β is more than the maximum unit price (β_{max}) of the resources, or less than the minimum unit price (β_{min}), stop and assign the requested amount of cloud resources to each service provider. Otherwise, send this updated value of β to the service controllers for solving the service provider level optimization problem. Increment l and jump to Step 2. This exchange of information is shown in Fig. 1.

3.4   Forecasting the Environmental Inputs at Each Service Provider:

These services are deployed in a dynamic and open distributed environment, where the incoming web requests are generated from external users (or clients) that cannot be controlled by the services. In addition, these web requests show a cyclic pattern in the arrival rate based upon the service popularity and time of the day [3]. These web requests vary significantly within a short duration of a few minutes. However, this variation in the arrival rate of the incoming web requests can be estimated within certain accuracy using Autoregressive Moving Average (ARIMA) filters [4] or Kalman filters [13], as done in earlier work [14,17]. In this paper, an ARIMA filter based prediction module is developed to estimate the future environmental input at each of the service providers $\hat{\omega}_i(k)$ (web requests) in Eq. 14, which is similar to the approach used in [14]. This module is shown in Fig. 2.

$$\hat{\omega}_i(k) = \theta(\omega_i(k-1, r)) = \gamma_{i1}\,\omega_i(k-1) + \gamma_{i2}\,\omega_i(k-2) + (1 - (\gamma_{i1} + \gamma_{i2}))\,\bar{\omega}_i(k-3, r) \tag{14}$$

where, γ_{i1} and γ_{i2} are user specified weights on the current and previous arrival rates. $\bar{\omega}(k-3, r)$ represents the average value of the environment inputs between time samples $k-3$ and $k-3-r$. This prediction module continuously monitors the arrival rate of the incoming web requests and estimates their future values at each sample.

4   Performance Management of Service Providers in a Cloud Computing Environment

The proposed interaction balance based resource allocation approach is simulated in Matlab for deriving an optimal resource allocation and manage the performance of four service providers that are hosting their respective service in a cloud computing environment. Details of the simulations are described in the following subsections.

4.1   Service Provider Level Control Setup

The service provider level controller dynamics is shown in Fig. 2. Each of the service providers receives incoming web requests $\omega_i(k)$ from the Dispatcher at the cloud broker during time sample k. Each service deployment processes the incoming web requests by using the allocated computational resource $u_i(k)$, which is a fraction $\alpha_i(k)$ of the computational resource available at the cloud broker. The controller module C receives the current system state $[q_i(k), r_i(k)]$ from the service deployment, future workload arrival rate $\hat{\omega}_i(k+1)$ from the traffic estimator, and the Lagrange multipliers β from the cloud broker. Now, controller module (C) uses the service provider model (M) and the available control algorithms to obtain the optimal value of resource share $\alpha_i(k+1)]$ by using Algorithm 1. The calculated resource share $\alpha_i(k+1)$ is sent back to the cloud broker to calculate the interaction error e.

4.2   Simulation Setup

The simulation settings and the coefficients used in the cost function are shown in Fig. 3(a). The Service provider 3 and 4 are assigned higher penalty for queue size and response time compared to the service provider 1 and 2. Therefore, the service provider 3 and 4 are expected to choose higher amount of computational resource compared to service provider 1 and 2. All of these service providers are assigned lower penalty for resource cost compared to the queue size and the response time, which will force all of these to focus more on the SLAs (queue size and response time) while calculating the optimal values of computational resources.

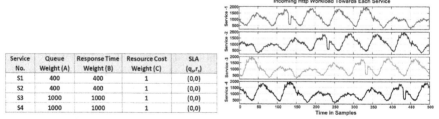

Service No.	Queue Weight (A)	Response Time Weight (B)	Resource Cost Weight (C)	SLA (q_o, r_o)
S1	400	400	1	(0,0)
S2	400	400	1	(0,0)
S3	1000	1000	1	(0,0)
S4	1000	1000	1	(0,0)

(a) The Parameter Values used for the Simulation Experiment.   (b) Simulated Incoming Web Requests Towards Services.

Fig. 3. Simulation parameters and generated web requests for each service provider

During this simulation, different web request workloads (see Fig. 3(b)) are generated for each services by utilizing the 1998 Football World Cup [3] traces. The tolerance value ϵ of the interaction error is set to 0.05 and the lookahead horizon H is set to 2. In addition, the minimum (β_{min}), maximum (β_{max}), and initial (β_{ini}) unit price of cloud computing resource is set to 1000, 10000, and 2500 pricing unit, respectively. The total available cloud resources for the simulation is constant as 16 Ghz during the entire simulation. These simulations can also be repeated with higher amount of total cloud resources, different pricing value, and higher rate of web requests for each service.

4.3 Simulation Results

This simulation is conducted to demonstrate the performance of the proposed performance management approach in a cloud computing environment for maximizing the profitability of the cloud broker while managing the SLAs of the service providers in a dynamic environment. During the simulation, extremely dynamic workloads (see Fig. 3(b)) are utilized for the service providers that facilitate competition among the service providers to acquire higher amount (or number) of cloud resources during few time samples due to an extremely high rate of incoming web requests. In contrast to this, during a few time samples, the total desired amount of resources is much smaller than the total amount of available resources at the cloud broker due to extremely low rate of incoming web requests towards the services. The results of this simulation are shown in Figs. 4, 5, and 6.

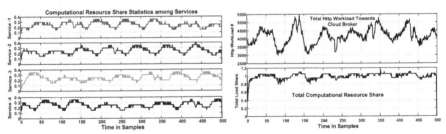

(a) Computational Resource Share Statistics at each Service Provider.

(b) Total Web Requests and Total Resource Share Statistics.

Fig. 4. Computational resource sharing among service providers and total workload analysis for the cloud broker

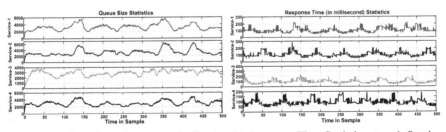

(a) Queue Size Statistics at each Service Provider.

(b) Response Time Statistics at each Service Provider.

Fig. 5. Queue size and response time statistics at each service provider

Computational Resource Statistics. Figure 4(a) shows the share of computational resource acquired by each of the service providers to maintain their respective SLAs. These service providers change their resource share based on the intensity of incoming web requests (see Fig. 3(b)). Initially, service provider 3 receives a higher number of web requests compared to other service providers, therefore in the beginning, service provider 3 acquires maximum share of computational resources. Similar phenomenon is observed in case of service provider 1, 2, and 4 during other time samples. Furthermore, the resource allocations adapts to the changes in the workload arrival rate by changing the resource distribution on the services to maintain their individual SLAs and maximizing the profitability of the cloud broker simultaneously.

Figure 4(b) shows the total web requests (sum of the workload of all the service providers) arrived at the cloud broker during a time sample, and the total share of cloud resources acquired by the service providers. Ideally, the total share of workload should always be 1, i.e., cloud broker should be able to change the unit price of the computational resource to facilitate 100 % allocation. However, in some scenarios when the total incoming web requests are too low (see Fig. 4(b), during time sample 160, 240, etc), the total allocation is lower than 100 % (less than 1). In a few time samples, this total resource allocation goes to as minimum as 80 % (or 0.8). On the contrary, when the total web requests are at the peak rate, the total share of desired workload increases beyond 1 (100 % allocation), because in these situations, the service providers compete for extra computational resources.

Queue Size and Response Time Statistics. Figure 5 shows the queue size and the response time observed at the service providers by using the proposed interaction balance based resource allocation approach. By comparing the observed queue size among service providers in Fig. 5(a), it is obvious that the queue size of the service providers 3 and 4 is lower than the queue size at the service providers 1 and 2, where incoming request rates are in similar range. The primary reason of this phenomenon is the higher penalty on SLAs (see Fig. 3(a)) in the cost function of service provider 3 and 4. Similar observation is also valid for the response time statistics in Fig. 5(b). This lower queue size and response time on service providers 3 and 4 do not hold true during a few time samples, when the incoming web request rate towards service provider 3 and 4 is much higher than the total towards service providers 1 and 2, such as time samples 0–50, 120–140, etc.

Interaction Count and Interaction Error. Figure 6(a) shows the number of interactions between the service providers and a cloud broker for determining the optimal unit price $\beta(k)$ of the cloud resources and the share of cloud resources $\alpha_i(k)$ assigned to each service provider for maximizing the cloud broker profit and maintaining the SLAs of the service provider. According to this figure, the number of interactions between the service providers and the cloud broker varies with the variation in total incoming web requests towards the cloud broker

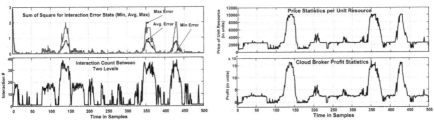

(a) Interactions between Cloud Broker and Service Providers.

(b) Unit Price and Profit Statistics at Cloud Broker.

Fig. 6. Interaction error and cloud broker's profitability statistics by using Eq. 6

(see Fig. 4). The number of interactions increase from 1 to 40 when the total incoming web requests are either minimum or maximum. In case of a low rate of incoming web requests, not all of the service providers require all the available computational resource, therefore a large number of interactions take place to decrease the unit price of the resource to facilitate the 100 % resource allocation. Similarly, when the incoming web request rate is extremely high, these interactions take place for increasing the unit price of a resource, which also reflects that these service providers are willing to pay more for acquiring more resources to maintain their SLAs.

Pricing of the Resource and Profitability. Figure 6(b) shows the unit price of the computational resources during simulation and profitability of the cloud broker, which is calculated using Eq. 6. By comparing Fig. 6(b) with Fig. 4(b), it is evident that the unit price of the computational resource increases when the total incoming web requests are increasing, and it finally results in an increased profit of the cloud broker. This observation can be explained by the basic mechanism of the proposed approach, that in case of limited resources, a cloud broker can increase the price, which will maximize its profit. All the service providers will either compete for the limited resources by paying the increased price or decrease their share to maintain the cost of operation. At a few instances of simulation, when the incoming request rate is too low, profitability of the cloud decreases because the unit price of the cloud resource is too low and some of the resources remain unassigned too.

5   Benefits of the Proposed Approach

In this paper, a cloud computing infrastructure is considered for optimally deploying a set of services, on a set of available cloud computing resources by using a cloud broker. According to the simulation results presented in the previous section, the proposed performance management approach derives an optimal resource allocation strategy to maintain the SLAs of the service providers, while at the same time maximizing the profitability of the cloud broker. The proposed approach is developed as a generic framework, which makes it a suitable candidate for being applied to a general class of services and resources. The proposed approach is also adaptive to the variations in the incoming web requests towards the hosted services. This approach is independent of the deployment environment and do not require any prior knowledge of the service provider performance behavior with respect to cloud resources at the cloud broker involved in dynamic resource allocation. Furthermore, the proposed approach is scalable in the number of service providers as these service providers only interact with the cloud broker.

The detailed performance and the overhead analysis of the proposed approach is already done by the authors [15]. In addition, the authors have demonstrated that the proposed approach supports dynamic addition of more services or deletion of existing services from the distributed environment while computing the optimal distribution of resources [15]. Moreover, this distributed control based approach has a lower computational overhead compared to the one of a centralized resource allocation approach that uses a large number of service providers [15]. In addition, this existing computational overhead can be further lowered by tuning the error tolerance ϵ and step length ξ at the cloud broker level control algorithm. At the service provider level, the computational overhead can be lowered by using more advanced tree search techniques (greedy, pruning, heuristics, and A^*) [1].

6   Conclusion and Future Work

In this paper, a distributed control-based performance management approach is introduced for efficiently managing the SLAs of a service deployed in a cloud computing environment and for maximizing the profitability of the cloud broker at the same time. The proposed approach is adaptive to the rate of the incoming web requests towards services and dynamically changes the resource allocation such that the service providers can maintain their SLAs. The proposed approach is novel in the terms of giving priority to the profit maximization for both the cloud broker and service providers while computing the optimal resource assignment. None of the research groups in academia or industry have published research or studies about applying the interaction balance method for optimal resource allocation through interactive bidding in cloud computing (or broker) environment.

In the future, the proposed approach will be extended on real cloud computing platforms for performance management of the service providers in a broker-based cloud computing environment, where the cloud resources will also have different reliability index with the varying unit price. The proposed approach will be used to derive an optimal deployment strategy for hosting a set of a wide range of services onto the most suitable set of cloud resources such that, in terms of efficiency and reliability, the overall performance of the system is optimized, while keeping the profitability considerations intact.

Acknowledgments. This work was supported in part by the National Science Foundation (NSF) under grant numbers NSF IIP-1127978 and NSF IIP-1034897 at the NSF Center for Cloud and Autonomic Computing, Mississippi State University, and by C-FAR, one of six centers of STARnet, a Semiconductor Research Corporation program sponsored by MARCO and DARPA at the University of Virginia, Charlottesville, VA.

References

1. Abdelwahed, S., Bai, J., Su, R., Kandasamy, N.: On the application of predictive control techniques for adaptive performance management of computing systems. IEEE Trans. Netw. Serv. Manag. **6**(4), 212–225 (2009)
2. Arianyan, E., Maleki, D., Yari, A., Arianyan, I.: Efficient resource allocation in cloud data centers through genetic algorithm. In: 2012 Sixth International Symposium on Telecommunications (IST), pp. 566–570, November 2012
3. Arlitt, M., Jin, T.: Workload characterization of the 1998 world cup web site. Technical report HPL-99-35R1, Hewlett-Packard Labs, September 1999
4. DeLurgio, S.A.: Forecasting Principles and Applications. McGraw-Hill, New York (1998)
5. Dinesh, K., Poornima, G., Kiruthika, K.: Efficient resources allocation for different jobs in cloud. Int. J. Comput. Appl. **56**, 30–35 (2012)
6. Amazon EC2. Amazon elastic compute cloud, March 2012. http://aws.amazon.com/ec2/
7. Google. Apps, March 2012. http://www.google.com/apps/intl/en/business/index.html
8. Gouda, K.C., Radhika, T.V., Akshatha, M.: Priority based resource allocation model for cloud computing. Int. J. Sci. Eng. Technol. Res. (IJSETR) **2**(1), 215–219 (2013)
9. Healey, M.: State of cloud 2011: Time for process maturation, January 2011. http://reports.informationweek.com/abstract/5/5116/Cloud-Computing/research-2011-state-of-cloud.html, March 2012
10. IBM. Smart cloud, March 2012. http://www.ibm.com/cloud-computing/us/en/
11. Jain, P., Rane, D., Patidar, S.: A novel cloud bursting brokerage and aggregation (cbba) algorithm for multi cloud environment. In: 2012 Second International Conference on Advanced Computing & Communication Technologies (ACCT), pp. 383–387. IEEE (2012)
12. Jebalia, M., Letaïfa, A.B., Hamdi, M., Tabbane, S.: A comparative study on game theoretic approaches for resource allocation in cloud computing architectures. In: IEEE 22nd International Workshop on Enabling Technologies: Infrastructure for Collaborative Enterprises (WETICE), 2013, pp. 336–341. IEEE (2013)
13. Kalman, R.E.: A new approach to linear filtering and prediction problems. Trans. ASME J. Basic Eng. **82**(D), 35–45 (1960)
14. Kandasamy, N., Abdelwahed, S., Khandekar, M.: A hierarchical optimization framework for autonomic performance management of distributed computing systems. In: Proceedings 26th IEEE International Conference on Distributed Computing Systems (ICDCS) (2006)
15. Mehrotra, R., Abdelwahed, S.: Towards autonomic performance management of large scale data centers using interaction balance principle. Cluster Comput. **17**(3), 979–999 (2014). doi:10.1007/s10586-013-0333-0

16. Mehrotra, R., Abdelwahed, S., Erradi, A.: A distributed control approach for autonomic performance management in cloud computing environment. In: Proceedings of the 2013 IEEE/ACM 6th International Conference on Utility and Cloud Computing, UCC '13, Washington, DC, USA, pp. 269–272. IEEE Computer Society (2013)
17. Mehrotra, R., Dubey, A., Abdelwahed, S., Tantawi, A.: A power-aware modeling and autonomic management framework for distributed computing systems. In: Ranka, S., Ahmad, I. (eds.) Handbook of Energy-Aware and Green Computing, p. 38. CRC Press, Boca Raton (2011)
18. Nair, S.K., Porwal, S., Dimitrakos, T., Ferrer, A.J., Tordsson, J., Sharif, T., Sheridan, C., Rajarajan, M., Khan, A.U.: Towards secure cloud bursting, brokerage and aggregation. In: 2010 IEEE 8th European Conference on Web Services (ECOWS), pp. 189–196. IEEE (2010)
19. Pawar, C.S., Wagh, R.B.: Priority based dynamic resource allocation in cloud computing. In: 2012 International Symposium on Cloud and Services Computing (ISCOS), pp. 1–6. IEEE (2012)
20. Search Cloud Provider. Cloud broker, April 2014. http://searchcloudprovider.techtarget.com/definition/cloud-broker
21. Rogers, O., Cliff, D.: A financial brokerage model for cloud computing. J. Cloud Comput. **1**(1), 1–12 (2012)
22. Roy, N., Dubey, A., Gokhale, A., Dowdy, L.: A capacity planning process for performance assurance of component-based distributed systems (abstracts only). SIGMETRICS Perform. Eval. Rev. **39**(3), 16–17 (2011)
23. Sadati, N.: A novel approach to coordination of large-scale systems; part ii interaction balance principle. In: IEEE International Conference on Industrial Technology, pp. 648–654, December 2005
24. Sundareswaran, S., Squicciarini, A., Lin, D.: A brokerage-based approach for cloud service selection. In: 2012 IEEE 5th International Conference on Cloud Computing (CLOUD), pp. 558–565. IEEE (2012)
25. Singh, M.G., Titli, A.: Systems Decomposition, Optimisation, and Control. Pergamon Press, Oxford (1978)
26. Windows. Azure, March 2012. http://www.windowsazure.com
27. Wu, L., Garg, S.K., Buyya, R.: Sla-based resource allocation for software as a service provider (saas) in cloud computing environments. In: 2011 11th IEEE/ACM International Symposium on Cluster, Cloud and Grid Computing (CCGrid), pp. 195–204. IEEE (2011)
28. Zaman, S., Grosu, D.: Combinatorial auction-based allocation of virtual machine instances in clouds. J. Parallel Distrib. Comput. **73**(4), 495–508 (2013)

Power-Efficient Assignment of Virtual Machines to Physical Machines

Jordi Arjona Aroca[1], Antonio Fernández Anta[2], Miguel A. Mosteiro[3](✉),
Christopher Thraves[4], and Lin Wang[5]

[1] Universidad Carlos III de Madrid, Madrid, Spain
jorge.arjona@imdea.org
[2] Institute IMDEA Networks, Madrid, Spain
antonio.fernandez@imdea.org
[3] Department of Computer Science, Kean University, Union, NJ, USA
mmosteir@kean.edu
[4] CNRS-LAAS and University of Toulouse - LAAS, Tolouse, France
cthraves@laas.fr
[5] Institute of Computing Technology, Chinese Academy of Sciences and
University of Chinese Academy of Sciences, Beijing, China
wanglin@ict.ac.cn

Abstract. Motivated by current trends in cloud computing, we study
a version of the generalized assignment problem where a set of virtual
processors has to be implemented by a set of *identical* processors. For
literature consistency, we say that a set of virtual machines (VMs) is
assigned to a set of physical machines (PMs). The optimization criteria
is to minimize the power consumed by all the PMs. We term the problem
Virtual Machine Assignment (VMA). Crucial differences with previous
work include a variable number of PMs, that each VM must be assigned
to exactly one PM (i.e., VMs cannot be implemented fractionally), and
a minimum power consumption for each active PM. Such infrastructure
may be strictly constrained in the number of PMs or in the PMs' capacity,
depending on how costly (in terms of power consumption) it is to add
a new PM to the system or to heavily load some of the existing PMs.
Low usage or ample budget yields models where PM capacity and/or the
number of PMs may be assumed unbounded for all practical purposes.
We study four VMA problems depending on whether the capacity or
the number of PMs is bounded or not. Specifically, we study hardness
and online competitiveness for a variety of cases. To the best of our
knowledge, this is the first comprehensive study of the VMA problem for
this cost function.

Keywords: Cloud computing · Generalized assignment · Scheduling ·
Load balancing · Power efficiency

This work has been supported in part by the Comunidad de Madrid grant
Cloud4BigData-CM, the MINECO grant TEC2011-29688-C02-01, the National Natural Science Foundation of China grant 61020106002, the National Science Foundation (CCF-0937829, CCF-1114930), and Kean University UFRI grant.

© Springer International Publishing Switzerland 2014
F. Pop and M. Potop-Butucaru (Eds.): ARMS-CC 2014, LNCS 8907, pp. 71–88, 2014.
DOI: 10.1007/978-3-319-13464-2_6

1   Introduction

The current pace of technology developments, and the continuous change in business requirements, may rapidly yield a given proprietary computational platform obsolete, oversized, or insufficient. Thus, outsourcing has recently become a popular approach to obtain computational services without incurring in amortization costs. Furthermore, in order to attain flexibility, such service is usually virtualized, so that the user may tune the computational platform to its particular needs. Users of such service need not to be aware of the particular implementation, they only need to specify the virtual machine they want to use. This conceptual approach to outsourced computing has been termed *cloud computing*, in reference to the cloud symbol used as an abstraction of a complex infrastructure in system diagrams. Current examples of cloud computing providers include Amazon Web Services [3], Rackspace [34], and Citrix [17].

Depending on what the specific service provided is, the cloud computing model comes in different flavors, such as *infrastructure as a service*, *platform as a service*, *storage as a service*, etc. In each of these models, the user may choose specific parameters of the computational resources provided. For instance, processing power, memory size, communication bandwidth, etc. Thus, in a cloud-computing service platform, various **virtual machines (VM)** with user-defined specifications must be implemented by, or **assigned to**[1], various **physical machines (PM)**[2]. Furthermore, such a platform must be scalable, allowing to add more PMs, should the business growth require such expansion. In this work, we call this problem the **Virtual Machine Assignment (VMA)** problem.

The optimization criteria for VMA depends on what the particular objective function sought is. From the previous discussion, it can be seen that, underlying VMA, there is some form of bin-packing problem. However, in VMA the number of PMs (i.e., bins for bin packing) may be increased if needed. Since CPU is generally the dominant power consumer in a server [7], VMA is usually carried out according to CPU workloads. With only the static power consumption of servers considered, previous work related to VMA has focused on minimizing the number of active PMs (cf. [11] and the references therein) in order to minimize the total static energy consumption. This is commonly known as VM consolidation [26,32]. However, despite the static power, the dynamic power consumption of a server, which has been shown to be superlinear on the **load** of a given computational resource [9,23], is also significant and cannot be ignored. Since the definition of load is not precise, we borrow the definition in [7] and define the load of a server as the amount of active cycles per second a task requires, an absolute metric independent of the operating frequency or the number of cores of a PM. The superlinearity property of the dynamic power consumption is also confirmed

---

[1] The cloud-computing literature uses instead the term *placement*. We choose here the term assignment for consistency with the literature on general assignment problems.

[2] We choose the notation VM and PM for simplicity and consistency, but notice that our study applies to any computational resource assignment problem, as long as the minimization function is the one modeled here.

by the results in [7]. As a result, when taking into account both parts of power consumption, the use of extra PMs may be more efficient energy-wise than a minimum number of heavily-loaded PMs. This inconsistency with the literature in VM consolidation has been supported by the results presented in [7] and, hence, we claim that the way consolidation has been traditionally performed has to be reconsidered. In this work, we combine both power-consumption factors and explore the most energy-efficient way for VMA. That is, for some parameters $\alpha > 1$ and $b > 0$, we seek to minimize the sum of the α powers of the PMs loads *plus* the fixed cost b of using each PM.

Physical resources are physically constrained. A PMs infrastructure may be strictly constrained in the number of PMs or in the PMs CPU capacity. However, if usage patterns indicate that the PMs will always be loaded well below their capacity, it may be assumed that the capacity is unlimited. Likewise, if the power budget is very big, the number of PMs may be assumed unconstrained for all practical purposes. These cases yield 4 VMA subproblems, depending on whether the capacity and the number of PMs is limited or not. We introduce these parameters denoting the problem as (C,m)-**VMA**, where C is the PM CPU capacity, m is the maximum number of PMs, and each of these parameters is replaced by a dot if unbounded.

In this work, we study the hardness and online competitiveness of the VMA problem. Specifically, we show that VMA is NP-hard *in the strong sense* (in particular, we observe that (C,m)-VMA is strongly NP-complete). Thus, VMA problems do not have a fully polynomial time approximation scheme (FPTAS). Nevertheless, using previous results derived for more general objective functions, we notice that $(\cdot, m)$- and $(\cdot, \cdot)$-VMA have a polynomial time approximation scheme (PTAS). We also show various lower and upper bounds on the offline approximation and the online competitiveness of VMA. Rather than attempting to obtain tight bounds for particular instances of the parameters of the problem (C, m, α, b) we focus on obtaining *general bounds*, whose parameters can be instantiated for the specific application. The bounds obtained show interesting trade-offs between the PM capacity and the fixed cost of adding a new PM to the system. To the best of our knowledge, this is the first VMA study that is focused on power consumption.

Roadmap. The paper is organized as follows. In what remains of this section, we define formally the $(\cdot, \cdot)$-VMA problem, we overview the related work, and we describe our results in detail. Section 2 includes some preliminary results that will be used throughout the paper. The offline and online analyses are included in Sects. 3 and 4 respectively. Section 5 discusses some practical issues and provides some useful insights regarding real implementation. For succinctness, many of the proofs are left to the full version of this paper in [8].

1.1 Problem Definition

We describe the $(\cdot, \cdot)$-VMA problem now. Given a set $S = \{s_1, \ldots, s_m\}$ of $m > 1$ identical physical machines (PMs) of capacity C; rational numbers μ, α and b, where $\mu > 0$, $\alpha > 1$ and $b > 0$; a set $D = \{d_1, \ldots, d_n\}$ of n virtual machines and a function $\ell : D \rightarrow \mathbb{R}$ that gives the CPU load each virtual machine incurs[3], we aim to obtain a partition $\pi = \{A_1, \ldots, A_m\}$ of D, such that $\ell(A_i) \leq C$, for all i. Our objective will be then minimizing the power consumption given by the function

$$P(\pi) = \sum_{i \in [1,m]: A_i \neq \emptyset} \left(\mu \left(\sum_{d_j \in A_i} \ell(d_j) \right)^\alpha + b \right). \tag{1}$$

Let us define the function $f(\cdot)$, such that $f(x) = 0$ if $x = 0$ and $f(x) = \mu x^\alpha + b$ otherwise. Then, the objective function is to minimize $P(\pi) = \sum_{i=1}^m f(\ell(A_i))$. The parameter μ is used for consistency with the literature. For clarity we will consider $\mu = 1$ in the rest of the paper. All the results presented apply for other values of μ.

We also study several special cases of the VMA problem, namely (C, m)-VMA, $(C, \cdot)$-VMA, $(\cdot, m)$-VMA and $(\cdot, \cdot)$-VMA. (C, m)-VMA refers to the case where both the number of available PMs and its capacity are fixed. $(\cdot, \cdot)$-VMA, where $(\cdot)$ denotes unboundedness, refers to the case where both the number of available PMs and its capacity are unbounded (i.e., C is larger than the total load of the VMs that can ever be in the system at any time, or m is larger than the number of VMs that can ever be in the system at any time). $(C, \cdot)$-VMA and $(\cdot, m)$-VMA are the cases where the number of available PMs and their capacity is unbounded, respectively.

1.2 Related Work

To the best of our knowledge, previous work on VMA has been only experimental [16,27,30,36] or has focused on different cost functions [1,11,15,18]. First, we provide an overview of previous theoretical work for related assignment problems (storage allocation, scheduling, network design, etc.). The cost functions considered in that work resemble or generalize the power cost function under consideration here. Secondly, we overview related experimental work.

Chandra and Wong [15], and Cody and Coffman [18] study a problem for storage allocation that is a variant of $(\cdot, m)$-VMA with $b = 0$ and $\alpha = 2$. Hence, this problem tries to minimize the sum of the squares of the machine-load vector for a fixed number of machines. They study the offline version of the problem and provide algorithms with constant approximation ratio. A significant leap was taken by Alon et al. [1], since they present a PTAS for the problem of minimizing the L_p norm of the load vector, for any $p \geq 1$. This problem has the previous one as special case, and is also a variant of the $(\cdot, m)$-VMA problem when $p = \alpha$ and $b = 0$. Similarly, Alon et al. [2] extended this work for a more general set of functions, that include $f(\cdot)$ as defined above. Hence, their results can be directly applied in the $(\cdot, m)$-VMA problem. Later, Epstein et al. [20] extended [2] further for the uniformly related machines case. We will use these results in Sect. 3 in the analysis of the offline case of $(\cdot, m)$-VMA and $(\cdot, \cdot)$-VMA.

---

3 For convenience, we overload the function $\ell(\cdot)$ to be applied over sets of virtual machines, so that for any set $A \subseteq D, \ell(A) = \sum_{d_j \in A} \ell(d_j)$.

Bansal, Chan, and Pruhs minimize arbitrary power functions for speed scaling in job scheduling [9]. The problem is to schedule the execution of n computational jobs on a *single* processor, whose speed may vary within a countable collection of intervals. Each job has a release time, a processing work to be done, a weight characterizing its importance, and its execution can be suspended and restarted later without penalty. A scheduler algorithm must specify, for each time, a job to execute and a speed for the processor. The goal is to minimize the weighted sum of the flow times over all jobs plus the energy consumption, where the flow time of a job is the time elapsed from release to completion and the energy consumption is given by s^α where s is the processor speed and $\alpha > 1$ is some constant. For the online algorithm *shortest remaining processing time first*, the authors prove a $(3 + \epsilon)$ competitive ratio for the objective of total weighted flow plus energy. Whereas for the online algorithm *highest density first (HDF)*, where the density of a job is its weight-to-work ratio, they prove a $(2 + \epsilon)$ competitive ratio for the objective of fractional weighted flow plus energy.

Recently, Im, Moseley, and Pruhs studied online scheduling for general cost functions of the flow time, with the only restriction that such function is non-decreasing [24]. In their model, a collection of jobs, each characterized by a release time, a processing work, and a weight, must be processed by a *single* server whose speed is variable. A job can be suspended and restarted later without penalty. The authors show that HDF is $(2+\epsilon)$-speed $O(1)$-competitive against the optimal algorithm on a unit speed-processor, for all non-decreasing cost functions of the flow time. Furthermore, they also show that this ratio cannot be improved significantly proving impossibility results if the cost function is not uniform among jobs or the speed cannot be significantly increased.

A generalization of the above problem is studied by Gupta, Krishnaswamy, and Pruhs in [23]. The question addressed is how to assign jobs, *possibly fractionally*, to unrelated parallel machines in an online fashion in order to minimize the sum of the α-powers of the machine loads plus the assignment costs. Upon arrival of a job, the algorithm learns the increase on the load and the cost of assigning a unit of such job to a machine. Jobs cannot be suspended and/or reassigned. The authors model a greedy algorithm that assigns a job so that the cost is minimized as solving a mathematical program with constraints arriving online. They show a competitive ratio of α^α with respect to the solution of the dual program which is a lower bound for the optimal. They also show how to adapt the algorithm to integral assignments with a $O(\alpha)^\alpha$ competitive ratio, which applies directly to our $(\cdot, m)$-VMA problem. References to previous work on the particular case of minimizing energy with deadlines can be found in this paper.

Similar cost functions have been considered for the minimum cost network-design problem. In this problem, packets have to be routed through a (possibly multihop) network of speed scalable routers. There is a cost associated to assigning a packet to a link and to the speed or load of the router. The goal is to route all packets minimizing the aggregated cost. In [4,5] the authors show offline algorithms for this problem with undirected graph and homogeneous link cost functions that achieve polynomial and poly-logarithmic approximation, respectively.

The cost function is the α-th power of the link load plus a link assignment cost, for any constant $\alpha > 1$. The same problem and cost function is studied in [23]. Bansal *et al.* [10] study a minimum-cost virtual circuit multicast routing problem with speed scalable links. They give a polynomial-time $O(\alpha)$-approximation offline algorithm and a polylog-competitive online algorithm, both for the case with homogeneous power functions. They also show that the problem is APX-hard in the case with heterogeneous power functions and there is no polylog-approximation when the graph is directed. Recently, Antoniadis *et al.* [6] improved the results by providing a simple combinatorial algorithm that is $O(\log^\alpha n)$-approximate, from which we can construct an $\widetilde{O}(\log^{3\alpha+1} n)$-competitive online algorithm. The $(\cdot, m)$-VMA problem can be seen as a especial case of the problem considered in these papers in which there are only two nodes, source and destination, and m parallel links connecting them.

To the best of our knowledge, the problem of minimizing the power consumption (given in Eq. 1) with capacity constraints (i.e., the (C, m)-VMA and $(C, \cdot)$-VMA problems) has received very limited attention, in the realm of both VMA and network design, although the approaches in [5,10] are related to or based on the solutions for the capacitated network-design problem [14].

The experimental work related to VMA is vast and its detailed overview is out of the scope of this paper. Some of this work does not minimize energy [13,28,31] or it applies to a model different than ours (VM migration [33,35], knowledge of future load [29,35], feasibility of allocation [11], multilevel architecture [25,30,33], interconnected VMs [12], etc.). On the other hand, some of the experimental work where minimization of energy is evaluated focus on a more restrictive cost function [25,38,40].

In [35], the authors focus on an energy-efficient VM placement problem with two requirements: CPU and disk. These requirements are assumed to change dynamically and the goal is to consolidate loads among servers, possibly using migration at no cost. In our model VMs assignment is based on a CPU requirement that does not change and migration is not allowed. Should any other resource be the dominating energy cost, the same results apply for that requirement. Also, if loads change and migration is free, an offline algorithm can be used each time that a load changes or a new VM arrives. In [35] it is shown experimentally that energy-efficient VMA does not merely reduce to a packing problem. That is, to minimize the number of PMs used even if their load is close to their maximum capacity. For our model, we show here that the optimal load of a given server is a function only of the fixed cost of being active (b) and the exponential rate of power increase on the load (α). That is, the optimal load is not related to the maximum capacity of a PM.

1.3   Our Results

In this work, we study offline and online versions of the four versions of the VMA problem. For the offline problems, the first fact we observe is that there is a hard decision version of (C, m)-VMA: Is there a feasible partition π of the set D of VMs? By reduction from the 3-Partition problem, it can be shown that this decision problem is strongly NP-complete.

We then show that the $(\cdot, \cdot)$-VMA, $(C, \cdot)$-VMA, and $(\cdot, m)$-VMA problems are NP-hard in the strong sense, even if α is constant. This result implies that these problems do not have FPTAS, even if α is constant. However, we show that the $(\cdot, \cdot)$-VMA and $(\cdot, m)$-VMA problems have PTAS, while the $(C, \cdot)$-VMA problem can not be approximated beyond a ratio of $\frac{3}{2} \cdot \frac{\alpha - 1 + (\frac{2}{3})^\alpha}{\alpha}$ (unless P = NP). On the positive side, we show how to use an existing Asymptotic PTAS [21] to obtain algorithms that approximate the optimal solution of $(C, \cdot)$-VMA. (See Table 1.)

Then we move on to online VMA algorithms. We show various upper and lower bounds on the competitive ratio of the four versions of the problem. (See Table 1.) Observe that the results are often different depending on whether x^* is smaller than C or not. In fact, when $x^* < C$, there is a lower bound of $\frac{(3/2)2^\alpha - 1}{2^\alpha - 1}$

Table 1. Summary of bounds on the approximation/competitive ratio ρ. All lower bounds are existential. The number of PMs in an optimal $(C, \cdot)$-VMA solution is denoted as m^*. The number of PMs in an optimal Bin Packing solution is denoted as $\overline{m}$. The load that minimizes the ratio power consumption against load is denoted as x^*. The subset of VMs with load smaller than x^* is denoted as D_s.

VMA subprob.	$x^* < C$	$x^* \geq C$
$(C, \cdot)$ offline	$\rho \geq \frac{3}{2} \frac{\alpha - 1 + (2/3)^\alpha}{\alpha}$	$\rho \geq \frac{3}{2} \frac{\alpha - 1 + (2/3)^\alpha}{\alpha}$
	$\rho < \frac{\overline{m}}{m^*}\left(1 + \epsilon + \frac{1}{\alpha - 1} + \frac{1}{m}\right)$	$\rho < 1 + \epsilon + \frac{C^\alpha}{b} + \frac{1}{m}$
$(C, \cdot)$ online	$\rho \geq \frac{(3/2)2^\alpha - 1}{2^\alpha - 1}$	$\rho \geq \frac{C^\alpha + 2b}{b + \max\{C^\alpha, 2(C/2)^\alpha + b\}}$
	$\rho = 1$ if $D_s = \emptyset$, else $\rho \leq \left(1 - \frac{1}{\alpha}\left(1 - \frac{1}{2^\alpha}\right)\right)\left(2 + \frac{x^*}{\ell(D_s)}\right)$	$\rho \leq \frac{2b}{C}\left(1 + \frac{1}{(\alpha - 1)2^\alpha}\right)\left(2 + \frac{C}{\ell(D)}\right)$
(C, m) online	$\rho \geq \frac{(3/2)2^\alpha - 1}{2^\alpha - 1}$	$\rho \geq \frac{C^\alpha + 2b}{b + \max\{C^\alpha, 2(C/2)^\alpha + b\}}$
$(\cdot, \cdot)$ online	$\rho \geq \frac{(3/2)2^\alpha - 1}{2^\alpha - 1}$	not applicable
	$\rho = 1$ if $D_s = \emptyset$, else $\rho \leq \left(1 - \frac{1}{\alpha}\left(1 - \frac{1}{2^\alpha}\right)\right)\left(2 + \frac{x^*}{\ell(D_s)}\right)$	
$(\cdot, m)$ online	$\rho \geq \max\{\frac{(3/2)2^\alpha - 1}{2^\alpha - 1}, \frac{3^\alpha}{2^{\alpha+2} + \epsilon}\}$	not applicable
	$\rho \leq O(\alpha)^\alpha$ In [23]	
$(\cdot, 2)$ online	$\rho \geq \max\{\frac{3^\alpha}{2^{\alpha+1}}, \frac{(3/2)2^\alpha - 1}{2^\alpha - 1}, \frac{3^\alpha}{2^{\alpha+2} + \epsilon}\}$	not applicable
	$\rho = 1$ if $\ell(D) \leq \sqrt[\alpha]{b/(2^\alpha - 2)}$, else $\rho \leq \max\{2, \left(\frac{3}{2}\right)^{\alpha - 1}\}$	

Table 2. Summary of bounds on the approximation/competitive ratio ρ for $\alpha = 3$, $b = 2$, and $C = 2$ on the left and $C = 1$ on the right. All lower bounds are existential. The number of PMs in an optimal $(C, \cdot)$-VMA solution is denoted as m^*. The number of PMs in an optimal Bin Packing solution is denoted as $\overline{m}$. The load that minimizes the ratio power consumption against load is denoted as x^*. The subset of VMs with load smaller than x^* is denoted as D_s.

VMA subprob.	$x^* < C$	$x^* \geq C$
$(C, \cdot)$ offline	$\rho \geq \frac{11}{9}$	$\rho \geq \frac{11}{9}$
	$\rho < \frac{\overline{m}}{m^*}\left(\frac{3}{2} + \epsilon + \frac{1}{\overline{m}}\right)$	$\rho < \frac{3}{2} + \epsilon + \frac{1}{\overline{m}}$
$(C, \cdot)$ online	$\rho \geq \frac{11}{7}$	$\rho \geq \frac{20}{17}$
	$\rho \leq \frac{17}{12}\left(1 + \frac{1}{2\ell(D_s)}\right)$	$\rho \leq \frac{17}{2}\left(1 + \frac{1}{2\ell(D)}\right)$
(C, m) online	$\rho \geq \frac{11}{7}$	$\rho \geq \frac{20}{17}$
$(\cdot, \cdot)$ online	$\rho \geq \frac{11}{7}$	not applicable
	$\rho \leq \frac{17}{12}\left(1 + \frac{1}{2\ell(D_s)}\right)$	
$(\cdot, m)$ online	$\rho \geq \frac{11}{7}$	not applicable
$(\cdot, 2)$ online	$\rho \geq \frac{11}{7}$	not applicable
	$\rho \leq \frac{9}{4}$	

that applies to all versions of the problem. The bounds are given as a function of the input parameters of the problem, in order to allow for tighter expressions. To provide intuition on how tight the bounds are, we instantiate them for a realistic[4] value of $\alpha = 3$, and normalized values of $b = 2$ and $C \in \{1, 2\}$. The resulting bounds are shown in Table 2. As can be observed, the resulting upper and lower bounds are not very far in general.

2   Preliminaries

The following claims will be used in the analysis. We call **power rate** the power consumed per unit of load in a PM. Let x be the load of a PM. Then, its power rate is computed as $f(x)/x$. The load at which the power rate is minimized, denoted x^*, is the **optimal load**, and the corresponding rate is the **optimal power rate** $\varphi^* = f(x^*)/x^*$. Using calculus we get the following observation.

---

[4] The values for α in the servers studied in [7] (denoted as Erdos and Nemesis) are close to 1.5 and 3 and x^* values of $0.76C$ and $0.9C$ respectively.

Observation 1. *The optimal load is $x^* = (b/(\alpha - 1))^{1/\alpha}$. Additionaly, for any $x \neq x^*$, $f(x)/x > \varphi^*$.*

The following lemmas will be used in the analysis.

Lemma 1. *Consider two solutions $\pi = \{A_1, \ldots, A_m\}$ and $\pi' = \{A'_1, \ldots, A'_m\}$ of an instance of the VMA problem, such that for some $x, y \in [1, m]$ it holds that*

- *$A_x \neq \emptyset$ and $A_y \neq \emptyset$;*
- *$A'_x = A_x \cup A_y$, $A'_y = \emptyset$, and $A_i = A'_i$, for all $i \neq x$ and $i \neq y$; and*
- *$\ell(A_x) + \ell(A_y) \leq \min\{x^*, C\}$.*

Then, $P(\pi') < P(\pi)$.

From this lemma, it follows that the global power consumption can be reduced by having 2 VMs together in the same PM, when its aggregated load is smaller than $\min\{x^*, C\}$, instead of moving one VM to an unused PM. When we keep VMs together in a given partition we say that we are *using* Lemma 1.

Lemma 2. *Consider two solutions $\pi = \{A_1, \ldots, A_m\}$ and $\pi' = \{A'_1, \ldots, A'_m\}$ of an instance of the VMA problem, such that for some $x, y \in [1, m]$ it holds that*

- *$A_x \cup A_y = A'_x \cup A'_y$, while $A_i = A'_i$, for all $x \neq i \neq y$;*
- *none of A_x, A_y, A'_x, and A'_y is empty; and*
- *$|\ell(A_x) - \ell(A_y)| < |\ell(A'_x) - \ell(A'_y)|$.*

Then, $P(\pi) < P(\pi')$.

Corollary 1. *Consider a solution $\pi = \{A_1, \ldots, A_m\}$ of an instance of the VMA problem with total load $\ell(D)$, such that exactly k of the A_x sets, $x \in [1, m]$, are non-empty (hence it uses k PMs). Then, the power consumption is lower bounded by the power of the (maybe unfeasible) solution that balances the load evenly, i.e., $P(\pi) \geq kb + k(\ell(D)/k)^\alpha$.*

3   Offline Analysis

3.1   NP-Hardness

As was mentioned, it can be shown that deciding whether there is a feasible solution for an instance of the (C, m)-VMA problem is NP-complete or not, by a direct reduction from the 3-Partition problem. However, this result does not apply directly to the $(C, \cdot)$-VMA, $(\cdot, m)$-VMA, and $(\cdot, \cdot)$-VMA problems. We show now that these problems are NP-hard. We first prove the following lemma.

Lemma 3. *Given an instance of the VMA problem, any solution $\pi = \{A_1, \ldots, A_m\}$ where $\ell(A_i) \neq x^*$ for some $i \in [1, m] : A_i \neq \emptyset$, has power consumption $P(\pi) > \rho^* \ell(D) = \rho^* \sum_{d \in D} \ell(d)$.*

We show now in the following theorem that the different versions of the (C, m)-VMA problem with unbounded C or m are NP-hard.

Theorem 1. *The $(C, \cdot)$-VMA, $(\cdot, m)$-VMA and $(\cdot, \cdot)$-VMA problems are strongly NP-hard, even if α is constant.*

It is known that strongly NP-hard problems cannot have a fully polynomial-time approximation scheme (FPTAS) [37]. Hence, the following corollary.

Corollary 2. *The $(C, \cdot)$-VMA, $(\cdot, m)$-VMA and $(\cdot, \cdot)$-VMA problems do not have fully polynomial-time approximation schemes (FPTAS), even if α is constant.*

In the following sections we show that, while the $(\cdot, m)$-VMA and $(\cdot, \cdot)$-VMA problems have polynomial-time approximation schemes (PTAS), the $(C, \cdot)$-VMA problem cannot be approximated below $\frac{3}{2} \cdot \frac{\alpha - 1 + (2/3)^{\alpha}}{\alpha}$.

3.2 The $(\cdot, m)$-VMA and $(\cdot, \cdot)$-VMA Problems have PTAS

We have proved that the $(\cdot, m)$-VMA and $(\cdot, \cdot)$-VMA problems are NP-hard in the strong sense and that, hence, there exists no FPTAS for them. However, Alon et al. [2], proved that if a function $f(\cdot)$ satisfies a condition denoted $F*$, then the problem of scheduling jobs in m identical machines so that $\sum_i f(M_i)$ is minimized has a PTAS, where M_i is the load of the jobs allocated to machine i. This result implies that if our function $f(\cdot)$ satisfies condition $F*$, the same PTAS can be used for the $(\cdot, m)$-VMA and $(\cdot, \cdot)$-VMA problems. From Observation 6.1 in [20], it can be derived that, in fact, our power consumption function $f(\cdot)$ satisfies condition $F*$. Hence, the following theorem.

Theorem 2. *There are polynomial-time approximation schemes (PTAS) for the $(\cdot, m)$-VMA and $(\cdot, \cdot)$-VMA problems.*

3.3 Bounds on the Approximability of the $(C, \cdot)$-VMA Problem

We study now the $(C, \cdot)$-VMA problem, where we consider an unbounded number of machines with bounded capacity C. We will provide a lower bound on its approximation ratio, independently on the relation between x^* and C; and upper bounds for the cases when $x^* \geq C$ and $x^* < C$.

Lower Bound on the Approximation Ratio. The following theorem shows a lower bound on the approximation ratio of any offline algorithm for $(C, \cdot)$-VMA.

Theorem 3. *No algorithm achieves an approximation ratio smaller than $\frac{3}{2} \cdot \frac{\alpha - 1 + (\frac{2}{3})^{\alpha}}{\alpha}$ for the $(C, \cdot)$-VMA problem unless P $=$ NP.*

Upper Bound on the Approximation Ratio for $x^* \geq C$. We study now an upper bound on the competitive ratio of the $(C, \cdot)$-VMA problem for the case when $x^* \geq C$. Under this condition, the best is to load each PM to its full capacity. Intuitively, an optimal solution should load every machine up to its maximum capacity or, if not possible, should balance the load among PMs to maximize the average load. The following lemma formalizes this observation.

Lemma 4. *For any system with unbounded number of PMs where $x^* \geq C$ the power consumption of the optimal assignment π^* is lower bounded by the power consumption of a (possibly not feasible) solution where $\ell(D)$ is evenly distributed among $\overline{m}$ PMs, where $\overline{m}$ is the minimum number of PMs required to allocate all VMs (i.e., the optimal solution of the packing problem). That is, $P(\pi^*) \geq \overline{m} \cdot b + \overline{m}(\ell(D)/\overline{m})^\alpha$.*

Now we prove an upper bound on the approximation ratio showing a reduction to bin packing [22]. The reduction works as follows. Let each PM be seen as a bin of capacity C, and each VM be seen as an object to be placed in the bins, whose size is the VM load. Then, a solution for this bin packing problem instance yields a feasible (perhaps suboptimal) solution for the instance of $(C, \cdot)$-VMA. Moreover, using any bin-packing approximation algorithm, we obtain a feasible solution for $(C, \cdot)$-VMA that approximates the minimal number of PMs used. The power consumption of this solution approximates the power consumption of the optimal solution π^* of the instance of $(C, \cdot)$-VMA. In order to compute an upper bound on the approximation ratio of this algorithm, we will compare the power consumption of such solution against a lower bound on the power consumption of π^*. The following theorem shows the approximation ratio obtained.

Theorem 4. *For every $\epsilon > 0$, there exists an approximation algorithm for the $(C, \cdot)$-VMA problem when $x^* \geq C$ that achieves an approximation ratio of*

$$\rho < 1 + \epsilon + \frac{C^\alpha}{b} + \frac{1}{\overline{m}},$$

where $\overline{m}$ is the minimum number of PMs required to allocate all the VMs.

Upper Bound on the Approximation Ratio for $x^* < C$. We study now the $(C, \cdot)$-VMA problem when $x^* < C$. In this case, the optimal load per PM is less than its capacity, so an optimal solution would load every PM to x^* if possible, or try to balance the load close to x^*. In this case we slightly modify the bin packing algorithm described above, reducing the bin size from C to x^*. Then, using an approximation algorithm for this bin packing problem, the following theorem can be shown.

Theorem 5. *For every $\epsilon > 0$, there exists an approximation algorithm for the $(C, \cdot)$-VMA problem when $x^* < C$ that achieves an approximation ratio of*

$$\rho < \frac{\overline{m}}{m^*} \left((1 + \epsilon) + \frac{1}{\alpha - 1} \right) + \frac{1}{m^*},$$

where m^* is the number of PMs used by the optimal solution of $(C, \cdot)$-VMA, and $\overline{m}$ is the minimum number of PMs required to allocate all the VMs without exceeding load x^* (i.e., the optimal solution of the bin packing problem).

4 Online Analysis

In this section, we study the online version of the VMA problem, i.e., when the VMs are revealed one by one. We first study lower bounds and then provide online algorithms and prove upper bounds on their competitive ratio.

4.1 Lower Bounds

In this section, we compute lower bounds on the competitive ratio for $(\cdot,\cdot)$-VMA, $(C,\cdot)$-VMA, $(\cdot,m)$-VMA, (C,m)-VMA and $(\cdot,2)$-VMA problems. We start with one general construction that is used to obtain lower bounds on the first four cases. Then, we develop special constructions for $(\cdot,m)$-VMA and $(\cdot,2)$-VMA that improve the lower bounds for these two problems.

General Construction. We prove lower bounds on the competitive ratio of $(\cdot,\cdot)$-VMA, $(C,\cdot)$-VMA, $(\cdot,m)$-VMA and (C,m)-VMA problems. These lower bounds are shown in the following two theorems. In Theorem 6, we prove a lower bound on the competitive ratio that is valid in the cases when C is unbounded and when it is larger or equal than x^*. The case $C \leq x^*$ is covered in Theorem 7.

Theorem 6. *There exists an instance of problems $(\cdot,\cdot)$-VMA, $(\cdot,m)$-VMA, $(C,\cdot)$-VMA and (C,m)-VMA when $C > x^*$, such that no online algorithm can guarantee a competitive ratio smaller than $\frac{(3/2)2^\alpha - 1}{2^\alpha - 1}$.*

Theorem 7. *There exists an instance of problems $(C,\cdot)$-VMA and (C,m)-VMA when $C \leq x^*$ such that no online algorithm can guarantee a competitive ratio smaller than $(C^\alpha + 2b)/(b + \max(C^\alpha, 2(C/2)^\alpha + b))$.*

Special Constructions for $(\cdot,m)$-VMA and $(\cdot,2)$-VMA. We show first that for m PMs there is a lower bound on the competitive ratio that improves the previous lower bound when $\alpha > 4.5$. Secondly, we prove a particular lower bound for problem $(\cdot,2)$-VMA, that improves the previous lower bound when $\alpha > 3$.

Theorem 8. *There exists an instance of problem $(\cdot,m)$-VMA such that no online algorithm can guarantee a competitive ratio smaller than $3^\alpha/(2^{\alpha+2} + \epsilon)$ for any $\epsilon > 0$.*

Now, we show a stronger lower bound on the competitive ratio for $(\cdot,2)$-VMA problem.

Theorem 9. *There exists an instance of problem $(\cdot,2)$-VMA such that no online algorithm can guarantee a competitive ratio smaller than $3^\alpha/2^{\alpha+1}$.*

4.2   Upper Bounds

Now, we study upper bounds for $(\cdot, \cdot)$-VMA, $(C, \cdot)$-VMA, and $(\cdot, 2)$-VMA problems. We start giving an online VMA algorithm that can be used in $(\cdot, \cdot)$-VMA and $(C, \cdot)$-VMA problems. The algorithm uses the load of the new revealed VM in order to decide the PM where it will be assigned. If the load of the revealed VM is strictly larger than $\min\{x^*, C\}/2$, the algorithm assigns this VM to a new PM without any other VM already assigned to it. Otherwise, the algorithm schedules the revealed VM to any loaded PM whose current load is smaller or equal than $\frac{\min\{x^*, C\}}{2}$. Hence, when this new VM is assigned, the load of this PM remains smaller than $\min\{x^*, C\}$. If there is no such loaded PM, the revealed VM is assigned to a new PM. Note that, since the case under consideration assumes the existence of an unbounded number of PMs, there exists always one new PM. A detailed description of this algorithm is shown in Algorithm 1. As before, A_j denotes the set of VMs assigned to PM s_j at a given time.

Algorithm 1. Online algorithm for $(\cdot, \cdot)$-VMA and $(C, \cdot)$-VMA problems.

---

for *each VM d_i* **do**
  if $\ell(d_i) > \frac{\min\{x^*, C\}}{2}$ **then**
  | d_i is assigned to a new PM
  else
  | d_i is assigned to any loaded PM s_j where $\ell(A_j) \leq \frac{\min\{x^*, C\}}{2}$. If such loaded PM does not exist, d_i is assigned to a new PM

We prove the approximation ratio of Algorithm 1 in the following two theorems.

Theorem 10. *There exists an online algorithm for $(\cdot, \cdot)$-VMA and $(C, \cdot)$-VMA when $x^* < C$ that achieves the following competitive ratio:*

$$\rho = 1, \ \text{if no VM } d_i \text{ has load such that } \ell(d_i) < x^*,$$

$$\rho \leq \left(1 - \frac{1}{\alpha}\left(1 - \frac{1}{2^\alpha}\right)\right)\left(2 + \frac{x^*}{\ell(D_s)}\right), \ \text{otherwise.}$$

Theorem 11. *There exists an online algorithm for $(C, \cdot)$-VMA when $x^* \geq C$ that achieves competitive ratio $\rho \leq \frac{2b}{C}\left(1 + \frac{1}{(\alpha-1)2^\alpha}\right)\left(2 + \frac{C}{\ell(D)}\right)$.*

Proof. We proceed with the analysis of the competitive ratio of Algorithm 1 in the case when $x^* \geq C$. The analysis uses the same technique used in the proof for the previous theorem. Hence, we just show the difference.

On one hand, when $x^* \geq C$, it holds that $f(\ell(A_i))/\ell(A_i) \geq f(C)/C$ due to the fact that $f(x)/x$ is monotone decreasing in interval $(0, C]$. It is also obvious that all the PMs will be loaded no more C. As a result, the optimal power consumption for $(C, \cdot)$-VMA can be bounded by $P(\pi^*) \geq f(C)\ell(D)/C$. On the other hand, the solution given by Algorithm 1 can also be upper bounded. We consider the following two cases.

Case 1: $\ell(\hat{A}_i) \geq C/2$ for all i. In this case, every PM will be loaded between $C/2$ and C. Consequently,

$$P(\pi) = \sum_{\frac{C}{2} \leq \ell(\hat{A}_i) \leq C} f(\ell(\hat{A}_i)) \leq \frac{f(\frac{C}{2})}{\frac{C}{2}} \ell(D).$$

The competitive ratio ρ then satisfies

$$\rho \leq \frac{\frac{f(\frac{C}{2})}{\frac{C}{2}} \ell(D)}{\frac{f(C)}{C} \ell(D)} = 2 \frac{f(\frac{C}{2})}{f(C)} \leq \frac{2b}{C} \left(1 + \frac{1}{(\alpha-1)2^{\alpha}} \right).$$

Case 2: there exists s_i such that $\ell(\hat{A}_i) < C/2$. In this case, it holds:

$$P(\pi) = \sum_{\frac{C}{2} \leq \ell(\hat{A}_i) \leq C} f(\ell(\hat{A}_i)) + f(\ell(\hat{A}_{s'}))$$

$$\leq \frac{f(\frac{C}{2})}{\frac{C}{2}} \left(\sum_{d_i : \ell(d_i) \leq C} \ell(d_i) - \ell(\hat{A}_{s'}) \right) + f(\ell(\hat{A}_{s'}))$$

$$= \frac{f(\frac{C}{2})}{\frac{C}{2}} \left(\ell(D) - \ell(\hat{A}_{s'}) \right) + \ell(\hat{A}_{s'})^{\alpha} + b.$$

The competitive ratio ρ then satisfies

$$\rho \leq \frac{P(\pi)}{\frac{f(C)}{C} \ell(D)} \leq \frac{2b}{C} \left(1 + \frac{1}{(\alpha-1)2^{\alpha}} \right) + \frac{\ell(\hat{A}_{s'})^{\alpha} - \ell(\hat{A}_{s'}) \frac{f(\frac{C}{2})}{\frac{C}{2}} + b}{\frac{f(C)}{C} \ell(D)}$$

$$\leq \frac{2b}{C} \left(1 + \frac{1}{(\alpha-1)2^{\alpha}} \right) + \frac{\ell(\hat{A}_{s'})^{\alpha} + b}{\frac{f(C)}{C} \ell(D)}$$

$$\leq \frac{2b}{C} \left(1 + \frac{1}{(\alpha-1)2^{\alpha}} \right) + \frac{(\frac{C}{2})^{\alpha} + b}{\frac{f(C)}{C} \ell(D)}$$

$$= \frac{2b}{C} \left(1 + \frac{1}{(\alpha-1)2^{\alpha}} \right) \left(2 + \frac{C}{\ell(D)} \right).$$

Upper Bounds for $(\cdot, 2)$-VMA Problem. We now present an algorithm (detailed in Algorithm 2) for $(\cdot, 2)$-VMA problem and show an upper bound on its competitive ratio. A_1 and A_2 are the sets of VMs assigned to PMs s_1 and s_2, respectively, at any given time.

Algorithm 2. Online algorithm for $(\cdot, 2)$-VMA.

---

for *each VM d_i* **do**

    if $\ell(d_i) + \ell(A_1) \leq (b/(2^\alpha - 2))^{1/\alpha}$ *or* $\ell(A_1) \leq \ell(A_2)$ **then**

        d_i is assigned to s_1;

    else

        d_i is assigned to s_2;

We prove the approximation ratio of Algorithm 2 in the following theorem.

Theorem 12. *There exists an online algorithm for $(\cdot, 2)$-VMA that achieves the following competitive ratios.*

$$\rho = 1, \;\; for \; \ell(D) \leq \left(\tfrac{b}{2^\alpha - 2}\right)^{1/\alpha},$$

$$\rho \leq \max\left\{2, \left(\tfrac{3}{2}\right)^{\alpha-1}\right\}, \;\; for \; \ell(D) > \left(\tfrac{b}{2^\alpha - 2}\right)^{1/\alpha}.$$

5 Discussion

We discuss in this section practical issues that must be addressed to apply our results to production environments.

Heterogeneity of Servers. For the sake of simplicity, we assume in our model that all servers in a data center are identical. We believe this reasonable, considering that modern data centers are usually built with homogeneous commodity hardware. Nevertheless, the proposed model and derived results are also amenable to heterogeneous data center environments. In a heterogeneous data center, servers can be categorized into several groups with identical servers in each group. Then, different types of applications can be assigned to server groups according to their resource requirements. The VMA model presented here can be applied to the assignment problem of allocating tasks from the designated types of applications (especially CPU-intensive ones) to each group of servers. The approximation results we derive in this paper can be then combined with server-group assignment approximation bounds (out of the scope of this paper) for energy-efficient task assignment in real data centers, regardless of the homogeneity of servers.

Consolidation. Traditionally, consolidation has been understood as a bin packing problem [31,39], where VMs are assigned to PMs attempting to minimize the number of active PMs. However, the results we derived in this paper, as well as the results in [7], show that such approach is not energy-efficient. Indeed, we showed that PM's should be loaded up to x^* to reduce energy consumption, even if this requires having more active PMs.

VM arrival and departure. When a new VM arrives to the system, or an assigned VM departs, adjustments to the assignment may improve energy efficiency. Given that the cost of VM migration is nowadays decreasing dramatically, our offline positive results can also be accommodated by reassigning VMs whenever the set of VM demands changes. Should the cost of migration be high to reassign after each VM arrival or departure, time could be divided in epochs buffering newly arrived VM demands until the beginning of the next epoch, when all (new and old) VMs would be reassigned (if necessary) running our offline approximation algorithm.

Multi-resource scheduling. This work focuses on CPU-intensive jobs (VMs) such as MapReduce-like tasks [19] which are representative in production datacenters. As the CPU is generally the dominant energy consumer in a server, assigning VMs according to CPU workloads entails energy efficiency. However, there exist types of jobs demanding heavily other computational resources, such as memory and/or storage. Although these resources have limited impact on a server's energy consumption, VMs performance may be degraded if they become the bottleneck resource in the system. In this case, a joint optimization of multiple resources (out of the scope of this paper) is necessary for VMA.

References

1. Alon, N., Azar, Y., Woeginger, G.J., Yadid, T.: Approximation schemes for scheduling. In: Saks, M.E. (ed.) SODA, pp. 493–500. ACM/SIAM (1997)
2. Alon, N., Azar, Y., Woeginger, G.J., Yadid, T.: Approximation schemes for scheduling on parallel machines. J. Sched. **1**(1), 55–66 (1998)
3. Amazon. Amazon web services. http://aws.amazon.com. Accessed 27 August 2012
4. Andrews, M., Fernández Anta, A., Zhang, L., Zhao, W.: Routing for power minimization in the speed scaling model. IEEE/ACM Trans. Netw. **20**(1), 285–294 (2012)
5. Andrews, M., Antonakopoulos, S., Zhang, L.: Minimum-cost network design with (dis)economies of scale. In: Proceedings of 51-st Annual IEEE Symposium on Foundations of Computer Science, pp. 585–592 (2010)
6. Antoniadis, A., Im, S., Krishnaswamy, R., Moseley, B., Nagarajan, V., Pruhs, K., Stein, C.: Energy efficient circuit routing. In: SODA, Hallucination helps (2014)
7. Arjona Aroca, J., Chatzipapas, A., Fernández Anta, A., Mancuso, V.: A measurement-based analysis of the energy consumption of data center servers. In: e-Energy. ACM (2014)
8. Arjona Aroca, J., Fernández Anta, A., Mosteiro, M.A., Thraves, C., Wang, L.: Power-efficient assignment of virtual machines to physical machines (2013). arXiv:1304.7121v2 [cs.DS]. http://arxiv.org/abs/1304.7121
9. Bansal, N., Chan, H.-L., Pruhs, K.: Speed scaling with an arbitrary power function. In: Proceedings of 20-th Annual ACM-SIAM Symposium on Discrete Algorithms, pp. 693–701 (2009)
10. Bansal, N., Gupta, A., Krishnaswamy, R., Nagarajan, V., Pruhs, K., Stein, C.: Multicast routing for energy minimization using speed scaling. In: Even, G., Rawitz, D. (eds.) MedAlg 2012. LNCS, vol. 7659, pp. 37–51. Springer, Heidelberg (2012)
11. Bellur, U., Rao, C.S., Madhu Kumar, SD.: Optimal placement algorithms for virtual machines (2010). arXiv:1011.5064 (http://arxiv.org/abs/1011.5064)

12. Botero, J.F., Hesselbach, X., Duelli, M., Schlosser, D., Fischer, A., de Meer, H.: Energy efficient virtual network embedding. IEEE Commun. Lett. **16**(5), 756–759 (2012)

13. Cardosa, M., Singh, A., Pucha, H., Chandra, A.: Exploiting spatio-temporal trade-offs for energy-aware mapreduce in the cloud. In: 2011 IEEE International Conference on Cloud Computing (CLOUD), pp. 251–258 (2011)

14. Chakrabarty, D., Chekuri, C., Khanna, S., Korula, N.: Approximability of capacitated network design. In: Günlük, O., Woeginger, G.J. (eds.) IPCO 2011. LNCS, vol. 6655, pp. 78–91. Springer, Heidelberg (2011)

15. Chandra, K.A., Wong, C.K.: Worst-case analysis of a placement algorithm related to storage allocation. SIAM J. Comput. **4**(3), 249–263 (1975)

16. Chen, S.-C., Lee, C.-C., Chang, H.-Y., Lai, K.-C., Li, K.-C., Rong, C.: Energy-aware task consolidation technique for cloud computing. In: Proceedings of the IEEE Third International Conference on Cloud Computing Technology and Science, pp. 115–121 (2011)

17. Citrix. Citrix. http://www.citrix.com. Accessed 27 August 2012

18. Cody, R.A., Coffman Jr, E.G.: Record allocation for minimizing expected retrieval costs on drum-like storage devices. J. ACM **23**(1), 103–115 (1976)

19. Dean, J., Ghemawat, S.: Mapreduce: simplified data processing on large clusters. Commun. ACM **51**(1), 107–113 (2008)

20. Epstein, L., Sgall, J.: Approximation schemes for scheduling on uniformly related and identical parallel machines. Algorithmica **39**(1), 43–57 (2004)

21. Fernandez de la Vega, W., Lueker, G.S.: Bin packing can be solved within $1 + \epsilon$ in linear time. Combinatorica **1**(4), 349–355 (1981)

22. Garey, M.R., Johnson, D.S.: Computers and Intractability: A Guide to the Theory of NP-Completeness. W. H. Freeman & Co., New York (1979)

23. Gupta, A., Krishnaswamy, R., Pruhs, K.: Online primal-dual for non-linear optimization with applications to speed scaling. In: Erlebach, T., Persiano, G. (eds.) WAOA 2012. LNCS, vol. 7846, pp. 173–186. Springer, Heidelberg (2013)

24. Im, S., Moseley, B., Pruhs, K.: Online scheduling with general cost functions. In: Proceedings of 23-rd Annual ACM-SIAM Symposium on Discrete Algorithms, pp. 1254–1265 (2012)

25. Jansen, R., Brenner, P.R.: Energy efficient virtual machine allocation in the cloud. In: 2011 International Green Computing Conference and Workshops (IGCC), pp. 1–8 (2011)

26. Kusic, D., Kephart, J.O., Hanson, J.E., Kandasamy, N., Jiang, G.: Power and performance management of virtualized computing environments via lookahead control. Cluster Comput. **12**(1), 1–15 (2009)

27. Liu, N., Dong, Z., Rojas-Cessa, R.: Task and server assignment for reduction of energy consumption in datacenters. In: Proceedings of the IEEE 11-th International Symposium on Network Computing and Applications, pp. 171–174 (2012)

28. Machida, F., Kawato, M., Maeno, Y.: Redundant virtual machine placement for fault-tolerant consolidated server clusters. In: 2010 IEEE Network Operations and Management Symposium (NOMS), pp. 32–39 (2010)

29. Mark, C.C.T., Niyato, D., Chen-Khong, T.: Evolutionary optimal virtual machine placement and demand forecaster for cloud computing. In: 2011 IEEE International Conference on Advanced Information Networking and Applications (AINA), pp. 348–355 (2011)

30. Mills, K., Filliben, J., Dabrowski, C.: Comparing vm-placement algorithms for on-demand clouds. In: Proceedings of the IEEE Third International Conference on Cloud Computing Technology and Science, pp. 91–98 (2011)

31. Mishra, M., Sahoo, A.: On theory of vm placement: anomalies in existing methodologies and their mitigation using a novel vector based approach. In: 2011 IEEE International Conference on Cloud Computing (CLOUD), pp. 275–282 (2011)
32. Nathuji, R., Schwan, K.: Virtualpower: coordinated power management in virtualized enterprise systems. In: SOSP, pp. 265–278 (2007)
33. Van Nguyen, H., Tran, F.D., Menaud, J.-M.: Autonomic virtual resource management for service hosting platforms. In: Proceedings of the 2009 ICSE Workshop on Software Engineering Challenges of Cloud Computing, CLOUD '09, pp. 1–8. IEEE Computer Society (2009)
34. Rackspace. Rackspace. http://www.rackspace.com. Accessed 27 August 2012
35. Srikantaiah, S., Kansal, A., Zhao, F.: Energy aware consolidation for cloud computing. In: Proceedings of the 2008 Conference on Power Aware Computing and Systems, HotPower'08, p. 10. USENIX Association (2008)
36. Van den Bossche, R., Vanmechelen, K., Broeckhove, J.: Cost-efficient scheduling heuristics for deadline constrained workloads on hybrid clouds. In: Proceedings of the IEEE Third International Conference on Cloud Computing Technology and Science, pp. 320–327 (2011)
37. Vazirani, V.V.: Approximation Algorithms. Springer, Heidelberg (2004)
38. Viswanathan, H., Lee, E.K., Rodero, I., Pompili, D., Parashar, M., Gamell, M.: Energy-aware application-centric vm allocation for HPC workloads. In: 2011 IEEE International Symposium on Parallel and Distributed Processing Workshops and Phd Forum (IPDPSW), pp. 890–897 (2011)
39. Wang, M., Meng, X., Zhang, L.: Consolidating virtual machines with dynamic bandwidth demand in data centers. In: IEEE INFOCOM, pp. 71–75 (2011)
40. Xu, J., Fortes, J.: A multi-objective approach to virtual machine management in datacenters. In: Proceedings of the 8th ACM International Conference on Autonomic Computing, ICAC '11, pp. 225–234. ACM (2011)

Services and Applications

SLA-Driven Simulation of Multi-Tenant Scalable Cloud-Distributed Enterprise Information Systems

Alexandru-Florian Antonescu[1,2]($\boxtimes$) and Torsten Braun[1]

[1] Communication and Distributed Systems, University of Bern,
Neubrückstrasse 10, 3012 Bern, Switzerland
alexandru-florian.antonescu@sap.com, braun@iam.unibe.ch
[2] SAP Switzerland, Products and Innovation, Research,
Althardstrasse 80, 8105 Regensdorf, Switzerland

Abstract. Cloud Computing is an enabler for delivering large-scale, distributed enterprise applications with strict requirements in terms of performance. It is often the case that such applications have complex scaling and Service Level Agreement (SLA) management requirements. In this paper we present a simulation approach for validating and comparing SLA-aware scaling policies using the CloudSim simulator, using data from an actual Distributed Enterprise Information System (dEIS). We extend CloudSim with concurrent and multi-tenant task simulation capabilities. We then show how different scaling policies can be used for simulating multiple dEIS applications. We present multiple experiments depicting the impact of VM scaling on both datacenter energy consumption and dEIS performance indicators.

Keywords: Cloud computing · Service level agreement · Scaling

1 Introduction

Cloud Computing [1] is an enabler for delivering large-scale, distributed enterprise applications with strict requirements in terms of performance. It is often the case that such applications have complex scaling and Service Level Agreement (SLA) management requirements. As example, distributed Enterprise Information Systems [2] often interact with large-scale distributed databases, requiring distributed processing of results coming from multiple systems. Specific to cloud environments is the distribution of available cloud resources among multiple tenants, each running a specific set of applications with different workload patterns and SLA requirements.

The advent of Internet applications created new requirements for distributed software running in cloud environments, as the heterogeneity of physical computing infrastructure and application workloads increased. Thus, there is a need for testing the impact of different task allocation and resource scheduling

© Springer International Publishing Switzerland 2014
F. Pop and M. Potop-Butucaru (Eds.): ARMS-CC 2014, LNCS 8907, pp. 91–102, 2014.
DOI: 10.1007/978-3-319-13464-2_7

policies on the performance of distributed applications running in these distributed environments.

One way of achieving these goals of quantifying the performance impact of different resource allocation policies in cloud environments is by using simulations based on previously recorded performance monitoring traces. We extend our work in [3] by using the Distributed Enterprise Information System (dEIS) application model for simulating different SLA-based resource scaling policies in the CloudSim [7] simulator environment.

Our main contributions can be summarized as follows. We extend the CloudSim simulator with support for (1) multiple tenants with a dynamic number of VMs, and for (2) concurrent-tasks simulation at Virtual Machine (VM) level. We also present how to simulate different SLA scaling policies for multiple cloud tenants.

The rest of our paper is organized as follows. Section 2 presents the related work in the field of cloud simulators as well as modeling and simulation of distributed cloud applications.

Section 3 introduces the SLA scaling algorithms and CloudSim extensions required for supporting dynamic resource allocation and scaling. Section 4 presents the evaluation results, and finally, Sect. 5 draws conclusions and gives future research directions.

2   Related Work

There are many publications describing modeling approaches at simulation of cloud infrastructures and applications, focusing on both infrastructure modeling and resource utilization in virtual machines. We present a short overview of some of these works, along with a short description of CloudSim.

Sandhu et al. [4] present an approach at modeling dynamic workloads in CloudSim by considering both random-non-overlap and workload-based profile policies, similar to our approach for modeling dynamic enterprise workloads. However, we extend this work by considering SLA-based VM scaling, multiple tenants and concurrent execution/simulation of application tasks.

Buyya et al. [5] describe a model for simulating cloud resources using CloudSim. They focus on modeling physical and virtual cloud resources, such as physical servers, virtual machines, tasks, allocation and scheduling policies. However, they do not focus on describing application performance models, VM scaling policies or dynamic VM instantiation in CloudSim.

Long et al. [6] present the requirements for evaluating cloud infrastructures using CloudSim. They describe VM CPU utilization models using monitoring information gathered from a set of experiments, and use a power model of representing the energy consumption model in physical hosts. While we also employ a similar approach at modeling VM dynamic workload, we extend this by considering also the concurrent application workload, as well as considering a dynamic allocation of cloud resources by using SLA scaling.

2.1 CloudSim Cloud Simulator

As we used the CloudSim for running the allocation and scaling simulations, we describe briefly its architecture and main components.

CloudSim [7] positions itself as a simulator for both cloud applications and infrastructure. It accomplishes this by allowing modeling of hardware and software cloud resources. Among the modeled physical entities there are: hosts, network links and datacenters, while the modeled software entities are: virtual machines (VMs), brokers and cloudlets (tasks). This is achieved by offering the mentioned entities as Java classes that can be extended according to simulation requirements. The simulator is implemented using discrete events communication, fired at a specified minimum time interval. Cloud tasks (cloudlets) are created by *brokers*, which send them to VMs for execution on the resources of the hosts forming the datacenter. Upon completion of each cloudlet's execution, its parent broker is notified.

In CloudSim, a *datacenter* is composed of (1) a collection of *hosts*, (2) *storage* devices, (3) a policy controlling the allocation of *VMs* to hosts, and (4) resource utilization costs for comsumed computing time, memory, storage and network bandwidth. Each host is defined by (1) its number of *processing elements* and their Millions Instructions Per Second (MIPS) rating, (2) RAM memory size, (3) storage size, (4) network bandwidth, and (5) *VM scheduling policy*. As VM allocation policies it supports (1) time-shared, (2) space-shared, and (3) time-shared with over-subscription. The datacenter network is given using a BRITE [14] network topology specification.

VMs are described by their requirements in terms of (1) number of CPU cores and MIPS rating, (2) memory size, (3) network bandwidth, (4) virtual machine manager, and (5) cloudlet execution policy. There are four built-in cloudlet execution policies: (1) time-shared, (2) space-shared, (3) dynamic-workload, and (4) network space-shared. The CloudSim API allows for easy development of new cloudlet execution policies.

CloudSim models cloud tasks as *cloudlet* entities, defined by (1) computing requirements given as number of processing elements, and computing task length given in MIPS, (2) network bandwidth consumption for input and output, (3) CPU utilization model, (4) memory utilization model, and (5) network bandwidth utilization model.

Cloudlets are generated by *Datacenter Brokers*, which are equivalent to cloud services. Each broker controls one or more VMs and it implements a selection algorithm for choosing which VM to receive a given cloudlet. The broker also implements the algorithm for reacting to the completion of various cloudlets it has generated.

For simulating a distributed application, one must create one or more cloud brokers and implement the algorithms for generating cloudlets, as well as handling their completion. Also, at least one datacenter needs to be defined, including its hosts and network. In Sect. 2.2 we present the architecture of such a distributed enterprise application.

2.2 Distributed Enterprise Information System Architecture

A typical dEIS application consists of the following tiers, each contributing to the SLA management problem: consumer/thin client, load balancer, business logic and storage layer. Figure 1 provides an overview of the overall EIS topology. We shortly present the structure of the EIS system used, with more details found in [8,10]. This class of systems is representative for core enterprise management systems, such as ERP [13].

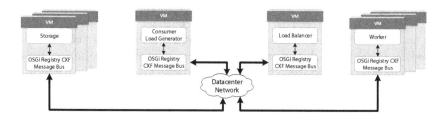

Fig. 1. dEIS architecture

As representative dEIS distributed application we used the one described in [3,8–11]. Targeted dEIS system is composed of four core services: one or more Thin Clients (CS), a Load Balancer (LB), one or more Worker services (WK), and one or more Database Storage services (ST). Each service runs in its own VM and communicates asynchronously with the other services using a distributed service messaging bus.

The CS service contains the graphical user interface, as well as logic for initiating data sessions and issuing requests. The LB service provides load balancing logic, while also maintaining session information about connected clients. The WK services implement data queries, analysis, transactional and arithmetic logic for the application. The ST service contains interfaces and mechanisms for creating, reading, updating and deleting store data. A detailed presentation of the performance model of dEIS can be found in [3].

3 SLA-Driven Distributed Systems Scaling

In this section we present the SLA-based scaling approach for managing VMs. We first describe the Parallel CloudSim Cloudlet Scheduler (PCCS) in Subsect. 3.1, and then, in Subsect. 3.2 we present the SLA scaling manager used for dynamically creating VMs based on SLA policies and application performance indicators.

3.1 Parallel CloudSim Cloudlet Scheduler

Out-of-the-box, the CloudSim simulator does not support either simulation of time-based application level tasks, nor parallel simulation of multiple tasks in a VM. For these reasons, we developed a new time-shared CloudSim cloudlet scheduler, which works as follows. First, the application task's duration is converted from milliseconds to MIPS by considering the MIPS rating of the CPU originally running the task and the average CPU utilization during its execution, as defined by Eq. 1

$$cl_{MIPS} = \frac{1000 \cdot cl_{ms}}{CPU_{MIPS}} \cdot \overline{CPU} \qquad (1)$$

where cl_{MIPS} is the calculated cloudlet's MIPS length, cl_{ms} is the cloudlet's duration in milliseconds when executed on a CPU with a MIPS rating of CPU_{MIPS} and an average utilization of $\overline{CPU}$.

Next, the PCCS will calculate the available CPU MIPS capacity cap of the current time slice ts using the formula presented in Eq. 2

$$cap = CPU_{MIPS}^{VM} \cdot cores \cdot ts \qquad (2)$$

where CPU_{MIPS}^{VM} is the MIPS capacity of the CPU belonging to the VM executing the cloudlet, and $cores$ is the number of cores of the CPU.

Finally, the PCCS will evenly distribute the available MIPS resources between all running cloudlets, each cloudlet receiving a MIPS amount equal to cap/n, where n is the number of active cloudlets in the considered time slice. During our simulations the scheduling time slice was equal to 1 millisecond.

3.2   SLA-Based Scaling Manager

The SLA Scaling Manager (SSM) is responsible for dynamically adjusting the number of VMs for each of the services of the distributed applications and for each of the cloud tenants. It accomplishes this using invariant conditions formed with terms obtained from the performance indicators of the services running in VMs. An example of an invariant condition can be: "average distributed transaction execution time is below one second". The threshold contained in the SLA invariant is then used by the SSM for determining the conditions for performing either a scale-out action [12] (creating one or more VMs), or a scale-in action (terminating one or more VMs).

The SSM operates according to Algorithm 1, mainly by calculating the SLA ratio sr as the factor by which the average over the moving time window W of SLA metric m is approaching its maximum threshold $max_{SLA}(m)$. If sr is above a given threshold S^{UP} (e.g. 0.9) and sr is increasing from the last check then a scale-out operation is flagged. Similarly, if sr is below a threshold S^{DOWN} (e.g. 0.6) and sr is decreasing, then a scale-in operation is flagged. Either scale-out or scale-in operations will be executed only if the number of such operations ss is below a given threshold ss^{MAX} (e.g. 2) in the last W_S seconds (e.g. 40 s, chosen as 1.5 times the time it takes for a VM to become fully operational), for ensuring system stability by preventing (1) fast-succeeding transitory scale-in and scale-out actions, and (2) oscillations in the number of VMs.

For the scale-in operation it is notable that the VM selected for shutdown (with lowest utilization value) is not immediately terminated, but first its broker

Algorithm 1. SSM Scaling algorithm

Data: per tenant: SLA scaling thresholds, monitoring information
Result: per tenant: scale-out, scale-in VM operations
while *not at end of simulation* **do**
    foreach *tenant e* **do**
        calculate average value $\overline{m_{SLA}}$ of SLA metric m over the sliding time window
        W $\overline{m_{SLA}} \leftarrow average\,(m(t), m(t-1), ..., m(t-W))$;
        calculate SLA ratio sr for metric m: $sr \leftarrow \frac{m_{SLA}}{max_{SLA}(m)}$;
        evaluate scale-out condition: $up \leftarrow (sr > s^{UP})AND(sr(t) > sr(t - W_S))$;
        evaluate scale-in condition:
        $down \leftarrow (sr < S^{DOWN})AND(sr(t) < sr(t - W_S))$;
        calculate scaling speed ss as the number of scale-out or scale-in operations in
        the last time window W_S;
        if $(up = true)\,AND\,(ss < ss^{MAX})$ **then**
            create new VM;
        else if $(down = true)\,AND\,(ss < ss^{MAX})\,AND(count(VM) > 1)$ **then**
            select vm for shutdown with lowest load;
            inform VM's broker of imminent shutdown for preventing sending to
            workload to VM;
            wait for T seconds before shutting-down the VM;
        end
    end
    schedule next scheduling check;
end

---

is informed about the scale-in operation for preventing new load being sent to the VM and then after a given time period T (e.g. 10 s), during which tasks running in the VM will get a chance to complete, the VM is finally terminated.

4   Evaluation Results

In order to evaluate the integration of the SLA Scaling Manager and Parallel Cloudlet Scheduler into CloudSim simulator we ran three different simulations testing both the handling of multiple cloud tenants and the ability to scale the number of VMs according to high-level SLAs.

4.1   Simulation 1

In this simulation we considered a single cloud tenant running a constant load of 20 concurrent distributed transactions, with the dEIS system configured to use only one VM for each service. We used this simulation as a base for comparing the others simulations where we will introduce multi-tenancy and varying scaling conditions.

In Fig. 2a we display the simulated load, which varied between 19 and 20 concurrent requests due to asynchronous sampling of the number of active dEIS

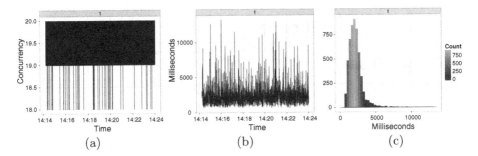

Fig. 2. Simulation 1 (a) CS concurrent load (b) CS response time (c) Histogram of CS response times

requests. Figure 2b shows the response time measured at the CS service for each distributed concurrent transaction, under the given workload. As the simulation model uses datasets from a real distributed application [3], it has a rather large variance. Figure 2c displays the distribution of response times at CS service. The average CS response time was 2200 ms at the considered workload level of 20 concurrent transactions per second.

In Fig. 3a we display the execution times at the WK service, respectively in Fig. 3b at the ST service. This shows the breakdown of total transaction execution time between WK and ST services, with an average WK execution time of 1652 ms and a standard deviation of 1025 ms, and an average of 533 ms and standard deviation of 329 ms for the ST service respectively.

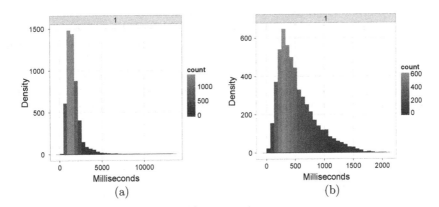

Fig. 3. Simulation 1 (a) Distribution of WK execution times (b) Distribution of ST execution times

Figure 4a displays the hosts' average CPU utilization as calculated from the VMs' CPU utilization, while Fig. 4b shows the energy consumption of the hosts, by considering a linear dependency model between the CPU utilization and

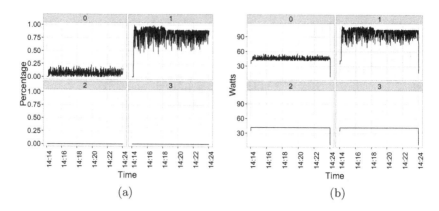

Fig. 4. Simulation 1 (a) Hosts CPU utilization (b) Hosts power consumption

host's power consumption. It is important to note the fact that hosts with no active utilization still consumed a large amount of energy.

Figure 9a shows the total power consumption at datacenter level, summed over every second, for the first simulation. The total simulated energy consumption had a value of 335.9 KJ, distributed evenly across the entire simulation duration, as a consequence of the constant workload.

4.2   Simulation 2

In the second simulation we considered two cloud tenants (client-organization), each executing a varying workload as shown in Fig. 5a, which increased from 1 to 20 concurrent transactions and then decreased back to 1. The first tenant (#0) executed its workload on a fixed virtual infrastructure (static number of VMs/no scaling), while the second tenant (#1) had scaling enabled at 1000 ms for WK the service, and at 400 ms for the ST service respectively.

As shown in Figs. 5b and c, tenant #1 (SLA scaling enabled) had a lower average transaction execution time of 965.8 ms, compared to tenant #0, who had

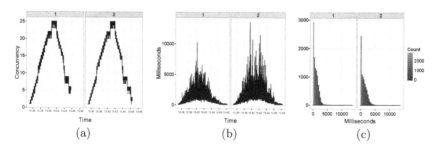

Fig. 5. Simulation 2 - per tenant, CS service (a) Concurrent load (b) Execution time (c) Histogram of execution times

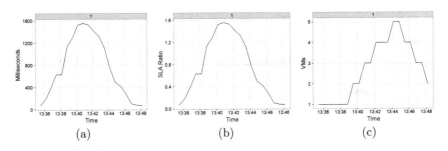

Fig. 6. Simulation 2 - WK service (a) Average execution (b) SLA scaling ratio (c) Number of VMs

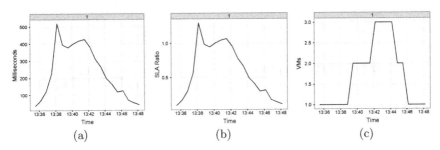

Fig. 7. Simulation 2 - ST service (a) Average execution time (b) SLA scaling ratio (c) Number of VMs

an average execution time of 1144.1 ms. This shows the advantages of running the cloud workload under SLA conditions on a dynamically scaled infrastructure, compared to running it on a fixed-sized virtual infrastructure.

The scaling behavior for tenant #1 is described separately for WK and ST services. Figure 6a shows the average execution time for the WK VMs calculated over a moving time window of 40 seconds, correlated with the concurrent workload presented in Fig. 5a. Figure 6b shows the SLA ratio between the average execution time and the SLA threshold of 1000 ms. As the SLA ratio approached the SLA scaling threshold (0.9 for scale-out, respectively 0.6 for scale-in), the SSM algorithm varied accordingly the number of VMs, as shown in Fig. 6c.

Similarly, the ST service was scaled based on the average execution time shown in Fig. 7a. The SLA scaling ratio for ST service is shown in Fig. 7b, while the actual number of ST VMs is displayed in Fig. 7c. The maximum number of ST VMs varied from 1 to 3 and then back to 1. It is important to note that the system did not oscillate as the SLA scaling ratio approached the scaling threshold, because of the scaling speed limitation mechanism described in Sect. 3.2.

The effect of scaling VMs on the average CPU utilization of hosts can be observed in Fig. 8a, while the energy consumption per host can be observed in Fig. 8b. The total datacenter's power consumption can be visualized in Fig. 9b and had a value of 538 KJ. As the VMs' utilization increases the effect on

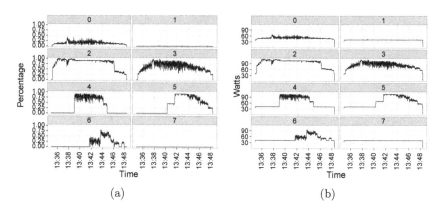

Fig. 8. Simulation 2 (a) Hosts CPU utilization. (b) Hosts power consumption.

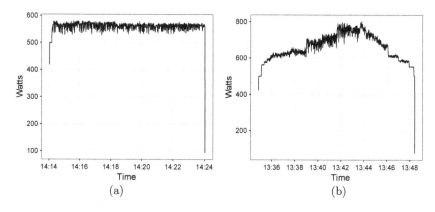

Fig. 9. Total datacenter power consumption. (a) Simulation 1. (b) Simulation 2

datacenter's power consumption is an increase with approx. 20 %, as the idle hosts still contribute significantly to the total power consumption.

4.3   Simulation 3

The third simulation consisted of two tenants, each with SLA scaling enabled. The SLA scaling thresholds were the same for both tenants, 1000 ms for the WK services, respectively 400 ms for ST services.

The workload executed by the first tenant was varying from 1 to 20 and back to 1 concurrent transactions, while the workload of the second tenant was constant at 20 concurrent transactions as shown in Fig. 10a. The execution time per request of each tenant at the CS service is displayed in Fig. 10b, and had an average value of 1017.4 ms for tenant 1, and 1802.2 ms for tenant 2 respectively. The measured average values are consistent with the ones obtained in simulations 1 and 2. The histogram of tenants' execution times measured at the CS service is displayed in Fig. 10c.

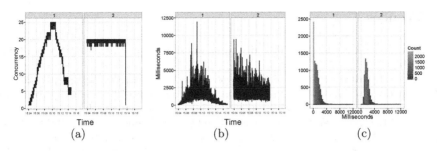

Fig. 10. Simulation 3 - CS service (a) Concurrent load (b) Response time (c) Histogram of response times

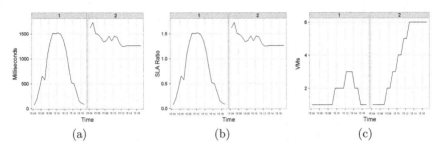

Fig. 11. Simulation 3 - (a) WK average execution (b) WK SLA scaling ratio (c) Number of VK VMs

The WK's average execution time per tenant is displayed in Fig. 11a, while the SLA ratios are displayed in Fig. 11b, and the number of WK's VMs is shown in Fig. 11c. The simulated values are consistent with the ones produced in the previous two simulations.

5   Conclusions

We have shown how CloudSim can be used as a simulation platform for testing SLA-based infrastructure scaling policies using application performance traces recorded from a small-scale cloud deployment. We described, implemented and validated a time-shared parallel cloudlet scheduler for CloudSim, which we used for building and evaluating a SLA scaling manager for VMs, by running three simulations of varying workloads in a multi-tenant cloud environment.

We have also proposed and validated a CloudSim model for translating application-level performance profiling information to VM-level CloudSim scheduler resource utilization level. We have also identified some possible optimization points in cloud infrastructure management, regarding energy consumption of idle servers. We have shown that SLA guarantees can be used for VM scaling purposes when it is possible to convert them to SLA ratios.

As future work we consider evaluating more complex scaling algorithms by using prediction of both the workload and the SLA usage ratios.

References

1. Mell, P., Grance, T.: The NIST definition of cloud computing. NIST Special Publication (2011)
2. Woods, D.: Enterprise Services: Architecture. O'Reilly Media, Sebastopol (2003)
3. Antonescu, A.F., Braun, T.: Modeling and simulation of concurrent workload processing in cloud-distributed enterprise information systems. In: Proceedings of ACM SIGCOMM Workshop on Distributed Cloud Computing (DCC 2014) (2014)
4. Sandhu, A., Kaur, M.: Modeling local broker policy based on workload profile in network cloud. Int. J. Sci. Res. (IJSR) 2(8), 372–376 (2013). India Online ISSN: 2319–7064
5. Buyya, R., et al.: Modeling and simulation of scalable cloud computing environments and the cloudsim toolkit: challenges and opportunities. In: 2009 International Conference on High Performance Computing and Simulation, HPCS'09, IEEE (2009)
6. Long, W., et al.: Using cloudsim to model and simulate cloud computing environment. In: 2013 9th International Conference on Computational Intelligence and Security (CIS) (2013)
7. Lab, G.: Cloud simulator cloudsim (2014). http://code.google.com/p/cloudsim
8. Antonescu, A.F., Braun, T.: Improving management of distributed services using correlations and predictions in SLA-driven cloud computing systems. In: Proceedings of IEEE/IFIP Network Operations and Management Symposium (NOMS), IEEE, Poland, Krakow, May 2014
9. Antonescu, A.F., Oprescu, A.M., et al.: Dynamic optimization of SLA-based services scaling rules. In: Proceedings of 5th IEEE International Conference on Cloud Computing Technology and Science (CloudCom), December 2013
10. Antonescu, A.F., Robinson, P., Braun, T.: Dynamic topology orchestration for distributed cloud-based applications. In: Proceedings of 2nd IEEE Symposium on Network Cloud Computing and Applications (NCCA) (2012)
11. Antonescu, A.F., Robinson, P., Braun, T.: Dynamic SLA management with forecasting using multi-objective optimizations. In: Proceedings of 13th IFIP/IEEE Symposium on Integrated Network Management (IM), May 2013
12. Ferre, M.R.: Vmware ESX server: scale up or scale out. IBM Redpaper (2004)
13. Leon, A.: Enterprise Resource Planning. Tata McGraw-Hill Education, New Delhi (2008)
14. Medina, A., et al.: BRITE: an approach to universal topology generation. In: 2001 Proceedings of Ninth International Symposium on Modeling, Analysis and Simulation of Computer and Telecommunication Systems (2001)

Towards Type-Based Optimizations in Distributed Applications Using ABS and JAVA 8

Vlad Serbanescu$^{(\boxtimes)}$, Chetan Nagarajagowda, Keyvan Azadbakht,
Frank de Boer, and Behrooz Nobakht

Centrum Wiskunde and Informatica, Amsterdam, The Netherlands
{vlad.serbanescu,nagaraja,k.azadbakht,frb,behrooz.nobakht}@cwi.nl

Abstract. In this paper we present an API to support modeling applications with Actors based on the paradigm of the Abstract Behavioural Specification (ABS) language. With the introduction of JAVA 8, we expose this API through a JAVA library to allow for a high-level actor-based methodology for programming distributed systems which supports the programming to interfaces discipline. We validate this solution through a case study where we obtain significant performance improvements as well as illustrating the ease with which simple high and low-level optimizations can be obtained by examining topologies and communication within an application. Using this API we show it is much easier to observe drawbacks of shared data-structures and communications methods in the design phase of a distributed application and apply the necessary corrections in order to obtain better results.

Keywords: Cloud computing · Programming models · Distributed applications · Formal methods · Optimization

1 Introduction

The Java language is one of the mainstream object oriented programming languages that supports a programming to interfaces discipline. It has evolved into a platform to design and implement standards in several domains of both research and industry, along with supporting its community with new language features and standards. With application reaching exascale dimensions in terms of data volumes and requiring a lot of computing power, focus has increased in researching numerous libraries and frameworks with an attempt to provide distribution and concurrency at the level of Java language. However, it is widely recognized that the thread-based model of concurrency in Java that is a well-known approach is not appropriate for realizing distributed systems because of its inherent synchronous communication model. A powerful concept on the other hand is the event-driven actor model of concurrency introduced in [9] which allows many applications to extend these actors to suit their behaviour. Examples of these domains include designing embedded systems [5], wireless sensor networks

© Springer International Publishing Switzerland 2014
F. Pop and M. Potop-Butucaru (Eds.): ARMS-CC 2014, LNCS 8907, pp. 103–112, 2014.
DOI: 10.1007/978-3-319-13464-2_8

[4], distributed web-services [19], multi-core programming [12,18] and delivering cloud services through SaaS or PaaS [14,17]. Furthermore, it provides the basis for increasingly popular languages in parallel and distributed computing like Scala [8]. However, such a language uses an explicit mechanism at application level to support message passing and handling, which diminishes the general object-oriented approach of method look-ups that forms the basis of programming to interfaces.

We introduce Java 8 API [15] to program distributed systems and to formalize actor-based programming which implies asynchronous message passing together with the evergrowing object-oriented software engineering approach. Using asynchronous message passing and a corresponding actor programming methodology which abstracts invocation from execution (e.g. thread-based deployment), we want to fully support and emphasize the programming to interfaces discipline. The main research question of this paper is to demonstrate that using this API, several type-based optimizations can be achieved at the design phase as well as detecting possible bottlenecks in distributed applications using the simple example of The Sieve of Eratosthenes [3,16]. This is the first step in researching how to use type-systems to automate optimizations in parallel and distributed applications.

2   The ABS Language

Our starting point for the actor programming model assumed in this paper is the Abstract Behavioral Specification language (ABS) introduced in [11]. ABS offers programmers several features such as asynchronous method calls, futures to control these calls, interfaces for encapsulation and cooperative scheduling of method invocations inside concurrent (active) objects. Specifically any object created in ABS represents an actor with encapsulated data. Similar to JAVA, their behaviour and state is defined by implementing interfaces with their corresponding methods. Thus they interact by making asynchronous calls to these methods which generate messages that are pushed into a queue specific to each actor. An actor progresses by taking a message out of its queue and processing it by executing its corresponding method. This feature combination results in a concurrent object-oriented model which is inherently compositional. The simplicity of ABS results from the fact that each actor is viewed as a separate processor making it very suitable for modeling distributed applications similar to MPI [6], with the added benefit of specifying a distinct behaviour for each actor without the connectivity issue. Finally asynchronous method calls use futures as dynamically generated references to return values.

3   The ABS-API Library

In this section we focus on the features in Java 8 that allow us to have an efficient and easy to use implementation of the actor model in ABS. First, methods in an interface are declared as Defender Methods using the **default** keyword. This allows actors to have a default behaviour and optionally override this behaviour to suit a specific function. For instance, in Java 8 java.util.comparator provides a default method named reversed() that creates a reversed-order comparator of the original one. Such default method eliminates the need for any implementing class to provide such behavior by inheritance. Second, the introduction of Java Functional Interfaces and lambda expressions is a fundamental change in Java 8. All interfaces that contain only one abstract method are now functional interfaces that at runtime can be turned into lambda expressions. This means that the same lambda expression can be statically cast to a different matching functional interface based on the context. This is a fundamental new feature in Java 8 that facilitates application of functional programming paradigm in an object-oriented language. This API makes use of these new features available in JAVA 8 because many of the interfaces found in the Java libraries are now marked as functional interfaces, most important of which in this context are java.lang.Runnable and java.util.concurrent.Callable. This means that a lambda expression can replace an instance of Runnable or Callable at runtime by JVM. Therefore a lambda expression equivalent of a Runnable or a Callable can be treated as a queued message of an actor and executed. Finally, Java Dynamic Invocation and execution with method handles enables JVM to support efficient and flexible execution of method invocations in the absence of static type information. This feature introduces a new API, available through java.lang.invoke.MethodHandles that allows translation of a lambda expression in Java 8 at runtime to be executed by JVM. Furthermore, this feature has been validated performance-wise over anonymous inner classes and the Java Reflection API. Thus, lambda expressions are compiled and translated into method handle invocations rather reflective code or anonymous inner classes.

The ABS-API library has a fundamental interface namely the Actor Interface. Using an interface for an actor allows an object to preserve its own interfaces, and also it allows for multiple interfaces to be implemented and composed. A Java API for the implementation of ABS models should have the following main features. First, one actor should be able to asynchronously send an arbitrary message in terms of a method invocation to a receiver actor. Second, sending a message can optionally generate the equivalent of an ABS future that the sending actor can use to refer to the return value. Finally, an object during the processing of a message should have a context reference to the sender of a message in order to reply to the message via another message. All these characteristics must co-exist without requiring any modification of the intended interface, for an object to act like an actor. The Actor interface provides a set of default methods, namely the run and send methods, as well as a queue that supports concurrent features of Java API 5. On one hand, the default run method takes a message from the queue, checks its type and executes the message correspondingly. On the other hand, the default (overloaded) send method stores the sent message in the corresponding queue. As mentioned before, in ABS we use futures to control synchronization. In the ABS-API we model messages that are expected to return a result as instances of Callable and a future is created by the send method which is returned to the caller, while those messages that need to run in parallel without a future reference to the outcome are modeled as instances of Runnable.

4 Case Study

Using our solution, we present in this section a parallelized implementation of the Sieve of Eratosthenes [3,16]. We aim to illustrate the benefit of using the Java language to program in an actor-based model while at the same time showing the performance improvement compared to other actor models, the benefit of observing certain behaviours in the programming phase, as well as showing that the actor-based model still performs well when compared to implementations that apply low-level optimizations. Generating prime numbers is a key factor in authentication algorithms. With distributed applications running on several cloud environments, the need to authenticate securely and transparently without a sizable overhead is constantly increasing. At the same time our case study is perfect for modeling partitions as actors as well as making it easy to simulate an application that can work on a multi-core platform using a shared memory or a distributed platform where communication between actors is key. The Sieve of Eratosthenes also allows us to illustrate several optimizations that result from the actor based model, as well as how certain well known optimizations are easy to apply in this model without significantly increasing the code size and therefore the design phase of a distributed application.

To model the algorithm using actors we use the well-known partitioning parallel algorithm and represent each partition as an actor. In this algorithm, the numbers are partitioned into smaller sequences of numbers with the same size. Based on this algorithm, the size of each partition must be equal or greater than(except probably for the last partition) $\lfloor \sqrt{n} \rfloor$, and the number of partitions must be equal or less than $\lceil n/\lfloor \sqrt{n} \rfloor \rceil$, where n is the target number. Following the above-mentioned constraints, the first partition contains all the prime numbers required to sieve, therefore the first actor in the model will be responsible for sending asynchronous messages to the others that will invoke the sieving process. With asynchronous messages written as regular method calls in Java, there is a significant improvement in the ease of programming compared to a similar solution that uses specialized directives like in MPI.

We decided to implement a data structure optimization, and therefore use a BitSet data structure and also half the amount of processing work by eliminating even numbers. These two optimizations clearly improve results and therefore needed to be applied before testing our model to other implementations which have at least these optimizations. We tested our solution on the SurfSara [13] cluster using a 16 CPU machine with 128 GB of memory. A small example of a sieve invocation and using a future to synchronize on the result for checking the correctness of the prime numbers found at the end of the program is given in the following.

```
for (Actor s : actors) {
//sieving process invocation for a new prime number
Future<Object> r = this.send(()->{s.sieve(prime)});
futures.add(r);
}
```

Our main result in this paper is that with just the two standard optimizations, we obtained instant results for candidates up to 10^8 and 2.6 s when testing with 10^9 candidates. We decided to compare our results to the fastest sieving algorithm that further has cache-friendly memory management, wheel factorization and segmented sieve [20]. Our model is only 10 times slower with the record program finishing for a target of 10^9 in 0.26 s. What we want to emphasize however is that the source code size for this record implementation is 505 K compared to 30 K, the size of the Actor-based model. This significantly improves the ease of programming even in a simple distributed application. Further comparisons with other Actor-based models will be discussed in the following section.

4.1 Type-Based Optimization

As discussed before, we aim to use this API to observe certain drawbacks or bottlenecks from the programming phase of the application. In this simple example it is easy to observe that the number of asynchronous messages sent between actors is very high. With the API exposed in the Java language we can easily use a shared data structure to eliminate the messages sent corresponding to each prime number used to sieve the partitions. While this is something very trivial, what we actually aim to extract from this ABS-API is the possibility to detect and automate such optimizations depending on the application that is modeled. We want to be able to analyze several applications which can be CPU-intensive, IO-intensive or with multiple memory accesses and be able to detect performance penalties just like the one above.

5 Experimental Methodologies and Results

The development of multicore CPUs rapidly provides a bigger need for parallel and concurrent programming. Currently there are multiple open source frameworks such as Akka, Erlang, Scala, Finagle, Storm, Hadoop, Ruby, Go Language, Hive and Pig available for distributed parallel and concurrent programming. Further Akka, Finagle, Storm and MapReduce are different elegant solutions for distributed computing and are based on functional programming languages. Pig programs are more complex, and can be compiled into an execution plan consisting of several stages of MapReduce jobs, some of which can run concurrently. Further Pig and Hive are script based data flow languages and thus more volatile and harder to debug during programming and provides a higher level of abstraction for MapReduce programming that is similar to SQL, but it is procedural code, not declarative. They can be extended with User Defined

Functions (UDFs) written in Java, Python, JavaScript, Ruby, or Groovy and includes tools for data execution but was not ideal for implementing the Sieve of Eratosthenes case demonstrated in the proposed paper.

Also there are various actor oriented libraries and languages in the existing techniques for implementing some variant of actor semantics and are based on object oriented programming languages. The actor oriented languages includes but are not limited to Erlang, SALSA, E language and AXUM that are based on message passing. Further one of the important programming models based on message passing is the Actor model. The Actor model is an inherently concurrent model based on asynchronous message passing. Moreover the Actor based model includes many important features such as encapsulation, fair scheduling, location transparency, locality of references which makes the actor model a suitable programming model for distributed parallel and concurrent programming. ABS is a concurrent, object-oriented modeling language that features functional data types. The ABS model uses asynchronous method calls, interfaces for encapsulation, and cooperative scheduling of method activations inside concurrent objects. In specific the ABS language is a class-based object-oriented language that features algebraic data types and side effect-free functions. Also Actors [22] implement a shared-nothing model for concurrency. A model represents a fragment of the state of sieve, specifically some subset of the primes discovered currently in the existing techniques. Further the existing open source frameworks are compared with the ABS model proposed in the paper for performance by implementing the Sieve of Eratosthenes case using the ABS API.

Currently there is a plurality of concurrent programming languages that use the Actor-based model approach for computing the primes using Sieve of Eratosthenes Algorithm. The results obtained from the existing concurrent programming languages such as Scala, Erlang and Go Programming Language are compared with the Actor based model approach implemented for Sieve of Eratosthenes Algorithm in the proposed paper. As discussed in the previous section, the Actor-based model approach proposed in the paper generates primes at $2.6\,\text{s}$ until 10^9 on 16 CPU machines using Sieve of Eratosthenes Algorithm.

In the existing implementation for Sieve of Eratosthenes Algorithm in Ruby using JRuby and Akka [23], both the controller and model actors are defined as distinct classes. The message sent between the actors is a list with a leading symbol and a payload contained in the remainder of the list. The model only considers a value prime if it does not equal or divide evenly into any previously observed primes. The Sieve of Eratosthenes algorithm implemented in Ruby using JRuby and Akka computes primes until 10^4 in $77.114\,\text{s}$. This method was not effective and the performance was really slow once we got past an upper bound of about 10,000 numbers.

This follows a similar implementation [21] for the Sieve of Eratosthenes Algorithm in Erlang where tuples are used for sending messages instead of lists. The Sieve of Eratosthenes algorithm implemented using Erlang calculates primes until 10^6 in $3.6\,\text{s}$. This method was effective for calculating primes until 10^6, but the performance was really slow for higher numbers between the range of 10^7 to 10^9.

Further there are other actor-based languages, like Scala which closely follows the object-oriented model of programming though it has many functional programming features included to support message passing and handling but this method diminishes the general object-oriented approach of method look-ups that forms the basis of programming to interfaces.

Further in the existing technique, the Sieve of Eratosthenes Algorithm is implemented using the Go programming language. Go programming language [2] is a compiled language that combines some of the syntax of C with some more dynamic aspects to form a next generation systems programming language. One interesting feature of the Go language is the built-in multithreading feature which is based on channels and goprocesses. For the Sieve of Eratosthenes implementation using GoLangauge, each time a candidate makes it through the sieve and is returned as a new prime number. Further a new goroutine is created to check future candidates and reject them if they divide evenly by the new prime. The implementation is not useful as a standalone application since it includes no termination condition and also there are other disadvantages in the model as each goroutine knows only about the prime it contains and the channel where candidates should be sent if they pass. Once the goroutine is created its state does not change and also new state is added by creating a new goroutine for a newly-discovered prime and the state is never deleted. Moreover once a prime is discovered, removing it from consideration is non-sensical due to all states being completely distributed and no entity in the system knows about all discovered primes. The Sieve of Eratosthenes algorithm implemented using Go programming language calculates primes until 10^7 in $1\,\mathrm{m}\,33.62\,\mathrm{s}$. This method was effective for calculating primes until 10^7 and could be further optimized using the Wheel Factorization optimization technique which in turn provided better time performance and calculated primes in $12\,\mathrm{s}$ for primes until 10^7.

Using the approach of the Go Programming Language, we tried the same modeling in ABS. We created an object which generated candidate numbers and created new objects with new found primes. The numbers were then sent through asynchronous messages to objects containing primes up until the last object which spawned a separate object with the newly found prime. Each object operated as a separate thread which verified candidate numbers and discarded them. In this manner we discovered that the JAVA backend of ABS was extremely costly performance-wise when sending asynchronous messages and creating new objects. Even after buffering several prime numbers into the same object and balancing the verification load we still obtained very slow results compared even to a naive sequential approach. These results are what prompted us to develop the ABS-API as a layer of translation between ABS and the JAVA backend to both reduce code size and improve performance.

We also looked at some optimizations possible from the API perspective. One interesting optimization was using instruction level parallelism by sieving with more than one prime number at a time. While this is a very trivial task for this application, we want to investigate the possibility of adjusting the overall work of an actor as a load balancing technique implemented directly in the coding phase using the ABS-API. Furthermore we want to introduce a notion of location-awareness to our ABS-API such that actors know when they can communicate using just reads and writes from a shared data structure and when actual asynchronous messages need to be passed in between them depending on the machine that the actors run on. This memory-management optimization is be a significant benefit to Cloud-distributed applications.

6   Related Work

Our Java ABS-API solution was constructed after looking at several works of research and development in the domain of actor modeling and implementation in different languages [10]. We discuss a few languages at the level of modeling and implementation with more focus on Java and JVM-based efforts. Erlang [1] is a programming language used to build massively scalable soft real-time systems with requirements on high availability. It is a functional language, which extends to its native actors support. Its runtime system has built-in support for concurrency, distribution and fault tolerance. Erlang provides language-level features for creating and managing processes with the aim of simplifying concurrent programming. The processes in Erlang communicate using message passing instead of shared variables, which removes the need for locks, but makes all synchronization explicit. Scala [8] is both a functional and object-oriented language that unifies thread-based and event-based programming model to fill the gap for concurrency programming. Like Java it provides the same features for handling concurrency, but it is not possible to manage and schedule priorities on messages sent to other actors. We also compared our results to Akka [7] implementation of the actor model. This toolkit allows to build highly concurrent, distributed, and fault tolerant event-driven applications on the JVM based on actor model.

7   Conclusions

In this paper, we discussed an implementation of the actor-based ABS modeling language in Java 8 which uses the basic object-oriented mechanisms, principles of method look-up and programming to interfaces. We have used the API to model a simple distributed application that remains performant without applying specific optimization and fares much better than other actor-based models. We also showed the functionality of using Java to program distributed applications as well as making it possible to detect possible optimizations at the design phase.

The underlying modeling language has an executable semantics and supports a variety of formal analysis techniques, including deadlock and schedulability analysis. Further it supports a formal behavioral specification of interfaces to be used as contracts. As discussed in Sect. 4.1 our research will focus on using type systems to automate optimization, extend our solution to identify resource usage of programs and communication topologies and apply a corresponding optimization table from which to eliminate drawbacks and bottlenecks during code generation. Our future work will also focus on modeling more difficult distributed applications at testing important cloud features such as reliability, resource-provisioning, multitenancy and scalability. We also aim to automatically generate ABS models from Java code which follows the ABS design methodology. Model extraction allows industry level applications be abstracted into models and analyzed for different goals such as deadlock analysis and concurrency optimization.

References

1. Armstrong, J., Virding, R., Wikström, C., Williams, M.: Concurrent Programming in Erlang. Morgan Kaufmann, San Francisco (1993)
2. Balbaert, I.: The Way to Go: A Thorough Introduction to the Go Programming Language. IUniverse, Bloomington (2012)
3. Bokhari, S.H.: Multiprocessing the sieve of Eratosthenes. Computer **20**(4), 50–58 (1987)
4. Cheong, E., Lee, E.A., Zhao, Y.: Viptos: a graphical development and simulation environment for TinyOS-based wireless sensor networks. In: SenSys, vol. 5, pp. 302–302 (2005)
5. Geoffray, N., Thomas, G., Folliot, B., Clément, C.: Towards a new isolation abstraction for OSGi. In: Proceedings of the 1st Workshop on Isolation and Integration in Embedded Systems, pp. 41–45. ACM (2008)
6. Gropp, W., Lusk, E., Skjellum, A.: Using MPI: Portable Parallel Programming with the Message-passing Interface, vol. 1. MIT press, Cambridge (1999)
7. Haller, P.: On the integration of the actor model in mainstream technologies: the scala perspective. In: Proceedings of the 2nd edition on Programming Systems, Languages and Applications Based on Actors, Agents, and Decentralized Control Abstractions, pp. 1–6. ACM (2012)
8. Haller, P., Odersky, M.: Scala actors: unifying thread-based and event-based programming. Theor. Comput. Sci. **410**(2), 202–220 (2009)
9. Hewitt, C.: Procedural embedding of knowledge in planner. In: IJCAI, pp. 167–184 (1971)
10. Imam, S.M., Sarkar, V.: Integrating task parallelism with actors. In: ACM SIGPLAN Notices, vol. 47, pp. 753–772. ACM (2012)
11. Johnsen, E.B., Hähnle, R., Schäfer, J., Schlatte, R., Steffen, M.: ABS: a core language for abstract behavioral specification. In: Aichernig, B.K., de Boer, F.S., Bonsangue, M.M. (eds.) Formal Methods for Components and Objects. LNCS, vol. 6957, pp. 142–164. Springer, Heidelberg (2011)
12. Karmani, R.K., Shali, A., Agha, G.: Actor frameworks for the JVM platform: a comparative analysis. In: Proceedings of the 7th International Conference on Principles and Practice of Programming in Java, pp. 11–20. ACM (2009)
13. https://surfsara.nl/
14. Nicolae, B., Antoniu, G., Bougé, L., Moise, D., Carpen-Amarie, A.: Blobseer: next-generation data management for large scale infrastructures. J. Parallel Distrib. Comput. **71**, 169–184 (2011). http://dx.doi.org/10.1016/j.jpdc.2010.08.004
15. Nobakht, B., de Boer, F.S.: Programming with actors in Java 8. In: Margaria, T., Steffen, B. (eds.) ISoLA 2014, Part II. LNCS, vol. 8803, pp. 37–53. Springer, Heidelberg (2014)

16. O'Neill, M.E.: The genuine sieve of Eratosthenes. J. Funct. Program. **19**(01), 95–106 (2009)
17. Pierre, G., Stratan, C.: ConPaaS: a platform for hosting elastic cloud applications. IEEE Internet Comput. **16**(5), 88–92 (2012)
18. Pop, F., Dobre, C., Cristea, V.: Evaluation of multi-objective decentralized scheduling for applications in grid environment. In: Proceedings of 2008 IEEE 4th International Conference on Intelligent Computer Communication and Processing, pp. 231–238. IEEE Computer Society, Cluj-Napoca, Romania (2008). ISBN: 978-1-4244-2673-7
19. Serbanescu, V.N., Pop, F., Cristea, V., Achim, O.M.: Web services allocation guided by reputation in distributed SOA-based environments. In: 2012 11th International Symposium on Parallel and Distributed Computing (ISPDC), pp. 127–134. IEEE (2012)
20. Sieve, F.: http://primesieve.org
21. Tasharofi, S.: Efficient testing of actor programs with non-deterministic behaviors. Ph.D. thesis, University of Illinois at Urbana-Champaign (2014)
22. http://heuristic-fencepost.blogspot.nl/2012/02/ruby-and-concurrency-maintaining-purity.html
23. http://absurdfarce.github.io/blog/2012/01/05/ruby-and-concurrency-design-with-actorsandakka/

A Parallel Genetic Algorithm Framework for Cloud Computing Applications

Elena Apostol[✉], Iulia Băluță, Alexandru Gorgoi, and Valentin Cristea

University Politehnica Bucharest, Bucharest, Romania
{elena.apostol,valentin.cristea}@cs.pub.ro,
{iulia.baluta,alexandru.gorgoi}@cti.pub.ro

Abstract. Genetic Algorithms (GA) are a subclass of evolutionary algorithms that use the principle of evolution in order to search for solutions to optimization problems. Evolutionary algorithms are by their nature very good candidates for parallelization, and genetic algorithms do not make an exception. Moreover, researchers have stated that genetic algorithms with larger populations tend to obtain better solutions with faster convergence. These are the main reasons why they can benefit from a MapReduce implementation. However, research in this area is still young, and there are only a few approaches for adapting genetic algorithms to the MapReduce model.

In this article we analyze the use of subpopulations for the GA MapReduce implementations. MapReduce naturally creates subpopulations, and if this characteristic is properly explored, we can find better solutions for genetic algorithm parallelization. In this context, we propose new models for two well know genetic algorithm implementations, namely island and neighborhood model. Our solutions are using the island model, with isolated subpopulations, and the neighborhood model, with overlapping subpopulations. We incorporate these solutions in a framework, that makes the development of Cloud applications using Genetic Algorithm easier.

Keywords: Cloud applications · Map-reduce · Parallel genetic algorithms · Sub-populations

1 Introduction

In the past few years, the increase in the information available on the Internet and the large volumes of information captured by complex scientific equipment in domains like High Energy Physics or Astronomy have determined researchers to explore the domain of data intensive computing. Data-intensive frameworks were developed to deal with these situations. Among them, the MapReduce framework and Hadoop - its open source implementation, are widely used in research these days.

The power of the MapReduce framework comes from the fact that it splits the data into smaller blocks that can be processed in parallel by the mappers

© Springer International Publishing Switzerland 2014
F. Pop and M. Potop-Butucaru (Eds.): ARMS-CC 2014, LNCS 8907, pp. 113–127, 2014.
DOI: 10.1007/978-3-319-13464-2_9

and then transmitted to the reducers for merge. This approach is similar to SIMD processors. For the user of the framework, the process is translated into two functions: a map function and a reduce function. The framework takes care of splitting the data into chunks and passing the results from the mappers to the reducers. The intensive parallel processing nature of this framework makes it a good candidate for execution of parallel algorithms.

Genetic algorithms are a subclass of evolutionary algorithms, and are based on the darwinian principles of evolution and natural selection. A genetic algorithm searches for a solution to a problem by evolving a population of individuals towards fitness maximization. The essential aspects of any genetic algorithm are: how to represent a solution to the problem as an individual (encoding), how to evaluate how good an individual is (fitness) and how to evolve better individuals from the existing ones (selection, crossover).

Evolutionary algorithms are by their nature very good candidates for parallelization, and genetic algorithms do not make an exception. Moreover, researchers have stated that genetic algorithms with larger populations tend to obtain better solutions with faster convergence [4, 10]. These are the main reasons why they can benefit from a MapReduce implementation. However, research in this area is still young, and there are only a few approaches for adapting genetic algorithms to the MapReduce model [2, 4, 6, 9]. These approaches, however, explore but a small part of the parallelization approaches existing in the field. Moreover, they do not discuss the use of subpopulations in their MapReduce implementations. This is an important discussion, as MapReduce naturally creates subpopulations, and if we manage to properly explore and exploit this characteristic we can find better solutions for genetic algorithm parallelization. We propose two alternative solutions to the implementation suggested in [9]: the island model, with isolated subpopulations, and the neighborhood model, with overlapping subpopulations. We proposed and implemented these methods as part of a framework for genetic algorithms in Hadoop. The purpose of the framework is to make the development of genetic algorithms easier and to enhance in this way the research in this area. The framework has two different approaches for adapting genetic algorithms to MapReduce: a coarse grained approach, that follows the island model and a distributed fitness evaluation approach, with three possible models: global population, island model and neighborhood model.

The rest of the paper is structured as follows. In Sect. 2 we present some relevant related work. In Sect. 3 we present the architecture of the framework. In Sect. 4 we describe the methods of applying map reduce. We then describe the distributed fitness evaluation mechanism and the three models that we developed using this method: the global population model, the island model and the neighborhood model. In the fifth section, we present the experiments that we have conducted for the distributed fitness evaluation method. We then evaluate and interpret those results, and, in the last section, we provide conclusions and some ideas for future work.

2   Related Work

Using map reduce for running genetic algorithms has been a subject of research in the last few years. In [2], an adapted model of map reduce with an additional reduce step, has been proposed in order to deal with iterative algorithms like evolutionary algorithms. However, there were some drawbacks regarding that method, mainly the fact that there was a lot of serial execution time and the fact that this model does not use the benefits that map reduce offers but instead forces a new model.

In [9], it is argued that there is no need for adapting the map reduce model for genetic algorithms, but instead we should try to adapt the genetic algorithms to fit into the model. The author succeeds in doing just that and introduces a new model of fine-grained parallel genetic algorithm adapted for MapReduce. In this model, each iteration of the algorithm is transformed into a map reduce job. He also extends his model for two classes of GAs: compact and extended compact genetic algorithms.

This work becomes the starting point of other projects, among which the most notable is [4]. In this article, the job shop scheduling problem is tested using the model in [9], slightly adapted and tuned. The main merit of this work is that it introduces the idea that map reduce might be fit to work with very large populations, that, correctly handled, can lead to faster convergence with very good solutions. It is common for map reduce to work with big data, so this approach suits it.

Our work differs from these previous works in that it incorporates these approaches in a more generic implementation, inside a framework for genetic algorithms in Hadoop. Another contribution that we brought was the discussion regarding the imminent separation of the global population into subpopulations handled by reducers, and the way that we could use this to implement some well-known models for parallel genetic algorithms. We note that implementing these models involve no additional costs, but provides good results for some classes of problems.

3   The Proposed GA Framework Architecture

In order to create a distributed genetic algorithm we must consider the independent elements of the algorithm which will be executed in parallel. Because on Hadoop each mapper takes independent tasks we considered the multiple population coarse grained GA model. Each mapper takes as input a subpopulation and for each individual computes the fitness function and takes care of crossover and mutation. The Reducer's job is to migrate individuals from one subpopulation to another. This way we enlarge the solution space by bringing novelty to populations. We denoted our framework as IGAF, which stands for "Improved Genetic Algorithm Framework".

IGAF is designed on three different levels regarding to the accessibility and configuration from the user's point of view. It consists of several interconnected modules, as depicted in Fig. 1.

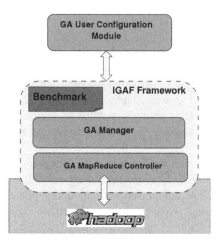

Fig. 1. IGAF framework architecture

At the upper layer stays the *GA User Configuration* module, which is the interface that the user has towards the configuration of the algorithm implementation. Here, the user can set the parameters of the algorithm for the next two levels of the implementation. The parameters that can be set using the configuration model can also be spread into two categories: genetic algorithms parameters, map reduce implementation parameters. The first category consists of the genetic parameters, such as: mutation, crossover, selection and other parameters needed for the tuning of the genetic algorithms: mutation rate, stop criteria, population size, etc. In the second category there are parameters specific to the chosen map reduce implementation: migration percentage, retain best individuals, distributed model, partitioner implementation, etc.

The next level is represented by the *GA Manager*, which contains the logic for the evolutionary algorithms. This module controls the different types of behaviors that can be impose to the Map Reduce stage, such as the *'distributed fitness evaluation'* or the *'island model'*.

In the third level, and the closest to the Hadoop core, there is the *GA MapReduce Controller* which contains two sub-modules. The first sub-module manages the mappers, the reducers and the partitioner. It provides different behaviors for those components and an interface in order to dynamically add new types of behaviors. The second sub-module manages the Map Reduce pipeline, verifies the stop criteria and writes the result in the HDFS at the end of the algorithm.

When dealing with Evolutionary and in particular with Genetic Algorithms there are many parameters to be taken into consideration in order to obtain the best results. These parameters may refer to how the initial populations will be generated, what genetic algorithm model to be used, the migration frequency and rate, the percentage of individual to be removed for the next generation and so on. The Benchmark module gives the user the possibility to adjust these parameters in order to achieve a certain performance regarding the execution time or the solution accuracy.

4   Framework Functionality

In this section we will describe the possible behaviors of the framework, based on the user configuration: the island behavior or the distributed fitness evaluation behavior. We adapted these models to better suit data-intensive Cloud applications. We will present a series of implementation details and the modifications we added to these models.

4.1   The Improved Island Model Coarse-Grained Implementation

The island model works at subpopulation level. Each subpopulation will evolve independently, without any kind of interaction. After all the subpopulations evolved, a migration process will start. The migration process is responsible of diversifying each subpopulation with individuals from other subpopulation.

The framework will pass a subpopulation to each mapper and then, each mapper will evolve its subpopulation. This approach can be seen as a number of genetic algorithms running in parallel and solving the same problem. Initially the solution space of each mapper is different. After the number of pipeline steps increases the solution space of the mappers begins to resemble and to converge.

In a pipeline step the mapper tries to evolve the subpopulation and after the maximum number of generations is reached or the subpopulation cannot evolve anymore, it writes the output (the evolved subpopulation) for the reducers. Each subpopulation has a specific identifier. The reducer decodes the subpopulations and starts the migration process. The default migration process consists of selecting the best $p\%$ chromosomes of the subpopulation i and replacing the worst $p\%$ chromosomes of the subpopulation $i+1$. This behavior can, however, be changed by the user through the configuration section.

Depending on the genetic problem the migration frequency may vary. For example, a genetic problem can have the migration frequency in such way that the migration will be performed in each pipeline step, in random pipeline steps or in every k step.

When migration is complete the reducers write all the subpopulations on the HDFS file system as a final result or for the next pipeline step. The framework analyzes the output received from the reducers and decides if the solution satisfies the input conditions. If more work is required the next pipeline step is prepared and launched on Hadoop.

Since each mapper process starts with a different subpopulation, generic drift will tend to drive these populations into different directions. By introducing migration, the island model is able to exploit differences in various subpopulations; this variation represents a source of genetic diversity. However, migrating a large number of individuals too often may lead to destroying the global diversity (the islands will be less different). On the other hand, if migration doesn't occur often, it may lead to premature convergence of the subpopulations. So when dealing with the island model some aspects need to be considered:

- each reducer must choose the right subpopulations when exchanging individuals
- the migration frequency - how often individuals are exchanged
- the migration rate - the number of individuals exchanged between subpopulations
- the individuals chosen for exchange
- the individuals removed after the new individuals are received [3]

The user can use the Benchmark module in order to obtain a set of configuration parameters that will better suit his/her implementation.

4.2 An Efficient Distributed Fitness Evaluation

This approach is suitable when the fitness function is hard to compute and a lot of data is required for processing. The framework splits the entire population equally to mappers and each mapper will compute the fitness for every individual.

For the implementation of this model, we followed the work of A. Verma [9], and added some improvements.

The main idea is that each iteration of the algorithm will be transformed in a MapReduce job. The mappers will evaluate the time consuming fitness function for each individual, and then the reducers will perform selection, crossover and mutation to produce a new population for the next generation. Figure 2 depicts how the populations are distributed among the mappers and the reducers. Besides these general lines, the mapper and reducer can have additional improvements, depending on the implemented problem.

Because our framework is meant to be generic enough to capture any problem and to allow the user to implement a genetic algorithm in his specific way, much of the mapper's functionality can be configured and changed without the user modifying the specific mapper class.

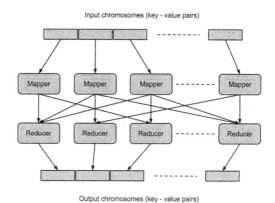

Fig. 2. Distributed fitness evaluation - global population

The Mapper. Each mapper receives a list of individuals and its main purpose is to evaluate the fitness function of each of them and to pass to the reducers the individuals with the fitness value set. Ideally, one mapper per individual would be used, and the calculated fitness should be enough computationally intensive to make the overhead of creating the mappers a small fraction of the total processing time.

Fitness evaluation is generally the first step performed in an iteration of the genetic algorithm, and it is also the part of the algorithm that is most suited for parallelization.

Besides the fitness evaluation, the mapper can include some local search mechanism in order to improve the chromosome that it receives. Also, the mapper can keep track of the best individual it has seen in order to treat it separately. In the implementation in [4], the best individuals are assigned a separate key, in order to be handled by a specific reducer that would determine the best individual at each generation. In our framework, we wanted to leave the decision regarding the handling of the best individuals to the user, by a parameter in the Configuration class indicating that the best individuals should be stored separately.

The Reducer. The reducer has the main purpose of selecting the chromosome for crossover and then performing crossover and mutation to obtain a set of individuals to pass to the next generation.

The selection mechanism, as well as crossover and mutation operators are up to the user. In other implementations of genetic algorithms that we have seen, variants of tournament selection seem to be the top choices. The user of the framework can choose to use this method or selection, as well as other methods with a default implementation offered by the framework, or to implement his own selection method. The same case also happens for the genetic operators of crossover and mutation.

The Partitioner. The partitioner is the one that assigns a certain (key-value) pair representing the output of a mapper to a reducer. By default, the partitioner in Hadoop assigns tasks according to the hash of the key.

In [9] it is argued that this implementation hurts the genetic algorithm, as it can make it converge slower or not converge at all. The reason for this is that the default partitioner sends all the individuals with the same key to the same reducer, creating in this way isolated partitions instead of simulating a global population. The proposed solution was to rewrite the partitioner to distribute randomly individuals from mappers to reducers, not taking in consideration the key assigned by the mapper. In our opinion, if a global population is wanted, then it can be achieved by making each mapper randomly generate a key for each chromosome from a list of keys with different hash values and leaving the default partitioner on. This requires that each mapper will know how many reducers are created, something that we can obtain in our mapper implementation from the Configuration object. Also, another reason why we can take this approach is that we considered IDs as keys, that are meaningful solely for the map-reduce process, as all the information about the individual is retained in the value field attached to the key.

However, the partitioner can be modified in order to handle the best individuals received from each mapper. In [4], the best individual of each mapper was assigned a special key: *null*. The partitioner wouldn't have known how to handle this key, so a new partitioner was implemented, that would group all the individuals with *null* keys to the same reducer, that would evaluate them. We can also note that in this implementation, the authors considered sending the best individuals to a reducer along with other individuals normally assigned by the partitioner to that reducer based on their hash value. However, other variations are possible: a reducer can handle only best individuals or they can be spread uniformly through the reducers. In order to know which way is better, one would have to consider all the possible ways of handling the best individuals and carefully select the one that would best suit its problem.

Population Initialization. The initialization of the population can be a real performance issue if it is done in a serial manner. This is the reason why in parallel implementations of genetic algorithms it is common to also parallelize this part of the algorithm. In the other map reduce implementations that we have study, the solution that was used was to make the initialization in a separate map reduce job, with the mappers generating the initial chromosomes. In this case the reduce phase is skipped and the output from the mappers is the final one. However, this approach creates a map reduce job just for initialization, which means additional overhead. We consider that this section can be incorporated in the first map reduce job. In this case, the mapper will receive a null value instead of an already generated chromosome. Also, before the evaluation of fitness, the mapper can generate a new individual that it will then evaluate normally.

4.3 Working with Subpopulations

The approach we presented so far follows the fine-grained model of parallel genetic algorithms. The original algorithm treats each individual independently and does not evolve subpopulations in isolation.

However, working at subpopulation level can be achieved by ensuring that at each generation, the mappers handling specific individuals and their offspring will always map the results to the same key, thus sending them to the same reducer for selection and mating. The exchange between the subpopulations can be done synchronously after a specific number of generations or asynchronously, each mapper at a random generation.

Isolated Subpopulations. In order to keep subpopulations isolated, we added a key attribute to all individuals, that will be also written in the representation in HDFS. Each reducer associates the key it receives to all individuals in its subpopulation and to all the offspring it creates from parents in the subpopulation.

In this way, all individuals in the same subpopulation will be recognized by the mappers and always sent together to a common reducer. The mapper randomly generates a key in the interval $[0, number\_of\_reducers - 1]$ for each individual in the first generation. In the next generations, since the individual already has a key, it uses that key to associate the individual with calculated fitness to a certain reducer.

Migration can happen, as we already mentioned, synchronously or asynchronously. Migration means that a mapper decides (based on a migration probability or at a certain generation) to send some individuals to another reducer than the one indicated by their associated key. In this case, the mapper generates another random key for a migrated individual and resets the key in its representation.

Migration causes certain reducers to receive more individuals than the normal configured subpopulation size. In this case, the individuals with the lowest fitness values are dropped, to maintain a constant subpopulation size (we can say that the newly received individuals replace the weaker ones in the existing subpopulation). Other reducers might receive less individuals than the subpopulation size. In this case, the receiver produces more offspring to compensate the migrated individuals (Fig. 3).

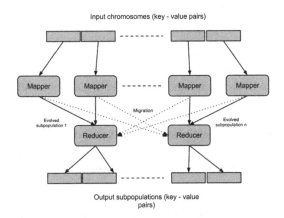

Fig. 3. Distributed fitness evaluation - isolated populations

Overlapping Subpopulations. Also, based on this approach, another well-known model of parallel GAs can be obtained: the neighborhood model, also known as fine grain model, with small overlapping subpopulations. This can be obtained by allowing each mapper to have a specific set of keys, thus communicating with a number of reducers common to other mappers in the neighborhood. In this way, each mapper will communicate through the reducers with only a fraction of the other mappers, the neighborhood of the mappers overlapping in such a way that would allow evolution in all population.

We keep the idea presented in the island model, and we give to each individual a subpopulation *id*. The set of keys for each mapper is constructed by creating a neighborhood of consecutive *ids* derived from the subpopulation *id* of the individual. So, for each individual, there are a number of reducers that will receive it. In this respect, the subpopulation *id* can also be seen as a node *id*, if we think of a grid representation (Fig. 4).

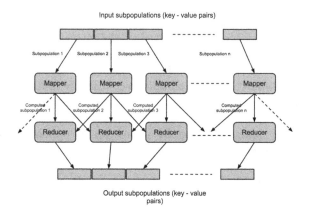

Fig. 4. Distributed fitness evaluation - overlapping subpopulations

Following this analogy, each node in the grid is represented as a mapper and a reducer. This means that the number of mappers will be equal to the number of reducers in this implementation. The mapper will handle the phase of spreading the value of the node in the neighborhood. The reducer will have the role of selecting among the individuals from the subpopulation represented by chromosomes that are locally stored in the node and those received from the neighborhood. After selection, crossover and mutation are performed and, in the end, only a number of individuals equal to the size of the node are kept for the next generation.

In the next generation, based on its *id*, each individual will be sent to the right reducers, so that the neighborhood relationships are kept. In the first iteration, the mapper is responsible for setting the subpopulation *id* of the newly generated chromosomes.

This technique of overlapping subpopulations can be efficient in some situations, as it follows the fine grained model of parallel genetic algorithms.

Parametrization. There are a few important decisions to take when implementing a genetic algorithm and when using distributed fitness evaluation. First of all, there are design decisions common for a genetic algorithm: choosing a chromosome representation, implementing a fitness function, determining the genetic operators: selection, crossover, mutation. The genetic operators must ensure the convergence of the algorithm, while also allowing diversity inside the population for a continuum improvement of the solution from one generation to another and thus to ensure the evolution of the population. Then there are some parameters that can be setup to improve the algorithm: stop criteria, mutation probability, chromosome sampling, population size or the use of a local optimizer.

Population size is especially important when using the distributed fitness evaluation approach, as the individuals of the population will be spread across the mappers for fitness evaluation and then grouped in subpopulations on each reducer for selection, crossover and mutation. It is important that each sub-population has enough individuals to ensure that the individuals selected for reproduction will be good enough to produce offspring that will improve the overall population. So, population size has to be carefully selected together with the number of mappers and the maximum number of reducers that will be created at each generation. The number of mappers and reducers are also dependent on the environment on which the algorithm is deployed.

Another important configuration option is the model that will be used in order to spread the individuals on the reducers. Naturally, the map reduce model creates subpopulations in the reduce step. However, the way subpopulations are used in the three models presented in the previous section are different and can impact the performance and convergence of the algorithm. In the results section, we try to compare the performances of these models on two different problems. However, choosing the best model depends on each problem and on the number of machines available in the environment.

Other decisions that can be taken in order to improve the algorithm for the distributed fitness evaluation approach are: to keep the best individuals on each mapper separately, to override the default partitioner in order to send the best individuals to one reducer or spread them to all reducers.

5   Experiments

5.1   Test Problems

In this section we will present the experiments that we conducted in order to test our framework. We will present the problems we choose for testing, the configurations for those problems and the results that we obtained. We tested our framework on two problems: the Traveling Salesman Problem and the Job Shop Scheduling Problem. Both of them are hard problems that are frequently used for benchmarking of genetic algorithm implementations.

The Traveling Salesman Problem (TSP) consists of finding the minimum path across N cities, starting from one city, visiting all cities exactly once and returning to the starting point. This is equivalent to finding a minimum Hamiltonian cycle in a complete graph with N nodes. For each instance of the problem, it is given the number of cities (N) and the distance between each two cities (or the coordinates of the cities).

For our tests, we used an instance of the problem with 38 cities, corresponding to the state of Djibouti, taken from [8].

The Job Shop Scheduling Problem (JSS) aims at scheduling N jobs, each with M tasks on M machines so that the makespan is minimized. The maskespan of a schedule is the time needed for all jobs to complete their execution, or more specific, the time that passes from the beginning of the first scheduled task until the completion of the last running task. Each task requires to be deployed on a specific machine. The tasks of a job must be executed in a specific order.

For testing we used a classical instance of the job shop scheduling problem: *FT*10. It consists of 10 jobs, each with 10 tasks that must be scheduled on 10 machines. The input data is taken from the *OR library* [1].

5.2   Conducted Experiments

We deployed our solution on the *Grid 5000's* distributed environment [5], using *Hadoop version 1.0.1*. We used *OpenNebula Cloud toolkit* [7] for deploying a Cloud infrastrucure on the *Grid 5000's* site.

We conducted several experiments in order to compare the three models for handling subpopulations: the global population model, the island model and the neighborhood model. We wanted to compare them in terms of result quality. In execution time we cannot see any significant variation, because the operations done by the mappers and reducers are almost the same, the only difference being the mechanism of handling subpopulation, which does not result in significant overhead.

The experiment consisted of varying population size while keeping the number of mappers and reducers constant, with all three models. For the first set of tests we chose as application the Job Shop Scheduling Problem (JSS). We used 50 mappers and 10 reducers, and subpopulations varying from 1000 to 10000 individuals for the first two models. For the neighborhood model, we need to have the same number of mappers and reducers, so we used 50 mappers and 50 reducers, with an overlapping window of 2. This means that a mapper will send its results to two reducers. Overall, the neighborhood model will have more reducers with smaller subpopulations, with the same population size.

The results we obtained are depicted in Fig. 5. We can see that, for all three models, the tendency is to obtain better results with bigger populations. Also, we can see that both the island model and the neighborhood model outperform the global population model. Moreover, the neighborhood model obtains with a population of 1000 better results than the other models obtain with a population of 7000, and the time therefore is considerably smaller. Besides that, we observed that the neighborhood model tends to converge faster than the other two models. The tests were made for 50 generations, and if the other two models were not converging after 50 generations, the neighborhood model was converging in 35 to 45 generations, which again was improving the time needed to run. On the other hand, a faster convergence presents the risk of converging to a local optima.

In order to properly evaluate the difference between the neighborhood model and the other two models, we tested the neighborhood model and the global population model for a more complex problem. We chose the instance of TSP with 38 cities.

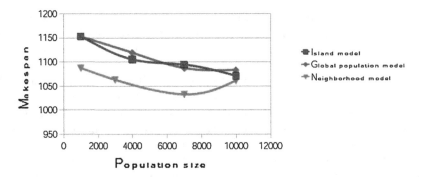

Fig. 5. Island vs. global population vs neighborhood model for JSS

We used 10 mappers and 5 reducers for the global population model and 10 mappers and 10 reducers for the neighborhood model. We kept the overlapping window at 2. The results are depicted in Fig. 6.

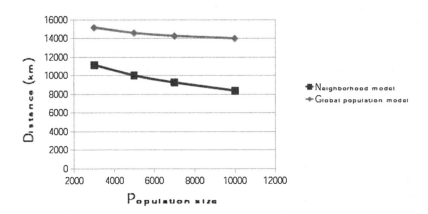

Fig. 6. Global population model vs neighborhood model for TSP

We can observe that in this case, too, the neighborhood model outperforms the global population model, and the difference is even bigger than for the previous test. Moreover, we can see that the global population model does not show much progress for larger populations, while the neighborhood model has a higher evolution rate.

6 Conclusions

Due to its powerful mechanism of handling large amounts of data and its massive parallelization technique, the MapReduce framework can be successfully used for running parallel algorithms. Genetic algorithms, due to their parallel nature and the need of using large populations to solve complex optimization problems, are one of the classes of algorithms that can benefit from this method of parallelization.

Research in the area of genetic algorithm parallelization using Hadoop is still in the beginning, and only a few works in adapting genetic algorithms to this model exist. The most convincing method used so far was to make each generation a MapReduce job. In this article, we used the same concept, but we enhanced it with different methods of handling subpopulations. We observed that is natural for the MapReduce model to form subpopulations, and thus the handling of subpopulations can be done with insignificant additional overhead. We used this characteristic to develop two alternative models: the island model and the neighborhood model. Both models rely on existing parallelization techniques for genetic algorithms, our contribution being to adapt these techniques to the MapReduce model and to add some modifications in order to improve the results.

Overall, we implemented three models for distributed fitness evaluation, with three methods of handling subpopulations: with a global population, isolated subpopulations and overlapping subpopulations. We tested all three implementations on two different problems: the job shop scheduling problem and the traveling salesman problem. There was no significant difference in execution time between the three models, but the quality of the solution was definitely higher for the neighborhood model over the other two models. The island model also outperformed the global population model. Moreover, as the complexity of the problem grows, the difference between the neighborhood model and the other models grows as well. This proved the fact that correctly handling the subpopulations formed by MapReduce can significantly improve the obtained results.

In our tests, we also measured the increase in execution time while increasing the size of the population. Also, we considered the variation in execution time when the number of mappers is increasing. We found that the number of mappers influences the execution time per iteration. The optimum number of mappers must be properly determined through tests. This is an important matter, as a too small number of mappers might get overloaded and a too large number of mappers might lead to additional overhead.

We implemented these models as part of a framework designed specifically for running genetic algorithms in Hadoop. The implementations are generic, so that each new problem could be easily implemented, with their specific parameters and genetic operators. We developed this framework having in mind the fact that, with a starting point and an easier way to develop genetic algorithms in Hadoop, research will grow and new improved models will be implemented.

As future work, we believe it is worth researching ways to reduce the overhead between mappers and reducers, by compressing the representations of individuals and thus reducing the I/O overhead.

Acknowledgments. The research presented in this paper is supported by the following projects: *"SideSTEP - Scheduling Methods for Dynamic Distributed Systems: a self-* approach"*, (PN-II-CT-RO-FR-2012-1-0084); "; *CyberWater* grant of the Romanian National Authority for Scientific Research, CNDI-UEFISCDI, project number 47/2012.

References

1. Beasley, J.: Or-library: distributing test problems by electronic mail. J. Oper. Res. Soc. **41**(11), 1069–1072 (1990)
2. Jin, R.B.C., Vecchiola, C.: Mrpga: an extension of mapreduce for parallelizing genetic algorithms. In: eScience, pp. 214–221, December 2008
3. Cantu-Paz, E.: A survey of parallel genetic algorithms. Calculateurs Paralleles, Reseaux et Syst. Repartis **10**(2), 141–171 (1998)
4. Huang, J.L.D.: Scaling populations of a genetic algorithm for job shop scheduling problems using mapreduce. In: Cloud Computing Technology and Science (2010)
5. Grid5000 home page (2014). Grid5000.Fr
6. Llorà, X., Verma, A., Campbell, R.H., Goldberg, D.E.: When huge is routine: scaling genetic algorithms and estimation of distribution algorithms via data-intensive computing. In: de Vega, F.F., Cantú-Paz, E. (eds.) Parallel and Distributed Computational Intelligence. SCI, vol. 269, pp. 11–41. Springer, Heidelberg (2010)
7. Open nebula home page (2014). OpenNebula.Org
8. The traveling salesman problem official site (2014). TSP.Gatech.Edu
9. Verma, A.: Scaling simple, compact and extended compact genetic algorithms using mapreduce. Master's thesis, University of Illinois at Urbana-Champaign, August 2010
10. Witt, C.: Population size versus runtime of a simple evolutionary algorithm. Theoret. Comput. Sci. **403**(1), 104–120 (2008)

Analysing Scalability Strategies for Service Choreographies on Cloud Environments

Raphael Gomes[1,2]([⊠]), Fabio Costa[1], and Ricardo Rocha[1]

[1] Instituto de Informática, Universidade Federal de Goiás, Goiânia, Brazil
{fmc,ricardo}@inf.ufg.br
[2] Instituto Federal de Goiás, Itumbiara, Brazil
raphael.gomes@ifg.edu.br

Abstract. Scalability is one of the major advantages brought by cloud computing environments. This advantage can be even more evident when considering the composition of services through choreographies. However, when dealing with applications that have quality of service concerns scalability needs to be performed in an efficient way considering both horizontal scaling - adding new virtual machines with additional resources, and vertical scaling - adding/removing resources from existing virtual machines. By efficiency we mean that non-functional properties must be offered in the choreographies while is made effective/improved resource usage. This paper discusses scalability strategies to enact service choreographies using cloud resources. We present efforts at the state of the art technology and an analysis of the outcomes in adopting different strategies of resource scaling. We also present experiments using a modified version of CloudSim to demonstrate the effectiveness of these strategies in terms of resource usage and the non-functional properties of choreographies.

Keywords: Cloud computing · Scalability · Choreography · Auto-scaling

1 Introduction

The provision of quality of service (QoS) is one of the main challenges in cloud computing [5], since this paradigm must provide assurances that go beyond the typical maintenance activities and must provide high reliability, scalability and autonomous behaviour. Many QoS aspects of an application are related with the scalability provided by the hardware resources used to deploy it. As a matter of fact, cloud environments are increasingly used due to their elasticity and the illusion of infinite resources. Increasing degrees of scalability are achieved through the automated management of resources, typically using horizontal scaling, which means changing the amount of resources used, by adding or removing virtual machines (VM) according to policies related to the use of such resources or non-functional properties of the application.

© Springer International Publishing Switzerland 2014
F. Pop and M. Potop-Butucaru (Eds.): ARMS-CC 2014, LNCS 8907, pp. 128–143, 2014.
DOI: 10.1007/978-3-319-13464-2_10

Another strategy for scalability is the use of vertical scaling, i.e. on-the-fly changing of the amount of resources allocated to an already running VM instance, for example, allocating more physical CPU time to a running virtual machine. In a complementary manner, we can have a hybrid approach where we increase both the number and the configuration of virtual machines.

Although there are different scalability strategies they must be used in an efficient way, regarding the consumption of resources. This is due to the fact that a poor management of resources can result in unnecessary spending in the case of public clouds, as well as problems related to energy consumption and loss of investment in the case of private clouds. Another issue that must be taken into account is the QoS offered to applications since some functionalities may not be useful if certain non-functional attributes are not guaranteed [8].

These challenges are even more evident in the so called Future Internet, which results from the evolution of the current Internet, in combination with the Internet of Content [9], the Internet of Services [24] and the Internet of Things [2]. In this new paradigm there are thousands of services belonging to different organizations that have to cooperate with each other in a distributed and large scale environment. This integrated view of services highlighted some problems that were not readily apparent in previous integration efforts, which hardly reached the scale that systems of web services now have [30].

Keeping centralized coordinators for these new types of applications is infeasible due to requirements like fault tolerance, availability, heterogeneity and adaptability. For this reason, the most promising solution may be the organization of decentralized and distributed services through choreographies. Choreographies are service compositions that implement distributed business processes, typically between organizations in order to reduce the number of exchanged messages and distribute business logic, without the need for centralized coordinators, since each service "knows" when to perform its operations and which other services it must interact with [3].

This paper discuss the state of the art in providing scalability for cloud-based service choreographies, considering both technologies and cloud providers. We discuss the outcomes of using cloud environments and the main advantages and disadvantages of adopting different scalability strategies to enact choreographies on cloud resources. We strengthen this discussion with some preliminary evaluation of these strategies. Although this article does not address aspects related to the implementation of choreographies, the analysis presented here can be used as input to different approaches regarding choreography execution in cloud, as well as general applications. The remaining of this paper is as follows: Sect. 2 presents a motivating example; Sect. 3 discusses how actual virtualization technologies and cloud providers handle scalability strategies, while Sect. 4 presents some results of the evaluation of these strategies in choreography enactment. Finally, Sect. 5 discusses related work and Sect. 6 presents the final remarks.

2   Motivating Example

Media sharing is one of the main Internet applications [21]. This type of application was driven by the increasing use of social networks and content sharing platforms such as YouTube, Instagram and Facebook, and its growth brings scalability problems, with increasing demands for data storage and transfer, and the pressure to deliver faster service and other quality attributes. Cloud computing is therefore an increasingly used alternative for resource providers to circumvent these problems. Therefore, in this section we will explore some scenarios to illustrate the complexities involved in the management of scalability issues.

Let us suppose a fictitious organization that uses a public cloud provider or a datacenter (using some virtualization technology) to obtain resources for its applications. One of the applications consists in a choreography of services for media sharing on the web. This application comprises a service for media upload that communicates with other two services: one to perform media storage and another to perform media indexing. There is also a service that provides the website front end.

The services of the application have associated quality of service requirements: initially the upload service must handle at least 100 concurrent requests; data storage must be performed in a secure environment; and indexing overhead should be less than 1 s for at least 90 % of the requests. Based on these requirements and on the expected demand, let us suppose that in order to enact the choreography, it is necessary to allocate one VM for the upload service, as well as using a scalable architecture for media storage, a relational database for data indexing, and another VM for the front end. The services and resources of the initial scenario are illustrated in Fig. 1(a).

After choreography deployment and application execution starts, suppose there is a considerable increase in demand. This behaviour is common in many web applications, which typically starts with only a handful of users but quickly grow to reach thousands and even millions of users. As an example, Facebook has an average growth of 250,000 new users per day [12].

In addition to increased demand, in our scenario another requirement was raised - the viewing of media in various formats. Accordingly, it is necessary to convert the original media, which is a intensive processing task. Thus, two new services must be added to the choreography: one to perform media processing before storage and another to control the queue for this. Furthermore, aiming to increase competitiveness, the upload QoS was modified, aiming to be able to handle ten times more requests concurrently. To meet this new scenario, it is necessary to review the initial resource allocation.

In the additional resource allocation we can adopt the strategies cited before: the first one is to do horizontal scaling. Accordingly, we can create other VM instances and get something like allocation A in Fig. 1(b). On the other hand, we can use vertical scaling and keep the number of resources but increasing their configuration, as in the allocation B in Fig. 1(b).

The main problem in this scenario is to decide which scalability strategy is the preferred option given the quality of service requirements and the cloud provider or technology features, e.g. performance, security, cost, etc. For instance, at a first glance horizontal scaling is a good choice for the media processing service due concurrency issues but what are the outcomes of adopting this strategy instead

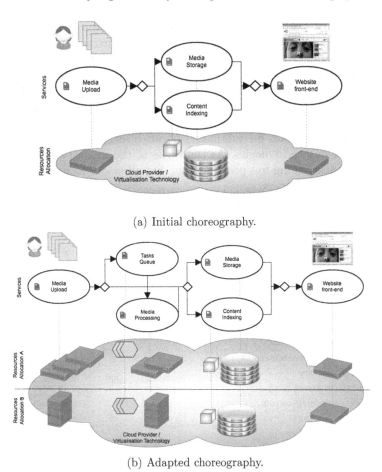

(a) Initial choreography.

(b) Adapted choreography.

Fig. 1. Choreography deployment for the media sharing application.

of vertical scaling? In addition we can even use both strategies by allocating more instances with an increased configuration. Another point is ability to determine the overhead as well as the ability to adopt each of these strategies when using a the given provider/technology.

3 Scalability Strategies in Cloud Platforms

Current virtualization technologies allow the addition of new VM instances as well as the re-dimensioning of running VMs. For horizontal scaling, experiments have shown different values for VM startup time [4,17], although on average it takes about 1 min, while vertical scaling allows to double the processing power in less than 1 s [34]. Gong et al. [15] indicate that changes in the amount of CPU take on average 120 ± 0.55 ms.

Another positive factor for the adoption of a hybrid approach rather than the commonly adopted practice of only scaling resources horizontally is that vertical scaling is quite advantageous in some cases, as Dawoud et al. [10] demonstrate. According to these authors, a web server running on a vertically scaled VM offers better performance than a web server running multiple VMs, i.e. a VM with 4 cores implies a lower response time compared to 4 VM instances running in parallel.

Table 1 presents details on automated resource scaling for some of the main providers and cloud technologies. As can be seen, the majority of them do not support automatic scaling but provide APIs that allow one to perform this task.

Table 1. Scalability in cloud providers/technologies.

Cloud Provider/Technology	Automatic horizontal scaling	Automatic vertical scaling
Amazon (aws.amazon.com)	yes	no
Windows Azure (www.windowsazure.com)	yes	no
Google App Engine (developers.google.com/appengine)	yes	no
Google Compute Engine (cloud.google.com/products/compute-engine)	yes	no
Rackspace (www.rackspace.com)	no	yes
Flexiscale (flexiscaletechnologies.co.uk)	no	yes
GoGrid (www.gogrid.com)	no	no
Joyent Cloud (www.joyent.com)	no	yes
Eucalyptus (www.eucalyptus.com)	no	no
Xen (www.xenproject.org)	no	yes

By using the *Auto Scaling* and *Cloud Watch* in Amazon EC2, it is possible define policies for VM creation and destruction. The average startup time for a new instance on this provider is between 2 and 10 min, though this time is close to 100 s for instances running Linux [20]. Similarly, VM startup time in Windows Azure is around 10 min, although different requests for VM creation may take up different amounts of time. Experiments in [17] indicate a delay of 4 min between the startup time of the first and fourth instance using Azure. Some cloud providers like Google App and Compute Engine[1] offer horizontal auto scaling, although it is not possible manage its operation.

Regarding vertical scaling, in Rackspace, Flexiscale and Joyent Cloud it is possible to do scaling of processor but this requires VM reboot. CPU scaling can be performed until it reaches the full capacity of the underlying physical machine [32]. In Xen we can also have scaling of memory, which is performed by a process known as *memory ballooning*, which allows changing of the amount of memory to a VM while it is running. A similar mechanism is offered for CPU scaling [27].

---

[1] In the Google Compute Engine horizontal auto scaling is implemented as an application from App Engine.

In addition to the APIs offered by cloud providers is possible to use frameworks to achieve automated scaling of resources. Table 2 [13] shows some of these frameworks, together with the providers they support and details on the scaling capacity.

Table 2. Frameworks for cloud resource management.

Framework	Supported providers	Scaling strategy
Cloudify (www. cloudifysource.org)	Amazon, OpenStack, Azure, HP Cloud, Rackspace	Automated scaling based on metrics related to VM configuration and number of instances
Cloud Foundry (www. cloudfoundry.com)	Amazon, OpenStack, Rackspace, Eucalyptus	Manual change in the number of VMs associated with an application
Scalr (www.scalr.com)	Amazon, OpenStack, Rack- space, Nimbula, Eucalyptus, IDC Frontier, CloudStack, Cloud Foundry	Automated scaling of infrastructure and database when they are overloaded or when scheduling is done
OnApp (onapp.com)	Xen, KVM, VMware and other smaller public provider	Vertical scaling with automated VM migration when the physical machine does not have enough resources

Besides scaling, it is necessary to take into account the time required to perform VM migration from one physical machine to another when the existing resources are insufficient. Considering Xen for instance, VM migration requires the transfer of all memory. However, the migration mechanism hides the latency by continuing running the application on the original VM while the memory contents are transferred. Experiments in [25] show that the migration of a VM with 800 MB of memory on a LAN using Xen caused unavailability of 165 ms to 210 ms and increased application execution time in 17–25 s. However, during this period throughput decreases only 12 %. The results in [31] show that, in an instance of an almost overloaded system (serving 600 concurrent users), migration causes significant downtime (about 3 s) but the 99th SLA percentile could be met, i.e. 99 % of more critical SLA could be met.

Based on the above, although there are no records of accurate results for all technologies in the literature, we can state that the achievement of scaling in two dimensions (vertical and horizontal) is feasible. Having said that, we now present some experiments to evaluate how these strategies work in the context of service choreographies.

4   Evaluating Scalability Strategies to Service Choreographies

We performed some preliminary experiments to analyse the scalability strategies and evaluate how it interferes in the resource usage and the QoS offered to choreographies. Through this experiment, we expect to answer the following research questions:

- Does the cost associated with the allocation of resources justify potential advantages obtained?
- Which one is the best strategy for resource scaling in a choreography enactment?
- How different scaling policies interfere in the usage of resources and nonfunctional characteristics of services choreographies?

The experiments were performed using simulations through a modified version of CloudSim [7]. Initially we present the modifications implemented and then we describe the experiments and their results. To design and describe the experiments we follow our structure proposed by Wohlin et al. [33].

4.1   Simulator

CloudSim [7] is an extensible toolkit that enables modelling and simulation of clouds, as well simulation of policies for resource provisioning. This simulator is usually used to investigate the infrastructure design decisions by analysing different configurations [6]. Cloud providers are modelled in the simulator as *Datacenters* receiving service requests. These requests are elements encapsulated in *VMs* that need to allocate shared processing power in a given *Host* in the datacenter. The *VMScheduler* component is responsible for scheduling the host that runs each VM.

Applications running in the cloud environment are represented as a set of *Cloudlets*, which store execution data as request size in millions of instructions (MI); and utilization modes of CPU, memory and bandwidth. The *Datacenter-Broker* component is responsible for simulation and management of cloudlets, and to configure their policies of resource management.

CloudSim has some limitations that hinder the simulation of our scenario. For example, it does not enable the simulation of automatic resource provisioning and it simulates just a single service. Thus, we implemented an extension of CloudSim to overcome these limitations and enable the simulation of choreography enactment. The implementation of auto scaling mechanism was made using a simplified version of the model proposed by Amazon for its services *Cloud-Watch* and *Auto Scaling*. According to this model, it is possible to establish metrics for resource monitoring, and policies for VM manipulation.

For representation of choreographies, we adopted the semantics of Web Service Choreography Description Language (WS-CDL) [19], an XML-based language to describe collaboration between multiple stakeholders in a process of business. WS-CDL is a W3C recommendation detailed at http://www.w3.org/TR/2005/CR-ws-cdl-10-20051109.

The modifications made in CloudSim not influence the core operation, since we added only metrics collection and resource allocation policies. Thus, the results remain equivalent to a real scenario.

4.2 Simulation of Resource Allocation Policies Applied to a Service Choreography

We performed simulations of running the media sharing application in a cloud environment adopting different policies for resource allocation. In those simulations, we aimed to analyse how those policies impact in resource usage and the application QoS.

Experiment Design. Our experiment evaluates how different resource scaling policies interfere in the usage of cloud resources and the resulting choreography's QoS.

Experiment Planning. We evaluate the scalability by simulating horizontal, vertical and hybrid scaling policies. The simulated scenario is the enactment of the media sharing choreography (Sect. 2) in a single cloud provider. The following variables were analysed:

- **Latency:** mean enactment time of the choreography.
- **Usage (VM):** mean and variance of the load in the virtual machines.
- **Usage (Host):** mean and variance of the load in the hosts (physical machines).
- **AWRT:** Average Weighted Response Time, as proposed by Grimme et al. [16], which measures how much, on average, users should expect to have their requests met.
- **Execution Overhead:** how much, on average, the execution time differs from an estimated optimal value. This value is taken assuming that the request in question is the only one in the cloud, i.e., no other concurrent requests share the same resource.

The size of the media used as input in the simulation was obtained randomly, whereas values between 0 and 10 GB. The activities duration, expressed in MI, that composes the choreography was estimated according to the size of the media, considering the average connection speed in Brazil and values obtained with benchmarks [22, 23, 26].

We evaluated scenarios with different requests per second rates: 1, 5, 10 and 30. For the horizontal scaling we performed scenarios with 1, 5, 10 and 30 running VMs. We used VM configurations equivalent to the types of Amazon EC2 *m1.small*, *m1.medium*, *m1.large* and *m1.xlarge* for the vertical scaling. In the hybrid approach, both the amount and configuration of VMs have changed. For each simulation, we consider a fixed amount of resources allocated. The simulated cloud consists of 10 hosts with same configuration: equivalent to a machine Intel® Xeon® Processor X5570, 8 GB of RAM.

Experiment Execution. This experiment is based on the modified version CloudSim described above. The choreographies submitted in the simulation were generated and stored so that the same input sets were used in the three scaling strategies.

There was no need of any treatment regarding the validity of the data.

Analysis and Interpretation of Results. Each experiment starts with the same scenario of one VM type *small* and load of one request/s. To evidentiate the difference among results, charts were plotted on a logarithmic scale, except for the chart of strategy costs (Fig. 3).

The first variable taken was the latency. As can be seen in Fig. 2(a), when there is 1 req/s the increase in VM number only brings high gains when going from 1 to 5 VMs, with a decrease of 52.8 % on average latency. With scaling to 10 VMs the gain decreases to 4.14 % and after that no more gains are obtained. This is due the fact that there are few requests, since a similar behaviour is observed in horizontal scaling when there are 5 req/s. Therefore, the horizontal scaling can only be justified for large-scale scenes, such as 30 req/s, where the gain is always greater than 50 % (Fig. 2(a)).

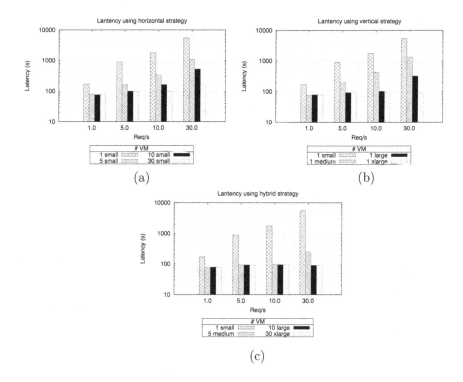

Fig. 2. Latency. (a) Horizontal strategy. (b) Vertical strategy. (c) Hybrid strategy.

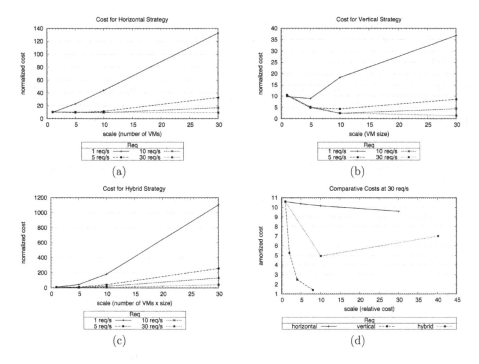

Fig. 3. Cost of scaling. (a) Horizontal strategy. (b) Vertical strategy. (c) Hybrid strategy. (d) Comparative among strategies.

Comparing the horizontal and vertical approaches (Figs. 2(a) and (b)), we can see that, regarding latency, to use only 1 VM type *medium* is almost as satisfying as using 5 VMs type *small*. For types *large* and *xlarge* the vertical strategy is more advantageous than the horizontal strategy. This shows that the allocation of a larger number of VMs is not the best approach in this scenario. This is mainly because of the cost: considering a public cloud, the most extreme case (30 req/s) would require the expenditure of $2.40 per hour in a horizontal approach and $0.64 using the vertical strategy[2].

The hybrid strategy (Fig. 2(c)) shows that increasing the amount and configuration of VMs only bring benefit in the first modification, i.e. move from one VM type *small* to 5 VMs type *medium*. The only exception is the case of 30 req/s, for which the second modification also brought gains. Comparing the vertical and hybrid approaches (Figs. 2(a) and (b)) we found that the hybrid strategy has not brought gains in some cases. This reinforces the argument that changing the configuration of VMs can be a better strategy than allocate a greater amount of VMs.

---

[2] This estimation is using Amazon EC2 resources in São Paulo (Brazil) availability zone in February/2014.

To compare each scaling strategy, we defined the cost of each scaling, called *normalized cost*, by the expression $cost\_per\_hour/(QoS \times load)$, where $cost\_per\_hour$ is the cost to implement the strategy, considering the number and type of VMs, QoS is the inverse of latency and *load* is the number of requests per seconds. Thus, a scaling strategy is better when the normalized cost decreases as the scale increases, for a same load. To a fair comparison among different strategies, we converted each strategy scale to a relative scale cost (per hour), considering that one small VM has a cost of one unit.

Figure 3 shows graphs of the normalized cost for each scaling strategy. Figure 3(d) shows a comparison between the cost of each strategy, on a load of 30 request/s. Figure 3(d) endorses the idea that the vertical strategy is the best strategy for the simulated scenario. Also, each strategy presents a point where it does not produce any benefit. As shown in Figs. 3(a) and (c), scaling in horizontal and hybrid approaches is only a beneficial approach at higher loads (close to 30 request/s).

The execution overhead and AWRT presented the same behaviour of latency, so the corresponding charts will not be shown or discussed. We also analyse the impact of scaling approaches on the use of resources, since the use of resources must be maximized in private clouds. Initially we analyse the use of physical machines. Since this factor depends solely on the amount and configuration of VMs created and there is no change in these attributes at runtime, the results are similar for all the requests rate and, so we put them together to facilitate comparison.

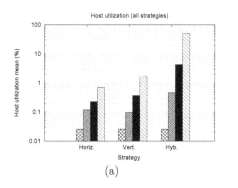
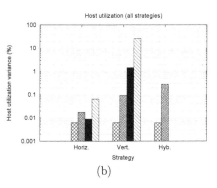

Fig. 4. Host usage. (a) Average. (b) Variance.

In Fig. 4 we can see the average and variance of utilization of physical machines. As showed in Fig. 4(a), the average host usage has no major changes when comparing the horizontal and vertical approaches, despite a much larger amount of VM created in the horizontal approach. Regarding the hybrid approach, only there was considerable use of resources in the latter case (30 VMs type *xlarge*), where the average utilization of physical machines was above 50 %. The low utilization rates for the other cases is due to the large number of available resources in the cloud.

The usage variance (Fig. 4(b)) shows that resources were allocated almost uniformly. The only exception occurred in the vertical approach using VM type *xlarge* for which variance was 26.31 %.

Regarding the VM usage, we note that even with a greater number of instances, the horizontal approach has a higher average utilization (Fig. 5(a)). This was expected since, by having a more limited setting, VMs need to conduct a more intensive processing to complete the activities. On the contrary, the creation of 30 VMs makes the average utilization of VMs lesser than 2 % for 1, 5 and 10 req/s. Even at 30 req/s the usage is no more than 25 %, which shows that most of these resources are idle, representing a loss. On the other hand, use only 1 or 5 VMs (with same configuration) causes the average utilization be near 100 % when there are many requests.

The vertical approach also seemed to be the best alternative with respect to the use of resources. Mean usage (Fig. 5(b)) with the type *medium* was around 50 % in almost all cases. For the type *large* this value was lower, not exceeding 25 %. The use of type *xlarge* makes the average utilization be very low, less than 4 % in all cases. For the hybrid case (Fig. 5(c)) the scaling only improves substantially the usage from the first to the second simulated case (5 VMs type *medium*), since allocation of more resources decrease the average usage to a low percentage, no more than 1 %.

In the analysis of usage variance it makes no sense to take into account the cases with only one VM running. As a result, according to Figs. 5(d) and (e) we can see that there are major differences only in extreme cases where the amount of VMs is greater than or equal to 10. This happens because in the other cases there is a limited number of VM, which makes usage occurs almost uniformly.

With this experiment we concluded that the allocation of a greater number of VMs is not the best strategy when considering services choreographies. Our results suggest that, due to dependencies between choreography activities, the use of a strategy that minimizes the execution time may produce improved results. However it is still necessary a mechanism to decide which strategy is the best in each scenario, using adaptive algorithms that learn with the execution historic. For services choreographies we can even use different strategies to each services set. In a future experiment, we plan to evaluate how a choreography style and architecture may influence the gain of each scaling strategy.

5   Related Work

There have been significant research efforts on the analysis of virtualization technologies [18,31] or cloud providers performance [11,17], mainly related to effects of horizontal or vertical scaling on the perceived latency.

Vaquero et al. [29] survey various approaches for application scalability in clouds at three different levels: server, network and platform; they also discriminate the two types of scalability: horizontal and vertical.

Suleiman et al. [28] identify a series of research challenges related to the scalability of existing solutions. Their work aims to determine how much to scale,

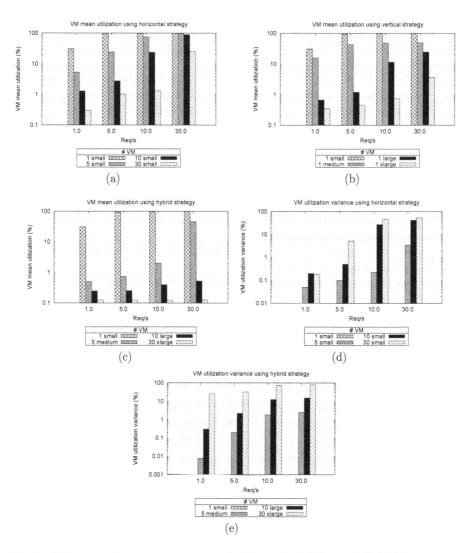

Fig. 5. VM usage. Average on horizontal (a), vertical (b) and hybrid (c) strategy. Variance on horizontal (d) and hybrid (e) strategy.

taking into account automated scaling mechanisms and the costs associated with licensing, as well as the flexibility enabled by the size and type of resources that can be scaled. They also analysed how to scale, and which scaling strategy to choose, conducting a trade-off analysis between horizontal and vertical solutions.

Nevertheless none of these works considers scalability in clouds to enact service choreographies. As we pointed out above, there are some particularities that must be taken into account, like dependencies between services or concurrency issues. To the best of our knowledge there is no other work that considers this subject.

6 Final Remarks

In this paper we discuss how the main cloud providers and virtualization technologies provide scalability. By means of experiments carried out through simulation, we investigate the impacts of using three scalability strategies do enact service choreographies on cloud resources.

While vertical scalability is possible in principle for all applications, it largely depends on the service provider to offer the mechanisms to implement this type of scaling dynamically. Horizontal scalability on the other hand mostly depends on the application components and the application as a whole to support it as an option [1]. As pointed out the overhead of each strategy also needs to be taken into account. Horizontal scaling, for instance, requires on average 10 min to start a new VM instance, which may not be feasible in scenarios that involve real-time applications.

We evaluated some scalability scenarios to enact service choreographies. In our analysis we concluded that vertical scaling is the best option in terms of cost, resource usage and application QoS attributes for the application considered. This result, although not be general for various application areas, it has applicability in resource allocation in approaches that use cloud computing in the general case. For instance, a model-driven development process can manage the relation between the infrastructure and the actual application non-functional requirements choosing the most suitable scalability strategy to meet these requirements [14].

Nevertheless important scenarios with scalability patterns still need to be evaluated. In addition, a more precise analysis must be performed in order to provide elements that will enable a more effective scalability strategy. In particular, it is necessary to characterize the nature and behaviour of choreographies, including the characteristics of each individual service, using this information to refine the evaluation of scalability strategies. In our work the main focus was application load but this analysis can take into account other aspects such as service load and the use of public vs. private clouds.

References

1. Andrikopoulos, V., Binz, T., Leymann, F., Strauch, S.: How to adapt applications for the Cloud environment. Computing **95**(6), 493–535 (2013)
2. Atzori, L., Iera, A., Morabito, G.: The internet of things: a survey. Comput. Netw. **54**(15), 2787–2805 (2010)
3. Barker, A., Walton, C., Robertson, D.: Choreographing web services. IEEE Trans. Serv. Comput. **2**(2), 152–166 (2009)
4. Bellenger, D., Bertram, J., Budina, A., Koschel, A., Pfänder, B., Serowy, C., Astrova, I., Grivas, S., Schaaf, M.: Scaling in cloud environments. Recent Researches in Computer Science (2011)
5. Blair, G., Kon, F., Cirne, W., Milojicic, D., Ramakrishnan, R., Reed, D., Silva, D.: Perspectives on cloud computing: interviews with five leading scientists from the cloud community. J. Internet Serv. Appl. **2**(1), 3–9 (2011)

6. Caglar, F., An, K., Shekhar, S., Gokhale, A.: Model-driven performance estimation, deployment, and resource management for cloud-hosted services. In: Proceedings of the 2013 ACM Workshop on Domain-Specific Modeling, pp. 21–26. ACM (2013)
7. Calheiros, R., Ranjan, R., Beloglazov, A., De Rose, C., Buyya, R.: CloudSim: a toolkit for modeling and simulation of cloud computing environments and evaluation of resource provisioning algorithms. Softw. Pract. Exper. 41(1), 23–50 (2011)
8. Chung, L., do Prado Leite, J.C.S.: On non-functional requirements in software engineering. In: Borgida, A.T., Chaudhri, V.K., Giorgini, P., Yu, E.S. (eds.) Conceptual Modeling: Foundations and Applications. LNCS, vol. 5600, pp. 363–379. Springer, Heidelberg (2009)
9. Daras, P., Williams, D., Guerrero, C., Kegel, I., Laso, I., Bouwen, J., Meunier, J., Niebert, N., Zahariadis, T.: Why do we need a content-centric future Internet? Proposals towards content-centric Internet architectures. Inf. Soc. Media J. (2009)
10. Dawoud, W., Takouna, I., Meinel, C.: Elastic virtual machine for fine-grained cloud resource provisioning. In: Krishna, P.V., Babu, M.R., Ariwa, E. (eds.) ObCom 2011, Part I. CCIS, vol. 269, pp. 11–25. Springer, Heidelberg (2012)
11. Dejun, J., Pierre, G., Chi, C.-H.: EC2 performance analysis for resource provisioning of service-oriented applications. In: Dan, A., Gittler, F., Toumani, F. (eds.) ICSOC/ServiceWave 2009. LNCS, vol. 6275, pp. 197–207. Springer, Heidelberg (2010)
12. Facebook: Statistics (2013). https://newsroom.fb.com
13. Ferry, N., Rossini, A., Chauvel, F., Morin, B., Solberg, A.: Towards model-driven provisioning, deployment, monitoring, and adaptation of multi-cloud systems. In: CLOUD 2013: IEEE 6th International Conference on Cloud Computing, pp. 887–894 (2013)
14. Gomes, R., Costa, F., Bencomo, N.: On modeling and satisfaction of non-functional requirements using cloud computing. In: Proceedings of the 2013 IEEE Latin America Conference on Cloud Computing and Communications (2013)
15. Gong, Z., Gu, X., Wilkes, J.: Press: predictive elastic resource scaling for cloud systems. In: 2010 International Conference on Network and Service Management (CNSM), pp. 9–16. IEEE (2010)
16. Grimme, C., Lepping, J., Papaspyrou, A.: Prospects of collaboration between compute providers by means of job interchange. In: Frachtenberg, E., Schwiegelshohn, U. (eds.) JSSPP 2007. LNCS, vol. 4942, pp. 132–151. Springer, Heidelberg (2008)
17. Hill, Z., Li, J., Mao, M., Ruiz-Alvarez, A., Humphrey, M.: Early observations on the performance of Windows Azure. In: Proceedings of the 19th ACM International Symposium on High Performance Distributed Computing, pp. 367–376. ACM (2010)
18. Huang, X., Bai, X., Lee, R.M.: An empirical study of VMM overhead, configuration performance and scalability. In: 2013 IEEE 7th International Symposium on Service Oriented System Engineering (SOSE), pp. 359–366 (2013)
19. Kavantzas, N., Burdett, D., Ritzinger, G., Fletcher, T., Lafon, Y., Barreto, C.: Web services choreography description language version 1.0. W3C candidate recommendation, 9 (2005)
20. Li, A., Yang, X., Kandula, S., Zhang, M.: CloudCmp: comparing public cloud providers. In: Proceedings of the 10th ACM SIGCOMM Conference on Internet Measurement, pp. 1–14. ACM (2010)
21. Miller, M.: Cloud Computing: Web-Based Applications that Change the Way You Work and Collaborate Online. Que Publishing, Indianapolis (2008)
22. Movavi: Faster Performance with Cutting-Edge Tech (2014). http://www.movavi.com/videoconverter/performance.html

23. MySQL: Estimating Query Performance (2014). http://dev.mysql.com/doc/refman/5.0/en/estimating-performance.html
24. Papadimitriou, D.: Future Internet - The cross-ETP vision document. European Technology Platform, Alcatel Lucent 8 (2009)
25. Ruth, P., Rhee, J., Xu, D., Goasguen, S., Kennell, R.: Autonomic live adaptation of virtual networked environments in a multidomain infrastructure. J. Internet Serv. Appl. **2**(2), 141–154 (2011)
26. Seagate: Savvio® 10K.5 SAS Product Manual (2012)
27. Senthil N.: Dynamic resource provisioning for virtual machine through vertical scaling and horizontal scaling. Ph.D. Dissertation. Department of Computer Science and Engineering, Indian Institute of Technology (2013)
28. Suleiman, B., Sakr, S., Jeffery, R., Liu, A.: On understanding the economics and elasticity challenges of deploying business applications on public cloud infrastructure. J. Internet Serv. Appl. **3**(2), 173–193 (2012)
29. Vaquero, L.M., Rodero-Merino, L., Buyya, R.: Dynamically scaling applications in the cloud. SIGCOMM Comput. Commun. Rev. **41**(1), 45–52 (2011)
30. Vincent, H., Issarny, V., Georgantas, N., Francesquini, E., Goldman, A., Kon, F.: CHOReOS: scaling choreographies for the internet of the future. In: Middleware'10 Posters and Demos Track, p. 8. ACM (2010)
31. Voorsluys, W., Broberg, J., Venugopal, S., Buyya, R.: Cost of virtual machine live migration in clouds: a performance evaluation. In: Jaatun, M.G., Zhao, G., Rong, C. (eds.) Cloud Computing. LNCS, vol. 5931, pp. 254–265. Springer, Heidelberg (2009)
32. Voorsluys, W., Broberg, J., Buyya, R.: Introduction to cloud computing. In: Cloud Computing, pp. 1–41 (2011)
33. Wohlin, C., Runeson, P., Höst, M., Ohlsson, M., Regnell, B., Wesslén, A.: Experimentation in Software Engineering: An Introduction. Kluwer Academic Publishers, Boston (2000)
34. Yazdanov, L., Fetzer, C.: Vertical scaling for prioritized VMs provisioning. In: 2012 Second International Conference on Cloud and Green Computing (CGC), pp. 118–125. IEEE (2012)

Foundational Models for Resource Management in Cloud

Towards Efficient Power Management in MapReduce: *Investigation of CPU-Frequencies Scaling on Power Efficiency in Hadoop*

Shadi Ibrahim[1]([⊠]), Diana Moise[2], Houssem-Eddine Chihoub[3],
Alexandra Carpen-Amarie[4], Luc Bougé[5], and Gabriel Antoniu[1]

[1] Inria, Rennes Bretagne Atlantique Research Center, Rennes, France
{shadi.ibrahim,gabriel.antoniu}@inria.fr
[2] InIT Cloud Computing Lab, ZHAW Winterthur, Winterthur, Switzerland
diana-maria.moise@zhaw.ch
[3] Inria, Sophia Antipolis Research Center, Sophia Antipolis, France
houssem-eddine.chihoub@inria.fr
[4] Vienna University of Technology, Vienna, Austria
carpenamarie@par.tuwien.ac.at
[5] ENS Rennes/IRISA, Rennes, France
luc.bouge@ens-rennes.fr

Abstract. With increasingly inexpensive cloud storage and increasingly powerful cloud processing, the cloud has rapidly become the environment to store and analyze data. Most of the large-scale data computations in the cloud heavily rely on the MapReduce paradigm and its Hadoop implementation. Nevertheless, this exponential growth in popularity has significantly impacted power consumption in cloud infrastructures. In this paper, we focus on MapReduce and we investigate the impact of dynamically scaling the frequency of compute nodes on the performance and energy consumption of a Hadoop cluster. To this end, a series of experiments are conducted to explore the implications of *Dynamic Voltage Frequency scaling* (DVFS) settings on power consumption in Hadoop-clusters. By adapting existing DVFS governors (i.e., *performance, powersave, ondemand, conservative* and *userspace*) in the Hadoop cluster, we observe significant variation in performance and power consumption of the cluster with different applications when applying these governors: the different DVFS settings are only sub-optimal for different MapReduce applications. Furthermore, our results reveal that the current CPU governors do not exactly reflect their design goal and may even become ineffective to manage the power consumption in Hadoop clusters. This study aims at providing more clear understanding of the interplay between performance and power management in Hadoop cluster and therefore offers useful insight into designing power-aware techniques for Hadoop systems.

Keywords: MapReduce · Hadoop · Power management · DVFS · Governors

© Springer International Publishing Switzerland 2014
F. Pop and M. Potop-Butucaru (Eds.): ARMS-CC 2014, LNCS 8907, pp. 147–164, 2014.
DOI: 10.1007/978-3-319-13464-2_11

1 Introduction

Power consumption has started to severely constrain the design and the way data-centers are operated. Power bills became a substantial part of the monetary cost for data-center operators. Hamilton [11] estimated that money spent on electrical power of servers and cooling units had exceeded 40 percent of total expenses of data-centers in 2008.

The surging costs of operating large data-centers have been mitigated by the advent of cloud computing, which allowed for better resource management, facilitated by the adoption of virtualization technologies. Nevertheless, overall energy consumption is continuously increasing as a result of the rapidly growing demand for computing resources. While various energy-saving mechanisms have been devised for large-scale infrastructures, not all of them are suitable in a cloud context, as they might impact the performance of the executed workloads. For instance, shutting down nodes to reduce power consumption may lead to aggressive virtual machine consolidation and resource over-provisioning, with dramatic effects on application performance. green cloud computing has thus emerged in an attempt to find a proper tradeoff between performance requirements and energy efficiency. To address this challenge, green clouds focus on the use of renewable energy sources, as well as on optimizing energy-saving mechanisms at the level of the data-center. Many research efforts have targeted power-saving techniques based on the Dynamic Voltage Frequency Scaling (DVFS) support in modern processors. In this paper, we aim at investigating the efficiency of such techniques in the context of large-scale data processing, which covers a major share of all cloud applications.

The most popular paradigm for data processing has been proposed by Google through their MapReduce model [6], which gained a wide adoption due to features including scalability, fault tolerance, and simplicity. Its most well-known open-source implementation, Hadoop [10], was designed to process hundreds of terabytes of data on thousands of cores at Yahoo!. As such large-scale deployments become a distinctive characteristic of cloud infrastructures, energy-efficient MapReduce is nowadays an essential concern in data-centers. Several studies have explored power saving in Hadoop clusters, through various techniques [2,4].

MapReduce systems span over a multitude of computing nodes that are frequency and voltage-scalable. Our study, conducted on a Grid'5000 cluster [17], investigates the CPU-usage variation for three representative MapReduce benchmarks (*Pi*, *Grep* and *Sort*). As shown in Fig. 1, the CPU load is high (more than 90 %) during almost 75 % of the job running time for the *Pi* application and is relatively high (more than 75 %) only during 65 % and 15 % of the job running time for *Grep* and *Sort* jobs, respectively. Thus, there is a significant potential for reducing energy consumption by scaling down the CPU when the peak CPU performance is not required by the workload.

The contribution of this paper is to investigate such opportunities for optimizing energy consumption in Hadoop clusters. We rely on a series of experiments to explore the implications of DVFS settings on power consumption in Hadoop clusters. As DVFS research has reached a certain maturity, several CPU Frequency Scaling tools and governors have been proposed and implemented in the Linux kernel. For instance, governors such as *ondemand* or *performance* tune the CPU frequency to optimize application execution time, while *powersave* is designed to lower energy consumption.

We study the impact of different governors on Hadoop's performance and power efficiency. Interestingly, our experimental results report not only a noticeable variation of the power consumption and performance with different applications and under different governors, but also demonstrate the opportunity to achieve a better tradeoff between performance and power consumption.

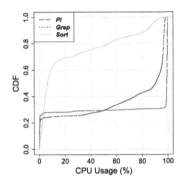

Fig. 1. CPU utilization when running *Pi*, *Grep* and *Sort* benchmarks with 7.5 GB of data in a 15-node Hadoop cluster: for the Pi and Grep applications, which represent CPU-intensive MapReduce applications, we observe that the CPU load is either high - more than 90 % and 80 % during 75 % and 55 % of the job running time - or low - less than 1 % for 21 % of the job running time, respectively. Conversely, for Sort application, a mostly I/O-intensive application, the CPU load has more variation.

The primary contributions of this paper are as follows:

1. It experimentally demonstrates that MapReduce applications experience variations in performance and power consumption under different CPU frequencies (similar to [32]) and also under different governors. A micro-analysis section is provided to explain this variation and its cause.
2. It illustrates in practice how the behavior of different governors influences the execution of MapReduce applications and how it shapes the performance of the entire cluster.

This study aims at providing a more clear understanding of the interplay between performance and power management in Hadoop clusters, with the purpose of deriving useful insights for designing power-aware techniques for Hadoop.

Paper Organization. The rest of this paper is organized as follows: Sect. 2 briefly presents Hadoop and the existing CPU power-management techniques. This section also discusses the related work. Section 3 describes an overview of our methodologies, followed by the experimental results in Sects. 4 and 5. Finally, we conclude the paper and propose our future work in Sect. 6.

2   Background and Related Work

In this section, we briefly introduce Hadoop and existing DVFS mechanisms. This section also presents related work on MapReduce energy consumption in data-centers and clouds.

2.1   Hadoop

Yahoo!'s Hadoop project [10] is a collection of various sub-projects for supporting scalable and reliable distributed computing. The two fundamental sub-projects feature a distributed file system (HDFS) and a Java-based open-source implementation of MapReduce through the Hadoop MapReduce framework. HDFS is a distributed file system that relies on a master/slave architecture to provide high-throughput access to application data [10]. The master server, called *namenode*, splits files into chunks and distributes them across the cluster with replication for fault tolerance. It holds all metadata information about stored files. The HDFS slaves are called *datanodes* and are designed to store data chunks, to serve read/write requests from clients and propagate replication tasks as directed by the *namenode*. Hadoop MapReduce is a software framework for distributed processing of large data sets on compute clusters. It runs on top of HDFS, thus collocating data storage with data processing. A centralized *Job Tracker* (JT) is responsible of: (a) querying the *namenode* for the block locations, (b) scheduling the tasks on *Task Trackers* (TT), based on the information retrieved from the *namenode*, and (c) monitoring the success and failures of the tasks.

2.2   Power Management at CPU Level

Modern processors offer the ability to tune the power mode of the CPU through the introduction of idle processor operating states (C-states) and CPU performance states (P-states). A C-state indicates whether the processor is currently active or not: processors in C_0 state are executing instructions while processors in higher C-states (C_i where $i = 1, 2$, *etc.*) are considered idle. Higher C-states reflect a deeper sleep mode, and thus increased power savings.

The P-states determine the processor frequencies and their associated voltage: Processors in the P_0 state run at the highest frequency and processors in the highest P-state run at lowest frequency. The number of available P-states varies by processor type.

Dynamic Voltage Frequency Scaling (DVFS) is a commonly used technique that improves CPU utilization and power management by tuning the CPU frequency according to the current load. The ideal DVFS mechanism can instantaneously change the voltage/frequency values. Since the 2.6.10 version of the

Table 1. CPU Governors

CpuFreq Goevrnor	Goal	Short description	Downsides
Performance	Maximize performance	Statically sets the CPU frequency to the highest available frequency	High power consumption
Powersave	Maximize power savings	Statically sets the CPU frequency to the lowest available frequency	Long response time
Ondemand	Power efficiency with reasonable performance	Dynamically adjusts the CPU frequency to the highest available frequency when the load is high and gradually degrades the CPU frequency when the load is low	Low performance/power saving benefits when the system switches between idle states and heavy load often
Conservative	Power efficiency with reasonable performance	Gradually upgrades the CPU frequency when the load is high and gradually degrades the CPU frequency when the load is low	Worse performance than Ondemand
Userspace	Support for user-defined frequencies	Statically sets the CPU frequency to a user-defined value	-

Linux kernel, there are five different governors available to dynamically scale the CPU frequency according to the CPU utilization. Each governor favors either performance or power efficiency, as shown in Table 1. More details can be found in [26]). Moreover, setting the governor to *userspace* allows users to use their own strategy in adjusting the CPU frequency. Additionally, modern CPUs provide a new feature called Turbo Boost which enhances the performance of a subset of a machine's cores by boosting their clock speed, while the rest of the available cores are in a sleep state.

2.3 Related Work

MapReduce has attracted much attention in the past few years [18]. Substantial research efforts have been dedicated to either adopting MapReduce in different environments such as multi-core [25], graphics processors (GPU)s [12], and virtual machines [15, 30] or to improving MapReduce performance through skew-handling [16, 21] and locality-execution [14, 33].

There have been several studies on evaluating and improving the MapReduce energy consumption in data-centers and clouds. Many of these studies focus on power-aware data-layout techniques [1, 19, 20, 23, 28, 29], which allow servers to be turned off without affecting data availability. GreenHDFS [19] separates the HDFS cluster into hot and cold zones and places the new or high-access data in the hot zone. Servers in the cold zone are transitioned to the power-saving mode and data are not replicated, thus only the server hosting the data will be woken up upon future access. Rabbit [1] is an energy-efficient distributed file system that maintains a primary replica on a small subset of always on nodes (active nodes). Remaining replicas are stored on a larger set of secondary nodes which are activated to scale up the performance or to tolerate primary failures. These data placement efforts could be combined with our approach to reduce the power consumption of powered servers. Instead of covering a set of nodes, Lang and Patel propose an all-in strategy (AIS) [22]. AIS saves energy in an all-or-nothing fashion: the entire MapReduce cluster is either on or off. All MapReduce jobs are queued until a certain threshold is reached and then all the jobs are executed with full cluster utilization.

Some works consider energy saving for MapReduce in the cloud [2, 34]. Cardosa *et al.* [2] present virtual machines (VMs) replacement algorithms that co-allocate VMs with similar runtime on the same physical machine in a way that the available resources are highly utilized. Consequently, this maximizes the number of idle servers that can be deactivated to save energy. Chen *et al.* [5] analyze how MapReduce parameters affect energy efficiency and discuss the computation versus I/O tradeoffs when using data compression in MapReduce clusters in terms of energy efficiency [4]. Chen *et al.* [3] present the *Berkeley Energy Efficient MapReduce* (BEEMR), an energy efficient MapReduce workload manager motivated by empirical analysis of real-life MapReduce with Interactive Analysis (MIA) traces at Facebook. They show that interactive jobs operate on just a small fraction of the data, and thus can be served by a small pool of dedicated machines with full power, while the less time-sensitive jobs can run in a batch fashion on the rest of the cluster. Recently, Goiri *et al.* [9] present GreenHadoop, a MapReduce framework for a data-center powered by renewable green sources of energy (e.g. solar or wind) and the electrical grid (as a backup). GreenHadoop schedules MapReduce jobs when green energy is available and only uses brown energy to avoid time violations.

Closely related works focus on achieving power efficiency in Hadoop clusters by using DVFS [27, 32]. Li *et al.* [27] discuss the implications of temperature (machine heat) on performance and energy tradeoffs of MapReduce. Based on the observation that higher temperature causes higher power consumption even with the same DVFS settings, they propose a temperature-aware power allocation (TAPA) that adjusts the CPUs frequencies according to their temperature. TAPA favors the maximum possible CPU frequency, thus maximizing computation capacity, without violating the power budget. Wirtz and Ge [32] compare the power consumption and the performance of Hadoop applications in three settings: (1) fixed frequencies, (2) setting the frequencies to maximum frequencies when executing the map or reduce otherwise minimum, and (3) performance-constraint frequency settings that tolerate some performance degradation while achieving better power consumption. Our work relies on the "Fine-grained" frequencies assignment, aiming to achieve the same performance while minimizing the power consumption.

Dynamic Voltage Frequency Scaling Techniques. There is a large body of work on techniques that control the DVFS mechanism for power-scalable PC cluster [7,8,13,24,31]. Some of these techniques control the CPU frequencies at runtime [13] and some scale the frequencies statically, based on extensive and expensive application profiling [7]. However, our approach differs from such works in the target applications (MapReduce applications).

3 Methodology Overview

The experimental investigation conducted in this paper focuses on exploring the implications of executing MapReduce applications in different DVFS settings. We conducted a series of experiments in order to assess the impact of various DVFS configurations on both power consumption and application performance. We further describe the experimental environment: the platform, deployment setup and used tools.

3.1 Platform

The experiments were carried out on the Grid'5000 [17] testbed. The Grid'5000 project provides the research community with a highly-configurable infrastructure that enables users to perform experiments at large scales. The platform is spread over 10 geographical sites located in France. For our experiments, we employed nodes belonging to the Nancy site on the Grid'5000. These nodes are outfitted with a 4-core Intel 2.53 GHz CPU and 16 GB of RAM. Intra-cluster communication is done through a 1 Gbps Ethernet network. It is worth mentioning that only 40 nodes of the Nancy site are equipped with power monitoring hardware consisting of 2 Power Distribution Units (PDUs), each hosting 20 outlets. Since each node is mapped to a specific outlet, we are able to acquire coarse and fine-grained power monitoring information using the Simple Network Management Protocol (SNMP). It is important to state that Grid'5000 allows us to create an isolated environment in order to have full control over the experiments and the obtained results.

3.2 Benchmarks

MapReduce applications are typically categorized as CPU-intensive, I/O bound, or both. For our analysis, we chose 3 applications that are commonly used for benchmarking MapReduce frameworks: *distributed grep, distributed sort* and *distributed pi*.

- **Distributed grep.** This application scans the input data in order to find the lines that match a specific pattern. The grep example can be easily expressed with MapReduce: the map function processes the input file line by line and matches each single line against the given pattern; if the matching is successful, then the line is emitted as intermediate data. The reduce function simply passes the intermediate data as final result.
- **Distributed sort.** The sort application consists in sorting key/value records based on key. With MapReduce, both the map and reduce functions are trivial computations, as they simply take the input data and emit it as output data. The sort MapReduce implementation takes advantage of the default optimizations performed by the framework that implicitly sorts both intermediate data and output data.
- **Distributed pi.** This benchmark estimates the value of pi based on sampling. The estimator first generates random points in a 1×1 area. The map phase checks whether each pair falls inside a 1-diameter circle; the reduce phase computes the ratio between the number of points inside the circle and the ones outside the circle. This ratio gives an estimate for the value of pi.

Of these 3 benchmarks, *pi* is purely CPU-intensive, while *grep* and *sort* are also I/O bound. However, *sort* is more data-intensive than *grep*, since it generates significantly more output data.

3.3 Hadoop Deployment

On the testbed described in Sect. 3.1, we configured and deployed a Hadoop cluster using the Hadoop 1.0.4 stable version [10]. The Hadoop instance consists of the namenode, the jobtracker and the Hadoop client, each deployed on a dedicated machine, leaving 13 nodes to serve as both datanodes and tasktrackers. The tasktrackers were configured with 4 slots for running map tasks and 2 slots for executing reduce tasks. At the level of HDFS, we use the default chunk size of 64 MB and the default replication factor of 3 for the input and output data. In addition to facilitating the tolerance of faults, data replication favors local execution of mappers and minimizes the number of remote map executions. Prior to running the benchmarks, we generated 900 chunks of text (adding up to 56 GB) to feed the *grep* and *sort* applications. This input size results in fairly long execution time which allows us to thoroughly monitor power consumption information.

3.4 Dynamic Voltage Frequencies Settings

The experiments involve running the benchmarks with various CPU settings and monitoring the power consumed by each node in this time frame. We distinguish a total of 15 scenarios corresponding to various values for CPU governors and frequencies. We were able to set the governor to conservative, on demand, performance, powersave, and userspace. With the governor set to userspace, we tune the CPU frequency to one of the following values: 1.2 GHz, 1.33 GHz, 1.47 GHz, 1.6 GHz, 1.73 GHZ, 1.87 GHZ, 2 GHz, 2.13 GHZ, 2.27 GHZ, 2.4 GHZ, 2.53 GHZ.

4 Macroscopic Analysis

In this section, we provide a high-level analysis of the experimental results we obtained. Our goal is to study the impact of various *governors* or CPU frequencies on the performance of several classes of MapReduce applications.

Figure 2 depicts the completion time and the energy consumption of each *governor* for our three applications: *pi*, *grep* and *sort*. Each point on the graphs stands for the application runtime and the total energy consumption of the Hadoop cluster during its execution for a specific CPU frequency or *governor*. We computed the total energy consumption for each application as the sum of the measured utilized power of each cluster node with a resolution of 1 second between measurements. In addition, Fig. 3 displays a comparative view of the average power consumption of a job for each of the three applications and DVFS settings.

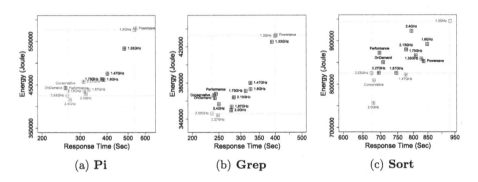

(a) Pi   (b) Grep   (c) Sort

Fig. 2. Application runtime vs Energy consumption under various DVFS settings

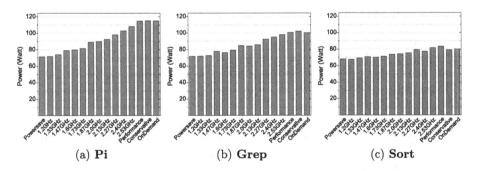

(a) Pi   (b) Grep   (c) Sort

Fig. 3. Average Power consumption under various DVFS settings

4.1   Performance Analysis

The results show the job completion time increases as the employed CPU frequency decreases, for each of the three applications. In the case of the *pi* and *grep* applications, the runtime increases by 104 % and 70 %, respectively, when replacing the highest frequency, that is 2.53 GHz, with the lowest one, namely 1.2 GHz. The explanation for this behavior comes from the fact that the runtime of these two applications mostly accounts for computation, as they produce very little output data. Thus, the CPU performance has a significant impact on application execution time. The *sort* application is IO-bound, generating the same amount of output data as the input data. As in our experiments we employed an input file of 900 chunks replicated 3 times, i.e. 56 GB of processed data and 168 GB of output data, *sort* spent a significant percentage of its execution time in reading data from and writing it to HDFS. Consequently, unlike *pi* and *grep*, the *sort* application exhibits a different behavior: reducing the CPU frequency from the highest to the lowest possible value only results in a 38 % runtime increase.

These results are consistent with the CDF of the CPU usage depicted in Fig. 1. *Pi* is a purely CPU-intensive application and consequently its CPU usage is the highest, amounting over 80 % for most of the CPU frequencies and governors. At the other end of the spectrum, the IO-bound workload of *sort* is the main factor that accounts for an average CPU usage between 20 % and 28 %.

4.2   Energy Consumption

The energy consumption on a Hadoop cluster depends on several parameters. One key factor is the CPU frequency, as low CPU frequencies also trigger low power consumption for a specific node. The application workload can however have an essential influence on the total energy utilized by the cluster. On the one hand, CPU-bound applications account for high CPU usage and thus for an increased energy consumption. Additionally, the application runtime directly impacts on the energy needed by the cluster, and thus attempts to improve application performance may result in better energy-efficiency. In this section we analyze the tradeoff between the aforementioned factors in the case of our three types of applications.

Figure 3(a) details the mean power consumption of a cluster node for each of the available fixed frequencies and all the governors, computed over the execution time of each application and the averaged across all cluster nodes. The average power consumption of a cluster node for *pi* is significantly lower for inferior CPU frequencies, as well as for the *powersave* governor. This observation would typically translate into an efficient total energy consumption at the level of the cluster for low frequencies. However, as Fig. 2(a) demonstrates, the highest CPU frequency, that is 2.53 GHz, achieves the best results both in terms of performance and energy-efficiency. This behavior can be explained by analyzing the workload: *pi* is a CPU-intensive application, which can achieve 104 % better performance by employing the highest CPU frequency, as shown in Section 4.1, whereas the average power consumption only increases by 48 %.

The same trend can be noticed for the *grep* and *sort* applications. Nevertheless, the energy savings induced by using the highest available frequency proportionally decrease with the percentage of CPU usage of the application. Thus, as *sort* uses the least amount of CPU power, its runtime is not significantly impacted by reducing the CPU frequency and the total energy consumption of the application only increases by 15 % between the highest and lowest CPU frequency values. The average power consumption for *sort* displayed in Fig. 3(c) confirms this behavior, as the low CPU utilization at high CPU frequencies such as 2.53 GHz leads to only a 22 % increase of the consumed power per node.

Consequently, the workload properties play an essential role in establishing the energy-consumption profile of an application. When the application runtime predominantly accounts for CPU usage, the most power-consuming CPU settings can surprisingly trigger a better total energy efficiency. Accordingly, applications that feature both IO- and CPU-intensive phases, can benefit from adaptive CPU frequency policies, aiming at maximizing the CPU performance only during the computation stages of the application. Such policies can ensure a reduced energy consumption at the level of the application in two steps. First, for the CPU-intensive phases the total energy can be decreased by reducing the execution time, as it is the case for *Pi*. Second, the duration of the IO-bound phases is not dependent of the CPU frequency settings and therefore, low CPU frequencies can be used to save energy.

5   Microscopic Analysis

In this section, we present a detailed comparative discussion of various CPU frequencies and policies and we explain their effects on the total energy consumption of applications.

5.1   Dynamic Frequency Scaling

The highest frequency that can be statically configured on the cluster nodes is 2.53 GHz, this being also the default frequency employed by the operating system. We consider this frequency as the baseline against which we study the two dynamic governors, as it provides the default application performance that can be achieved by the given machines. Both the *ondemand* and *conservative* governors are designed to dynamically adjust the CPU frequency to favour either performance or energy consumption.

CPU-Bound Applications. When running the *pi* benchmark, both governors achieve slightly better performance than the default CPU frequency, as shown in Fig. 2(a). This behavior can be explained by the fact that both governors attempt to increase the employed CPU frequency as much as possible when dealing with a CPU-intensive workload, as it is the case for *pi*.

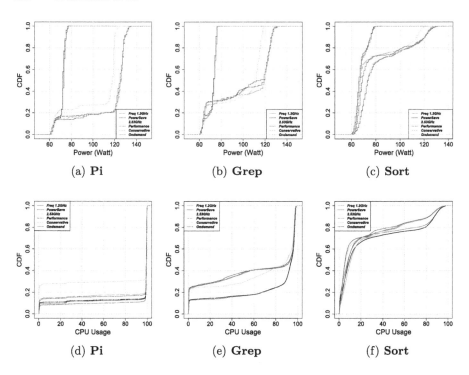

(a) **Pi**   (b) **Grep**   (c) **Sort**

(d) **Pi**   (e) **Grep**   (f) **Sort**

Fig. 4. CDF of the average power consumption and CPU usage across nodes during application execution for various frequency and scaling policy settings.

Figure 4 presents the cumulative distribution function (CDF) of the average power consumption and average CPU usage during benchmark execution across the cluster nodes, for the various CPU frequency settings and in each of the three scenarios we analyzed. The CPU utilization is higher than 98 % for more than 80 % of the execution time (as shown in Fig. 4d) for both governors. The CPU-bound nature of the *pi* application accounts for these values, as well as for the identical behavior of the two governors. Thus, as the CPU usage increases to almost 100 % when the application is executed, the *conservative* and *ondemand* governors switch to the highest available frequency and do not shift back to lower frequencies until the job has finished and the CPU is released.

Interestingly, Fig. 2(a) shows that the total energy consumption of the *pi* benchmark for the default frequency does not match the one corresponding to the performance-oriented governors, in spite of their similar execution times. The explanation lies in the processor ability to use the Turbo Boost capability when configured to employ an adaptive governor instead of a fixed frequency. The power consumption CDF for *pi* in Fig. 4(a) shows the used power for the default CPU frequency is almost constant to 120 Watts for 80 % of the job. As the CPU usage does not decrease during the execution of the *pi* application, this value represents the maximum power that the node can consume within a fixed frequency setting. However, the power consumption achieved by the two governors exceeds that of the default frequency, as emphasized by the *pi* CDF in Fig. 4(a). This outcome is only possible if the governors take advantage of the CPU Turbo Boost capability, that is they employ a frequency higher than 2.53 GHz and in turn consume an increased amount of energy. Figure 6 provides an insight into the percentage of the job execution time spent by each governor with an enabled Turbo feature for each of the three applications. As previously anticipated, in the case of *pi*, the *conservative* governor invokes Turbo frequencies for 70 % of the total time, while the *ondemand* governor requires Turbo for 65 % of the running time.

IO-Bound Applications. However, the *conservative* and *ondemand* governors behave differently for the *sort* application. As Fig. 2 shows, when using the *ondemand* governor, Hadoop requires more time to sort the input data than when it is configured with the *conservative* governor. This longer running time also results in higher power consumption. To better understand how these two governors function, we analyze the CPU usage as a function of execution time on a single datanode, during the *sort* benchmark (Fig. 5). Both governors start the execution at the default frequency (2.53 GHZ), but they adjust the CPU frequency according to the CPU usage and how it compares to predefined thresholds.

The *ondemand* governor uses as threshold a default value of 95 %: when the CPU usage is greater than 95 %, the CPU frequency is increased to the highest available frequency, i.e. 2.53 GHZ; if the CPU usage is less than this value, the governor gradually decreases the frequency to lower values. In the case of the *sort* benchmark, this policy allows Hadoop to run at the highest frequency in some points corresponding to the CPU usage peaks above the 95 % threshold (Fig. 5a). Nevertheless, the rest of the CPU-intensive phase of the *sort* application is executed at lower CPU frequencies, since the CPU usage during this phase is less than 95 %. The *conservative* governor employs two thresholds for tuning the CPU frequency: an up-threshold set to 80 % and a down-threshold of 20 %. The frequency is progressively increased and decreased by comparing the system usage to the two thresholds: CPU usage peaks above the up-threshold result in upgrading the frequency to the next available value;

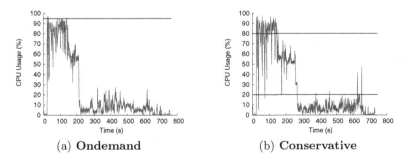

(a) **Ondemand**   (b) **Conservative**

Fig. 5. CPU usage on a Hadoop datanode during the execution of the *sort* application.

when the usage goes below the down-threshold, the CPU switches to the next lower frequency. Figure 5(b) shows that the computational-intensive phase of the *sort* benchmark exhibits CPU usage peaks greater than 80 %. This enables the conservative governor to keep the CPU at the highest frequency of 2.53 GHZ during most of this phase. Also, the down-threshold allows the I/O-bound part of the application to be executed at low CPU frequencies.

The internal implementation of the two governors is also responsible for the overall variation in performance and consumed energy between the static 2.53 GHZ setting and the dynamic governors detailed in Fig. 2(c). Thus, in the case of *sort*, the *conservative* governor achieves a better runtime than *ondemand*, despite the fact that the latter governor should favour performance. While the improvement accounts for less than 5 % of the execution time of the *ondemand* governor, it can be explained by the fact that the *conservative* governor spends more time at the highest frequency setting, speeding up the computational-intensive phases of *sort*. As most peaks in the CPU load do not reach the 95 % threshold required by the *ondemand* governor, it cannot take advantage of the highest available frequency, leading to a worse application runtime. Energy-wise, this behaviour translates into a total energy gain when using the fixed 2.53 GHZ frequency setting, on account on the longer execution time triggered by the *ondemand* governor. The *conservative* governor is in this case the best choice for saving energy, as it enables the application to take advantage of both high and low frequency settings, reducing the execution time of CPU-intensive phases and decreasing energy consumption during IO-intensive ones.

5.2   Statically-Configured Frequencies

In this section we focus on the *performance* and *powersave* governors, which set the CPU to a fixed frequency, either the maximum available one, that is 2.53 GHZ or the minimum 1.2 GIIZ, respectively. While they should exhibit similar behaviour with the fixed frequency, the *performance* governor features an interesting capability, that is to use Turbo Boost when executing heavy loads.

As far as the *pi* application is concerned, both *performance* and the fixed 2.53 GHZ frequency setting deliver relatively similar running times. The Turbo feature allows the *performance* governor to go past the 2.53 GHZ CPU frequency for 70 % of the job execution time and thus consume more power, as confirmed by the CDF in Fig. 4(a). A notable side effect is that the usage of the *performance* governor is less efficient from an energy standpoint (Fig. 2a). Figure 4(b) shows a similar behaviour in the case of *grep*, as it exhibits a sufficiently similar workload. Consequently, for CPU-bound applications, performance-oriented governors provide a convenient alternative over a fixed frequency, when the user tends to favor performance. To achieve energy savings without significantly sacrificing execution time, the default kernel setting, the fixed maximum frequency still provides the best alternative. As for *sort*, the generated CPU peaks account for a limited usage of the Turbo CPU feature, as detailed in Fig. 6. As a result, *sort* does not

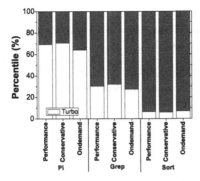

Fig. 6. Turbo Boost: The total usage of the Turbo feature for the duration of the application execution.

benefit from the *performance* governor in terms of energy, providing a better performance-energy tradeoff when using the 2.53 GHZ setting or the *conservative* governor.

6 Summary and Future Work

Energy efficiency has started to severely constrain the design and the way data-centers are operated, becoming a key research direction in the development of cloud infrastructures. As processing huge amounts of data is a typical task assigned to large-scale cloud platforms, several studies have been dedicated to improving power consumption for data-intensive cloud applications. In this study, we focus on MapReduce and we investigate the impact of dynamically scaling the frequency of compute nodes on the performance and energy consumption of a Hadoop cluster. We provide a detailed evaluation of a set of representative MapReduce workloads, highlighting a significant variation in both the performance and power consumption of the applications with different governors.

Furthermore, our results reveal that the current CPU governors do not exactly reflect their design goal and may even become ineffective at improving power consumption for Hadoop clusters. In addition, we unveil the correlations between the power efficiency of a Hadoop deployment, application performance and power-management mechanisms, such as DVFS or Turbo capabilities. We believe the insights drawn from this paper can serve as guidelines for efficiently deploying and executing data-intensive applications in large-scale data-centers.

As future work, we plan to extend our empirical evaluation for a wider diversity of MapReduce applications, such as scientific applications and the more complex pipeline MapReduce applications, and for various platforms (e.g., virtualized data-centers). In addition, we intend to explore different techniques and approaches to optimize power management in Hadoop clusters. As a first step, we are currently investigating the possibility of building dynamic frequency tuning tools specifically tailored to match MapReduce application types and execution stages.

Acknowledgments. This work is supported by the ANR MapReduce grant (ANR-10-SEGI-001) and the Héméra INRIA Large Wingspan-Project (see http://www.grid5000.fr/mediawiki/index.php/Hemera).

Experiments presented in this paper were carried out using the Grid'5000 test-bed, supported by a scientific interest group hosted by Inria and including CNRS, RENATER and several Universities as well as other organizations (see http://www.grid5000.fr/).

References

1. Amur, H., Cipar, J., Gupta, V., Ganger, G.R., Kozuch, M.A., Schwan, K.: Robust and flexible power-proportional storage. In: Proceedings of the 1st ACM Symposium on Cloud Computing, SoCC '10, pp. 217–228. ACM, New York (2010)
2. Cardosa, M., Singh, A., Pucha, H., Chandra, A.: Exploiting spatio-temporal trade-offs for energy-aware mapreduce in the cloud. In: Proceedings of the 2011 IEEE 4th International Conference on Cloud Computing, CLOUD '11, pp. 251–258, Washington, DC, USA (2011)
3. Chen, Y., Alspaugh, S., Borthakur, D., Katz, R.: Energy efficiency for large-scale mapreduce workloads with significant interactive analysis. In: Proceedings of the 7th ACM European Conference on Computer Systems (EuroSys '12), Bern, Switzerland (2012)
4. Chen, Y., Ganapathi, A., Katz, R.H.: To compress or not to compress - compute vs. io tradeoffs for mapreduce energy efficiency. In: Proceedings of the First ACM SIGCOMM Workshop on Green Networking, Green Networking '10, pp. 23–28. ACM, New York (2010)
5. Chen, Y., Keys, L., Katz, R.H.: Towards energy efficient mapreduce. Technical Report UCB/EECS-2009-109, EECS Department, University of California, Berkeley, Aug 2009
6. Dean, J., Ghemawat, S.: MapReduce: Simplified data processing on large clusters. Commun. ACM **51**(1), 107–113 (2008)
7. Freeh, V.W., Lowenthal, D.K.: Using multiple energy gears in mpi programs on a power-scalable cluster. In: Proceedings of the Tenth ACM SIGPLAN Symposium on Principles and Practice of Parallel Programming, PPoPP '05, pp. 164–173 (2005)
8. Ge, R., Feng, X., Song, S., Chang, H.-C., Li, D., Cameron, K.W.: Powerpack: Energy profiling and analysis of high-performance systems and applications. IEEE Trans. Parallel Distrib. Syst. **21**(5), 658–671 (2010)
9. Goiri, I., Le, K., Nguyen, T.D., Guitart, J., Torres, J., Bianchini, R.: Green-hadoop: Leveraging green energy in data-processing frameworks. In: Proceedings of the 7th ACM European Conference on Computer Systems (EuroSys '12), Bern, Switzerland (2012)
10. The Apache Hadoop Project (2014). http://www.hadoop.org
11. Hamilton, J.: Cost of Power in Large-Scale Data Centers (2008). http://perspectives.mvdirona.com/2008/11/28/CostOfPowerInLargeScaleDataCenters.aspx
12. He, B., Fang, W., Luo, Q., Govindaraju, N.K., Wang, T.: Mars: A mapreduce framework on graphics processors. In: Proceedings of the 17th International Conference on Parallel Architectures and Compilation Techniques, pp. 260–269, Toronto, Ontario, Canada (2008)

13. Hsu, C., Feng, W.: A power-aware run-time system for high-performance comput-
    ing. In: Proceedings of the 2005 ACM/IEEE Conference on Supercomputing, SC
    '05, p. 1. IEEE Computer Society, Washington, DC (2005)
14. Ibrahim, S., Hai, J., Lu, L., He, B., Antoniu, G., Song, W.: Maestro: Replica-
    aware map scheduling for mapreduce. In: Proceedings of the 12th IEEE/ACM
    International Symposium on Cluster. Cloud and Grid Computing (CCGrid 2012),
    pp. 59–72, Ottawa, Canada (2012)
15. Ibrahim, S., Jin, H., Lu, L., Qi, L., Wu, S., Shi, X.: Evaluating mapreduce on
    virtual machines: The hadoop case. In: Jaatun, M.G., Zhao, G., Rong, C. (eds.)
    Cloud Computing. LNCS, vol. 5931, pp. 519–528. Springer, Heidelberg (2009)
16. Ibrahim, S., Jin, H., Lu, L., Wu, S., He, B., Qi, L.: Leen: Locality/fairness-aware
    key partitioning for mapreduce in the cloud. In: Proceedings of the 2010 IEEE
    Second International Conference on Cloud Computing Technology and Science
    (CLOUDCOM'10), pp. 17–24, Indianapolis, USA (2010)
17. Jégou, Y., Lantéri, S., Leduc, J., Melab, N., Mornet, G., Namyst, R., Primet, P.,
    Quetier, B., Richard, O., Talbi, E.-G., Iréa, T.: Grid'5000: A large scale and highly
    reconfigurable experimental Grid testbed. Int. J. High Perform. Comput. Appl.
    20(4), 481–494 (2006)
18. Jin, H., Ibrahim, S., Qi, L., Cao, H., Wu, S., Shi, X.: The Mapreduce Programming
    Model and Implementations: Cloud Computing: Principles and Paradigms, pp.
    373–390. Wiley, Hoboken (2011)
19. Kaushik, R.T., Bhandarkar, M.: Greenhdfs: Towards an energy-conserving,
    storage-efficient, hybrid hadoop compute cluster. In: Proceedings of the 2010 Inter-
    national Conference on Power Aware Computing and Systems, HotPower'10, pp.
    1–9. USENIX Association, Berkeley (2010)
20. Kim, J., Chou, J., Rotem, D.: Energy proportionality and performance in data
    parallel computing clusters. In: Bayard Cushing, J., French, J., Bowers, S. (eds.)
    SSDBM 2011. LNCS, vol. 6809, pp. 414–431. Springer, Heidelberg (2011)
21. Kwon, Y.C., Balazinska, M., Howe, B., Rolia, J.: Skew-resistant parallel processing
    of feature-extracting scientific user-defined functions. In: Proceedings of the 1st
    ACM Symposium on Cloud Computing, pp. 75–86, Indianapolis, Indiana, USA
    (2010)
22. Lang, W., Patel, J.M.: Energy management for mapreduce clusters. Proc. VLDB
    Endow. **3**(1–2), 129–139 (2010)
23. Leverich, J., Kozyrakis, C.: On the energy (in)efficiency of hadoop clusters.
    SIGOPS Oper. Syst. Rev. **44**(1), 61–65 (2010)
24. Mhedheb, Y., Jrad, F., Tao, J., Zhao, J., Kołodziej, J., Streit, A.: Load and thermal-
    aware VM scheduling on the cloud. In: Kołodziej, J., Martino, B., Talia, D., Xiong,
    K. (eds.) ICA3PP 2013, Part I. LNCS, vol. 8285, pp. 101–114. Springer, Heidelberg
    (2013)
25. Ranger, C., Raghuraman, R., Penmetsa, A., Bradski, G., Kozyrakis, C.: Evaluating
    mapreduce for multi-core and multiprocessor systems. In: Proceedings of the 2007
    IEEE 13th International Symposium on High Performance Computer Architecture
    (HPCA-13), pp. 13–24, Phoenix, Arizona, USA (2007)
26. Redhat: Using CPUfreq Governors (2014). https://access.redhat.com/site/
    documentation/en-US/Red_Hat_Enterprise_Linux/6/html/Power_Management_
    Guide/cpufreq_governors.html
27. Li, S., Abdelzaher, T., Yuan, M.: Tapa: Temperature aware power allocation in data
    center with map-reduce. In: Proceedings of 2011 International Green Computing
    Conference and Workshops (IGCC'11), Green Networking '10, pP. 1–8. IEEE, New
    York (2011)

28. Thereska, E., Donnelly, A., Narayanan, D.: Sierra: Practical power-proportionality for data center storage. In: Proceedings of the Sixth Conference on Computer Systems, EuroSys '11, pp. 169–182. ACM, New York (2011)
29. Vasić, N., Barisits, M., Salzgeber, V., Kostic, D.: Making cluster applications energy-aware. In: Proceedings of the 1st Workshop on Automated Control for Datacenters and Clouds, ACDC '09, pp. 37–42. ACM, New York (2009)
30. Wang, L., Tao, J., Ranjan, R., Marten, H., Streit, A., Chen, J., Chen, D.: G-hadoop: Mapreduce across distributed data centers for data-intensive computing. Future Gener. Comput. Syst. **29**(3), 739–750 (2013)
31. Wang, X., Fu, X., Liu, X., Gu, Z.: Power-aware cpu utilization control for distributed real-time systems. In: Proceedings of the 2009 15th IEEE Symposium on Real-Time and Embedded Technology and Applications, RTAS '09, pp. 233–242. IEEE Computer Society (2009)
32. Wirtz, T., Ge, R.: Improving mapreduce energy efficiency for computation intensive workloads. In: Proceedings of 2011 International Green Computing Conference and Workshops (IGCC'11), Green Networking '10, pp. 1–8. IEEE, New York (2011)
33. Zaharia, M., Borthakur, D., Sarma, J.S., Elmeleegy, K., Shenker, S., Stoica, I.: Delay scheduling: A simple technique for achieving locality and fairness in cluster scheduling. In: Proceedings of the 5th ACM European Conference on Computer Systems (EuroSys'10), pp. 265–278, Paris, France (2010)
34. Zhu, N., Rao, L., Liu, X., Liu, J., Guan, H.: Taming power peaks in mapreduce clusters. In: Proceedings of the ACM SIGCOMM 2011 Conference, SIGCOMM '11, pp. 416–417. ACM, New York (2011)

Self-management of Live Streaming Application in Distributed Cloud Infrastructure

Patricia Endo[1,2(✉)], Marcelo Santos[1], Jônatas Vitalino[1],
Glauco Gonçalves[3], Moisés Rodrigues[1], Djamel F.H. Sadok[1],
Judith Kelner[1], and Azimeh Sefidcon[4]

[1] Federal University of Pernambuco, Av. Prof. Moraes Rego,
Recife 1235, Brazil
{patricia,marcelo,jonatas,moises,
jamel,jk}@gprt.ufpe.br
[2] University of Pernambuco, BR 104, s/n, Caruaru, Brazil
[3] Federal Rural University of Pernambuco, Rua Dom Manoel de Medeiros,
Recife, Brazil
glauco@deinfo.ufrpe.br
[4] Ericsson Research, Torshamnsgatan 21, Kista, Sweden
azimeh.sefidcon@ericsson.com

Abstract. Currently, live streaming traffic is responsible for more than half of aggregated traffic from fixed access networks in North America. But, due to traffic redundancy, it does not suitably utilize bandwidth and network resources. To cope with this problem in the context of Distributed Clouds (DClouds) we present RBSA4LS, an autonomic strategy that manages the dynamic creation of reflectors for reducing redundant traffic in live streaming applications. Under this strategy, nodes continually assess the utilization level by live streaming flows. When necessary, the network nodes communicate and self-appoint a new reflector node, which switches to multicasting video flows hence alleviating network links. We evaluated RBSA4LS through extensive simulations and the results showed that such a simple strategy can provide as much as 40 % of reduction in redundant traffic even for random topologies and reaches 85 % of bandwidth gain in a scenario with a large ISP topology.

Keywords: Cloud computing · Self-management · Live streaming · Simulation

1 Introduction

The Internet supports content dissemination towards the network edges. Its users may consume and produce shareable contents that should travel quickly over the core network. According to the Global Internet Phenomena Report [1], taking into consideration North America, the real-time entertainment traffic is responsible for around 61.45 % and 37.53 % of aggregated traffic in peak periods from fixed access network and mobile access network (Fig. 1a and b, respectively).

In [2], Kurt Michel, Director of Product Marketing at Akamai, stated that *"live video streaming has become an increasingly important part of the web content*

© Springer International Publishing Switzerland 2014
F. Pop and M. Potop-Butucaru (Eds.): ARMS-CC 2014, LNCS 8907, pp. 165–179, 2014.
DOI: 10.1007/978-3-319-13464-2_12

universe, as a variety of businesses and organizations attempt to capture a 'share of eyeball' and deliver richer, more HDTV-like experiences". In [3], authors also say that live streaming is becoming increasingly popular, and it is expected to be more pervasive in the near future. At the same time, the quality expectations of these ever-increasing audiences continue to grow. HD quality is becoming the de facto standard for all viewing experiences, from HDTV home viewing to "anywhere" viewing on mobile devices [2].

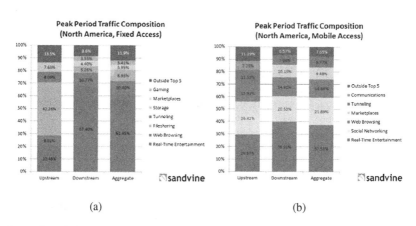

(a)   (b)

Fig. 1. Peak period aggregate traffic composition from (a) fixed access network and (b) mobile access network [1].

In the other side, the Internet yet presents challenges for live streaming delivery due to its own architectural design concept including the lack of end-to-end reliability or performance guarantees. Furthermore, traffic redundancy is a particular problem resultant from the way live streaming applications individually transfer information over the network to independent subscribers. Basically, when serving live video content the content provider creates single unicast flows from the video source to each client resulting in the transport of several copies of the same content packets over the network. Due to such traffic redundancy, expensive bandwidth and network resources are not adequately utilized [4].

A solution to address some of these challenges lies in the caching strategy commonly utilized by Content Delivery Network (CDN) providers [5]. According to [1], originally the CDN concept improved application performance by caching static and popular content at the edge of the Internet, close to end users, in order to avoid "middle mile" bottlenecks and minimize traffic redundancy as much as possible. However, applications like live multimedia streaming often generate dynamic and non-cacheable content, and therefore it is necessary to rethink the solution, just as major CDN providers (such as Akamai, Limelight, and Internap) have already evolved to support live streaming delivery [3].

Alternatively, Cloud Computing can be seen as a solution to support live streaming applications, since it is possible to rent virtual servers hence offering a scalable backend infrastructure to support a variable number of live video viewers. One can also make use of a Distributed Cloud (DCloud) [6–10] that represents a Cloud provider composed of small and distributed datacenters located at different geographical regions, to provide live streaming. But despite this, it is still necessary to implement solutions to deal with video distribution by mitigating traffic redundancy.

Since classical caching mechanisms and IP multicast present many issues to support live streaming application, looking for a new scalable autonomic strategy that focuses on reducing redundant traffic in a DCloud infrastructure can be seen as a potential field for research, development and innovation.

In this paper, we present an autonomic strategy based on a **Role-Based Self-Appointment** (RBSA) framework proposed in [11]. In a nutshell, RBSA is a generic framework that can be used for several management purposes in which nodes interact with their neighbors to exchange information, and decide by themselves which role they should perform. We adopted this framework in a scenario for managing live streaming application and called the resulting architecture RBSA4LS. RBSA4LS can be used by the DCloud infrastructure provider to offer video a streaming application while also optimizing its network resources usage autonomously. The main goal of this paper is to describe in detail how **RBSA4LS** optimizes link usage through an infrastructure provider that offers a live video streaming application by establishing, at the heart of our proposal, reflector and router roles. Moreover, we simulate RBSA4LS for different scenarios in order to gain insights on and discuss how it performs in terms of bandwidth reduction.

This paper is organized as follows: in Sect. 2, we describe the DClouds infrastructure in order to clarify the advantages obtained for working in this environment; Sect. 3 describes the RBSA instantiation special case to support a live streaming application; in Sect. 4 we present results from conducted simulations; we discuss RBSA4LS performance in Sect. 5; related works are described in Sect. 6, and final considerations and future works are delineated in Sect. 6.

2   Distributed Cloud

Current Cloud Computing providers mainly rely on large and consolidated datacenters in order to offer their services. The physical infrastructure is composed of many nodes (processing elements and network entities) to which users gain access through some virtualization technology. At the same time, small and geographically distributed datacenters can also be attractive for Cloud providers since this type of datacenters can offer a cheaper and low-power consumption alternative that reduces the costs of large and centralized ones. These small and distributed datacenters can be built at different geographical regions and can be connected to form a Distributed Cloud (DCloud). We believe that this scenario gives a good opportunity to develop mechanisms to optimize the usage of resources appropriated to this type of application in an innovative way.

We decided to use DClouds because we obtain more flexibility to deal with the resources within the infrastructure. We require such flexibility as we are looking for applying an autonomic management strategy.

The main objective of a video streaming application is to carry video signals to viewers while assuring minimum quality. Such objective can be supported by well-dimensioned Streaming Servers (SS) and a content distribution network that transports video information through several geographically distributed servers in a timely fashion. One can consider three distinct stakeholders in this scenario: the Application Provider, the DCloud Infrastructure Provider, and the Viewer.

(1) **Application Provider:** is the entity that requests to the DCloud Infrastructure Provider (computational and network) resources to host a video streaming application. The streaming application is characterized by the Streaming Server (SS) harnessed to a specific geographical region. Beyond this, the Application Provider is responsible for producing the content of the video streaming application;

(2) **DCloud Infrastructure Provider:** represents the provider responsible for accommodating different types of services on its physical infrastructure. The DCloud Provider can make use of virtualization technologies to deal with this heterogeneity of services. These services can be an IaaS, PaaS, or SaaS. However, the focus of this paper is a DCloud Infrastructure Provider selling a specific network configuration for use by video streaming applications; and

(3) **Viewer:** is the end-user of the video streaming application that is served by the DCloud Infrastructure Provider. The viewer (or service subscriber) accesses the application though an edge router.

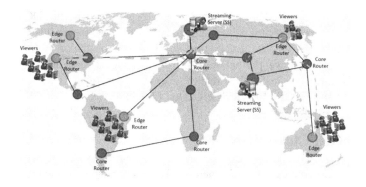

Fig. 2. Live streaming application over DCloud.

Figure 2 shows an example of a DCloud hosting service using virtualization technology. The SSs are responsible for providing the origin server and for leading with video signals. DCloud is responsible for the actual distribution of such signals to the subscribers who are accessing the SSs through edge routers. Any node in the infrastructure can be assigned as an edge router; if all nodes are edge routers, then this means that all viewers can directly access the head-end through any node in the network. If a node is not an edge router or an SS, then it is a core router. In Fig. 2, we are considering five edge routers, two SSs providing different live videos, and eight core routers. The flows from SSs to viewers are assigned in yellow; the width of the flow represents the network traffic in the path taken.

This scenario supports several alternatives for managing the video streaming application. Among these is the creation of a virtual overlay network in the DCloud infrastructure. In this case, the virtual network would be seen as a virtual forest-like structure: the SS would be the root server of this forest while the core and edge routers would form the live streaming delivery tree. In the next Section, we describe an autonomic mechanism based on RBSA, where nodes are able to appoint themselves, when needed, roles autonomously depending on network and service performance.

3 Role-Based Self-appointment for Live Streaming (RBSA4LS)

The proposed RBSA [11] is a mechanism executed by a node in order to choose by itself a suitable new role it should play in order to optimally manage resources in a distributed networked environment, such as Distributed Cloud.

In a general way, we can describe the node's behavior as follows: nodes monitor their resources continuously and, when predetermined conditions are met, for example through trigger fires or other observed indicators, a communication process is initiated in order to achieve an optimized state performing aggregation over video flows. A trigger is considered as an event that indicates context state changes. These could reflect possible operational problems, such as bottleneck, or performance loss. Next, nodes exchange messages and analyze their states. Processing of the interchanged information takes then place to autonomously reach decisions upon which to act. In the context of our approach, a node may even chose to spin a new role or maintain its current one based on the acquired intelligence. Roles are then mapped into local actions, according to pre-established rules. Since nodes do not have a global knowledge about the whole system they only take decisions that have local scope effects. One may describe the resulting behavior where a node assumes a specific role without seeking prior agreement from the others as self-appointment, a special type of self-configuration.

Authors in [11] provide some examples of RBSA applicability such as live streaming optimization, caching in CDN, and virtual machine management. In this Section, we will describe an RBSA instantiation scenario (called RBSA4LS) used to deal with our special problem: to provide a live streaming application that focuses on the reduction of network resource usage.

To this end, we introduce a new processing role some nodes may tale, namely, that of a **reflector**. The reflector acts as a flow concentrator with the sole responsibility of reducing redundant flows generated from for the same video server in the network. The main idea is that a node with many redundant flows from the same video streaming should be able to aggregate their traffic and redirect it to its subscribers. For this, our nodes in a network are constantly running RBSA4LS that will decide when to become a reflector based on two variables: (a) the amount of redundant flows crossing itself; and (b) the distance in hops to the server.

Table 1 shows the adaptation made in RBSA to comply with the requirements of the video streaming application. We established that the desired global behavior is to reduce the redundant traffic in the network. When the number of flows passing through a node reaches a specific value (called **threshold**), the node becomes a candidate for aggregating such flows and announces itself as one, i.e., it will send messages informing that it wants to be a reflector. The metric used to choose the best candidate is the distance in hops to the video server. The distance value can be obtained through some existing routing protocol and nodes do not need to know the distance of all others. Hence towards the end of the communication period (called **cycle**, i.e., the maximum amount of time units used to take a decision after messages were exchange was started), the candidate node to become reflector will be the one that experiences "considerable" load and is the farthest away from the existing servers.

Hence towards the end of the communication period (called cycle, i.e., the maximum amount of time units used to take a decision after messages were exchange was started), the candidate node to become reflector will be the one that experiences "considerable" load and is the farthest away from the existing servers.

When this node starts on its new role as a reflector, one expects to see a local reduction in streaming traffic hence alleviating network bandwidth resources. It is important to highlight that we are not interested in ensuring mutual exclusion; then it means that more than one node can become reflector at same time, and improve the bandwidth together.

In the same way nodes decide to become a reflector, they also can decide to return to router role. When nodes observed that the number of flows is less than the defined threshold, they can autonomously become a router and work normally.

Table 1. RBSA instantiation for a live streaming application

Global behavior	Reduce redundant traffic and alleviate links in the network
Monitored variable	Number of flows of a video streaming from the same video server passing through a node
Metric	Distance in hops to the original video server
Roles	Router: it routes live streaming flows normally
	Reflector: it aggregates redundant flows and performs multicast

4   Evaluation and Results

In order to analyze the RBSA4LS, we choose to use the NetLogo[1] simulator that is a multi-agent programmable modeling environment as our underlying simulation tool. We divided the analysis in two parts: the first set of simulations was carried out with the initial simple goal to configure the RBSA4LS. To achieve this, we used a random topology network composed of 50 nodes and executed as many as 25000 simulations of random topologies. The second set of simulations was conducted by using a real topology of a Tier 1 Internet Service Provider. The objective of the simulations now is

---

[1] http://ccl.northwestern.edu/netlogo/

to evaluate the RBSA4LS behavior; more specifically, we intend to evaluate the following metrics:

(1) **Bandwidth:** the goal is to measure the efficiency and gain in the reduction of link load. The bandwidth is measured as the sum of flows over each link in the network per time unit; and

(2) **Messages:** the main idea is to evaluate the overhead caused by exchanging messages between nodes to give these sufficient information to self-organize in an optimal way. This metric is calculated as the mean of all messages per time unit.

4.1   Configuration Scenario

The configuration scenario was used as a calibration phase to analyze the influence of the threshold and the cycle parameters that are previously configured. The topology is a random network composed of 50 nodes plus five edge nodes and one video server that are allocated randomly in each simulation. We built 50 different topologies generated according to the Barabási-Albert approach with only one initial node and $\Delta m = 1$ [12] generating a tree-based topology. Each combination of these factors composes an experiment that was subsequently repeated 50 times for each combination of the present factors and their levels shown in Table 3 (totalizing 22600 simulations) to obtain statistical confidence.

A scenario is simulated as follows. The clients arrive to the system and are attached randomly (using a uniform distribution) to one of the five edge nodes. Each client starts one video flow and remains viewing the video to its end. The video server sends video streams (a flow per subscriber) to clients located near the edge nodes. The time unit in NetLogo is measured in ticks. Table 2 shows the parameters used in the simulations and their respective values.

Table 2. Simulation parameters and respective values

Parameter	Level
Number of nodes	50
Number of edge nodes	5
Number of video streaming server	1
Cost between links	1
Mean of video streaming duration (exponential distribution)	5 ticks

Table 3. Simulation factors and levels

Parameter	Level
Threshold	15, 20, 25 flows
Cycle	5, 7, 10, and 15 ticks
Arrival rate (Poisson distribution)	10 and 20 clients per tick

The stop condition was calculated based on the statistical error accuracy considering 95 % of confidence on our two metrics: the average consumed bandwidth per tick and the average number of messages exchanged between nodes per tick.

The bandwidth error accuracy is calculated as $\frac{1.96*s_x}{\bar{X}*\sqrt{n}}$, where 1.96 is the value of the 0.975 percentile of the normal distribution, $\bar{X}$ is a moving average made over the consumed bandwidth, s_x is the standard deviation of this average, and n is the size of the time window used to compute the average that is chosen to be 500 times the cycle length. The message accuracy error is calculated similarly, but the statistics are made over the number of messages exchanged between nodes. Thus, to obtain a low variance, the simulation finishes when the error accuracy drops below 5 % for both metrics.

Regarding consumed bandwidth, we concentrated all results in Figs. 3 and 4 and compare with the reference baseline case, i.e., without RBSA self-appointment. Each point of the graphics represents a mean of all simulations made for each topology, with its respective factors and levels in the legend. The confidence interval was omitted because it is very small and does not offer additional insights to the analysis.

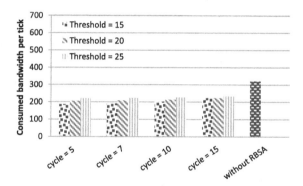

Fig. 3. Mean bandwidth for arrival rate 10.

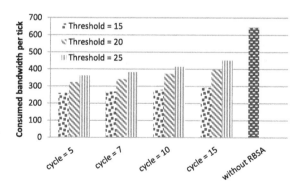

Fig. 4. Mean bandwidth for arrival rate 20.

The results show a reduction of overall bandwidth consumption provided by the usage of RBSA4LS and such reduction is more accentuated when more clients enter the system. As expected, doubling the clients' arrival rate (from 10 to 20 clients per tick for example), also doubles the usage of the links in the network when RBSA4LS is not used. Thus, one expects to see a sharper resource savings than with the scenario with a smaller arrival rate 10. Note that the results show that a best case scenario gain is obtained for the configuration (cycle = 5 ticks, threshold = 15 flows, and arrival rate = 20 clients per tick). Here the reduction was as much as 60 %.

A second aspect to be noted is that for all the values of cycle length, the bandwidth consumption of RBSA4LS with threshold 15 is statistically lower than RBSA4LS with threshold 20 and RBSA4LS with threshold 25. This occurs because the lower the threshold value is, the earlier nodes start to exchange messages and to decide when to become a reflector. In other words, if the threshold value is set high, the nodes would have to transfer more flow loads before triggering the self-appointment selection process and hence would inject more redundant streaming traffic in the network.

Regarding the number of locally exchanged messages, we focused our study to the results in Figs. 5 and 6 while comparing these against the worst case scenario. We are

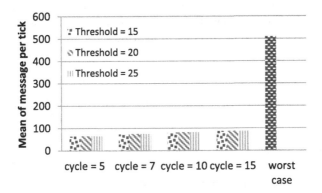

Fig. 5. Mean of messages for arrival rate 10.

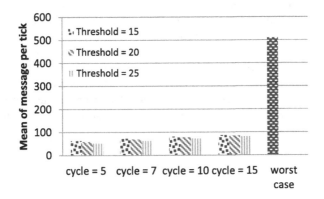

Fig. 6. Mean of messages for arrival rate 20.

considering that under the worst case scenario all nodes send messages to all their neighbors at the beginning of a cycle. Each bar of the graphics represents a mean of all simulations made for all experimented topologies, with its respective factors and levels listed in the legend.

With a 10 clients per tick arrival rate one note that, for fixed cycle value, when the threshold value increases, the mean of messages per tick decreases. See that this occurs for all cycles (5, 7, 10, and 15 ticks). As mentioned earlier, this means that the threshold causes a direct impact over the number of messages exchanged. This result was expected since it represents the amount of time to take a decision once message exchange is started by some node.

However, when the arrival rate is 20 clients per tick we can see that the threshold value has a low impact on the amount of exchanged messages per tick. This occurs because when arrival rate is 20 clients per tick, we have more active video flows in the network, consequently nodes will reach the defined threshold value quickly. Anyway, it is clear that the cycle length influences the number of messages.

We note that there is a variation when the cycle length is increased. This increase is expected since the cycle length represents how long nodes have to wait to take the decision to become a reflector, i.e., the higher the cycle length, the higher the time to initiate the message exchange phase and, consequently, the higher is the number of messages exchanged in the system. For all values of cycle and threshold, the number of messages is always much better than the worst case.

4.2   Cogent Topology

Cogent[2] is a multinational Tier 1 Internet Service Provider ranked, according to its website, as one of the top five networks in the world. Its network covers 37 countries in North America, Europe, and Asia. In this scenario, we use a version of the 2010's Cogent topology available at the Topology Zoo site.[3] Such topology covered only America and Europe and it consisted of 197 connection points and 243 links. Such representation was treated to remove duplicated links and redundant paths using out proposed self-appointment technique.

We located the server in a node with just one link, and located edge nodes by using the same rule, totalizing 22 edge nodes. Since a server could be located at any of the different nodes, we repeated the experiment 50 times to obtain statistical confidence. Other parameters and levels were maintained as in the last scenario. However, the factors were adjusted and considering the results, their configuration followed Table 4: the threshold is 20, the cycle length is 5 ticks, and the arrival rate is set to 20 clients per tick.

The stop condition was calculated based on the statistical error of 5 % on our two metrics: the average consumed bandwidth and the average number of messages exchanged between nodes (in the same way as in the first set of simulations); or 10000 ticks of simulation.

---

[2] http://www.cogentco.com/

[3] http://www.topology-zoo.org/

Table 4. Parameters and its respective values for the Cogent topology simulation

Parameter	Value
Number of nodes	197
Number of edge nodes	22
Number of video streaming server	1
Cost between links	1
Mean of video streaming duration (exponential distribution)	5 ticks
Threshold	20 flows
Cycle	5 ticks
Arrival rate (Poisson distribution)	20 clients per tick

For comparison, this time we created a static solution (called static reflectors), in which reflectors are previously located in the Cogent topology since the creation of the network and remain active throughout the simulation lifetime with no new reflectors being spawn.

```
program StaticReflectorsSolutionAlgorithm (topology)
    foreach node in topology
        if (node.isEdge()) then
            reflector.add(node)
        else if (node.amountLinks - 1 > threshold) then
            reflector.add(node)
        end
    return(reflector)
end
```

This algorithm uses a centralized strategy to allocate reflectors in static way by in an initial scenario. The rationale behind this algorithm is that reflectors created near of edge nodes can minimize bandwidth consumption for more links in the path between reflectors and the video server. Furthermore, the algorithm also considers that nodes very connected may become a bottleneck and should be alleviated in preference to others. Please recall that this solution is not adaptive.

Figure 7 shows the mean of consumed bandwidth representing both the total of consumed network bandwidth and the one occupied in the core of the network while disregarding the edge links. RBSA4LS successfully decreases the consumed bandwidth by as much as 85 % when compared with the scenario without the presence of RBSA4LS reflectors. Note that even the static solution decreases resource occupation by as much as 77 % when compared with the baseline configuration.

Since the static reflectors solution do not engage in the exchange of messages by definition, we show no comparisons here but the mean of messages per tick when RBSA4LS was used in the Cogent topology reached 89.43 message per tick.

In this last scenario, besides observing bandwidth and messages exchange, we introduced a new metric: that of the number of reflectors present by cycle. The goal of this metric is to evaluate the number of nodes performing the reflector role per cycle compared to the static case. This metric is important because reflectors represent a cost (hardware and software) and it could turn the solution impracticable due to the total

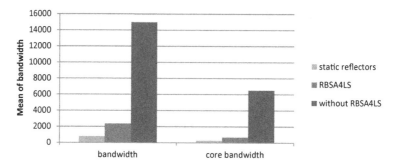

Fig. 7. Mean of bandwidth in Cogent topology.

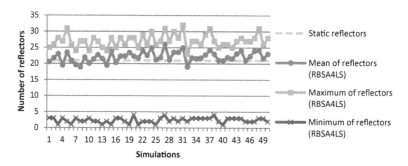

Fig. 8. Mean of reflectors per cycle in Cogent topology.

cost. Figure 8 represents the mean of such number per simulation (RBSA4LS and static reflectors solution) as well as the maximum and the minimum number of reflectors per simulation using RBSA4LS.

5   Discussion

RBSA has many configurable parameters such as the cycle value it defines and the threshold condition continuously tested. We analyzed through simulations the impact of each one on our observable output metrics, namely, bandwidth and additional message exchange overhead.

When we increased the cycle length value, we noted an increase in the number of exchanged messages. As mentioned earlier, this behavior is expected since the cycle length represents the time in which RBSA4LS exchanges messages to take a decision. The results also showed that a low threshold has a significant impact on consumed bandwidth. A low threshold reduces the consumed bandwidth because the entire system can react earlier and waiting a long time to introduce a new reflector into the network.

In bandwidth consumption, a low threshold will activate the message exchange earlier and it will promote the reduction in bandwidth consumption earlier. In the other hand, with a low threshold, message exchange will be activated more times hence increasing their overhead.

In a real topology, we compared the RBSA4LS with a scenario where static reflectors were pre-configured. Despite the algorithms bandwidth gain was lower as opposed to the gain against the scenario without RBSA4LS, the mean number of simultaneous reflectors per cycle for RBSA4LS remained close to that of the static case.

These results point the trade-off between centralized and autonomic distributed solutions. Centralized solutions can have a better performance, but require knowledge about all the elements of the network. Sometimes, the decision time is crucial and it is difficult to collect such information of all elements in the system. Anyway, the important key concept advocated by RBSA4LS is role creation, and we can show that it provides a good performance close to the static solution.

Finally, the technical feasibility for RBSA4LS implementation is currently provided by technologies such as Network Virtualization (NV) and Software Defined Networking (SDN) due to its capacity of managing flows over network. Using these approaches one can construct prototypes for future testing with RBSA4LS.

6 Related Work

According to [13], multicast is a key enabler to transfer high-bandwidth multimedia broadcasts and seminars on IP networks, since multicast promotes reduction of network traffic and video server load. However, there are factors that contribute to turn IP-layer multicast into an unfeasible solution for live streaming. For instance, its commercial deployment has been very limited, mainly because in order to support IP multicast all components in the infrastructure (video source servers, video client devices, and intermediate routers) should be made multicast-aware. Thus the video clients and servers must have support to IP multicast reception in the TCP/IP protocol stack, and the network routers must be able to build packet distribution trees that allow sources to send packets to all clients [14]. Authors in [Rajkumar and Swaminathan 2013] also say that IP multicast and Application Layer multicast create duplicate packets which deteriorates the redundant network traffic.

Another technical aspect contributing to the unfeasibility of IP-layer multicast is that the traditional multicast routing protocols, such as Distance Vector Multicast Routing Protocol (DVMRP), Multicast Open Shortest Path first (MOSPF), Protocol Independent Multicast Dense-Mode (PIM-DM), and Protocol Independent Multicast Sparse-Mode (PIM-SM) suffer from scaling problems [15]: DVMRP and PIM-DM initially send data everywhere and also require routers out of the distribution tree to hold prune state to prevent this flooding from persisting; MOSPF requires all routers to know where all receivers are located; and PIM-SM needs pre-distribution of information about the set of core routers called Rendezvous Point (RP). Since traffic needs to flow to the RP, a RP cannot handle too many groups simultaneously; therefore many RPs are needed globally.

Despite the existence of academic works having proposed infrastructure dedicated for the support of live streaming using CDNs (such as [3, 16]), none of them is focused on a Cloud virtualized infrastructure. Furthermore, there are proposals for the usage of centralized strategies for creating overlay multicast with the surrogates or servers that are part of the CDN infrastructure. Our main contribution in this paper was the proposal of an autonomic management of live streaming application over DCloud infrastructure, focusing on minimizing redundant traffic and on creating of reflectors.

7 Final Considerations and Future Work

In this paper, we presented RBSA4LS an autonomic strategy to manage creation of reflectors for reducing redundant traffic in a live streaming application over Distributed Cloud infrastructures. Such strategy is based on the RBSA framework that provides self-organizing solutions for node autonomic management in a network.

In RBSA4LS the network nodes continually sense the network and check forwarding packets to assess if the live streaming flows of a content source have achieved a high utilization level. If so, the nodes communicate and appoint a new reflector node, which will transparently start to multicast video flows to clients while alleviating the network links that goes through the content servers and reducing the redundant flows in the network.

We evaluated RBSA4LS through extensive simulations and the results showed that such simple strategy can reduce 40 % of the redundant traffic in random topologies with 50 nodes. We also simulated RBSA4LS in a large ISP topology obtaining a reduction of 85 % in the redundant traffic, which is close to the best result obtained by a static strategy that positions reflectors in the border of the network. Nevertheless, RBSA4LS autonomously appoints reflectors where they are needed and adapts such roles according to viewers' fluctuations.

As future work we are planning to take in consideration the cost of nodes and the cost of changing roles. We would like to study when reflector´s should cease to exist as streaming traffic diminishes in the network as well as their life migration impact. We are also prototyping the RBSA4LS in a physical and virtual testbed in order to verify the applicability of the proposal in a real environment. Moreover, we intend to apply the RBSA framework in other contexts, such as autonomic caching in CDNs.

References

1. Global Internet Phenomena Report (2013). https://www.sandvine.com/downloads/general/global-internet-phenomena/2013/2h-2013-global-internet-phenomena-report.pdf. Accessed Jan 2014
2. Michel, K.: Live Video Streaming that Can Handle Traffic Spikes - The Challenge. https://blogs.akamai.com/2013/01/live-video-streaming-that-can-handle-traffic-spikes-the-challenge.html. Accessed Jan 2014
3. Zhuang, Z., Guo, C.: Optimizing CDN infrastructure for live streaming with constrained server chaining. In: IEEE ISPA (2011)
4. Rajkumar, K., Swaminathan, P.: Eliminating redundant link traffic for live multimedia data over distributed system. Int. J. Eng. Technol. 5, 1202–1206 (2013)
5. Nygren, E., Sitaraman, K., Jennifer, S.: The akamai network: a platform for high-performance internet applications. In: ACM Operating Systems Review (SIGOPS), pp. 2–19 (2010)

6. Gonçalves, G., Endo, P.T., Palhares, A., Santos, M., Kelner, J., Sadok. D.: On the load balancing of virtual networks in distributed clouds. In: ACM SAC, pp. 625–631 (2012)
7. Church, K., Greenbreg, A., Hamilton, J.: On delivering embarrassingly distributed cloud services. In: Seventh Workshop on Hot Topics in Networks (HotNets), Citeseer (2008)
8. Alicherry, M., Lakshman, T.V.: Network aware resource allocation in distributed clouds. In: IEEE INFOCOM, pp. 963–971 (2012)
9. Endo, P.T., Palhares, A.V.A., Pereira, N.N., Gonçalves, G.E., Sadok, D., Kelner, J., Melander, B., Mangs, J.E.: Resource allocation for distributed cloud: concepts and research challenges. IEEE Netw. Mag. **25**, 42–46 (2011)
10. Valancius, V., Laoutaris, N., Massoulie, L., Diot, C., Rodriguez, P.: Greening the internet with nano data centers. In: International Conference on Emerging Networking Experiments and Technologies, pp. 37–48 (2009)
11. Endo, P., Palhares, A., Santos, M., Gonçalves, G., Sadok, D., Kelner, J., Sefidcon, A., Fetahi, W.: Role-based self-appointment for autonomic management of resources. In: IEEE NetMM (2014)
12. Lewis, T.G.: Network Science: Theory and Applications. Wiley, New York (2009)
13. Sharma, P., Perry, E., Malpani, R.: IP multicast operational network management: design, challenges, and experiences. IEEE Netw. **17**, 49–55 (2003)
14. Cisco Systems, IP Multicast Deployment Fundamentals, Design Implementation Guide (1999). http://www.cisco.com/en/US/tech/tk828/tech_brief09186a00800e9952.html. Accessed May 2013
15. Handley, M., Crowcroft, J.: Internet multicast today. Internet Protoc. J. **2**(4), 2–19 (1999)
16. LI, B., Wang, Z., Liu, J., Zhu, W.: Two decades of internet video streaming: a retrospective view. ACM Trans. Multimedia Comput. Commun. Appl. **2**(4), 2–19 (2013)

Towards the Impact of Design Flaws on the Resources Used by an Application

Cristina Marinescu[1,2]([⊠]), Şerban Stoenescu[2], and Teodor-Florin Fortiş[1]([⊠])

[1] HPC Center, West University of Timişoara, bvd. V. Pârvan 4, Timişoara, Romania
cristinam@hpc.uvt.ro, fortis@info.uvt.ro
[2] Department of Computer Science, "Politehnica" University Timişoara,
bvd. V. Pârvan 2, Timişoara, Romania

Abstract. One major research direction in cloud computing deals with the reduction of energy consumption. This can be seen as an optimization problem that must be addressed both at the hardware and the application (*i.e.*, software) level. At the software level, optimizing energy consumption is usually related with scaling down the resources required for running an application (*e.g.*, memory, CPU usage). In this context we can make the assumption that the presence of design flaws in the implementation of a software system may lead to a suboptimal resource usage. Our investigations on the impact of several design flaws on the amount of resources used by an application indicate that the presence of design flaws has an influence on memory consumption and CPU time and that proper refactoring can have a beneficial influence on resource usage.

Keywords: Design flaws · Resource usage · Energy optimization · Energy consumption · Cloud computing

1 Introduction

Over the last years, cloud computing has become an increasingly widespread approach for deploying software systems. Consequently, an ever growing number of applications have been deployed on cloud infrastructures. However, hiring computing power for running an application in a cloud raises different issues related with energy consumption [25]. In this context, an important research direction in cloud computing deals with the issue of minimizing energy consumption, by optimizing resource usage [15].

Energy consumption may be reduced by optimizing the hardware side (*e.g.*, by using more energy efficient cooling systems). However, in many cases the optimization can be even more cost-effective if, additionally, it addresses the software side, too. This can be done by reducing the used resources (*e.g.*, memory, CPU time) claimed by the applications which run in the cloud since it seems that energy consumption is affected by these resources [5].

The optimal usage of computing resources is an important factor of external quality. Therefore, in order to assess and control it, this quality factor must be

© Springer International Publishing Switzerland 2014
F. Pop and M. Potop-Butucaru (Eds.): ARMS-CC 2014, LNCS 8907, pp. 180–192, 2014.
DOI: 10.1007/978-3-319-13464-2_13

put in relation with the internal quality criteria [11]. One approach for quantifying the internal quality of an application is the Factor-Strategy Model [17]. This model captures deviations from design rules and principles of software design in terms of design flaws (see [6,23]).

Over the last years various empirical studies have shown that code entities affected by design flaws are harder to maintain [4], change more often [12] and exhibit more defects [16,20] than other entities which do not reveal design flaws. Therefore, a legitimate hypothesis is that one of the factors that may influence the amount of computing resources used by an application is the quality of its design.

In this paper we start an investigation for the following research question: *does the existence of design flaws in the implementation of a software system lead to a suboptimal resource usage?* This research question is particularly relevant considering the increasing number of cloud providers that offer solutions for deploying object-oriented applications to the cloud. Additionally, there is potential interest in the HPC area, as energy efficiency is a must for achieving *"petaFLOPS computational speeds and beyond"* [24].

To the best of our knowledge there are no previous results that investigate if the presence of design flaws is correlated with an increased usage of computing resources.

The paper is structured as follows: in Sect. 2 we relate our investigation to previous work. In the first part of Sect. 3 we present the addressed research question, as well as the impact of a well-known design flaw towards the resource usages of a very simple program. We continue with an investigation towards the impact of design flaws against a well know open source software system. We end the section by pointing out the results of the study. The threats to the validity are presented in Sect. 4. In the last section (Sect. 5) we summarize the results and hint towards future work.

2   Related Work

In this section we relate our work to the two domains we are investigating: energy optimization and design flaws. Additionally, an overview of cloud-specific approaches on energy efficiency is offered.

2.1   Energy Optimization

Energy optimization at the application-level is a topic that has lately gained much attention from both the research community, as well as the industry. According to [5] energy consumption scales linearly with resource utilization. Therefore, we can consider the memory and CPU time used by an application as valuable metrics in the context of energy reduction.

Hindle [10] has performed a study that investigates the correlation between software changes and power consumption. His results show performance optimization across the versions of the investigated systems. The major difference to the work presented in our paper is that we manually refactored the available source code in order to reduce the number of the exhibited design flaws. By contrast, in the work of Hindle various measurements were performed on different versions of the analyzed systems without isolating changes made for system improvement.

Grosskop and Visser [9] proposed an energy model of an application and suggested some optimizations at the application level. However, none of the proposed optimization are related to the presence of design flaws in the source code of the application.

```
class Employee {
    private int age, zip;
    private String address,
        occupation;

    // Setters & getters
    // Moving functionality --->

    public String toString () {
    return age + " " +
        address + " " +
        zip + " " + occupation;
    }
}


class Main1 {
    public static void
        main (String[] args) {
    int dim = 1000;
    if (args.length == 1)
        dim =
        Integer.parseInt(args[0]);

    Employee employees[] =
        new Employee[dim];
    String s;
    for (int i=0; i<dim; i++) {
        employees[i] =
        new Employee();
        employees[i].setAge(i);
        employees[i].setAddress(
        new String("Street"));
        employees[i].setZip(200000);
        employees[i].setOccupation(
        new String("Programmer"));

        s = employees[i].toString();
    }
    }
}
```

```
class EmployeeUser {
    private Employee emp;
    ...

    public String print () {
    return emp.getAge() + " " +
        emp.getAddress() + " " +
        emp.getZip() + " " +
        emp.getOccupation();
    }
}
// <----- Moved functionality

class Main2 {
    public static void
        main (String[] args) {
    int dim = 1000;
    if (args.length == 1)
        dim =
        Integer.parseInt(args[0]);
    Employee employees[] =
        new Employee[dim];
    EmployeeUser emp[] =
        new EmployeeUser[dim];
    String s;
    for (int i=0; i<dim; i++) {
        employees[i] =
        new Employee();
        employees[i].setAge(i);
        employees[i].setAddress(
        new String("Street"));
        employees[i].setZip(200000);
        employees[i].setOcupation(
        new String("Programmer"));

        emp[i] = new EmployeeUser(
        employees[i]);
        s = emp[i].print();
    }
    }
}
```

(a) Scenario 1   (b) Scenario 2

Fig. 1. The two experimentation scenarios.

2.2   Design Flaws

Design flaws are deviations from the principles, patterns and best practices of software design, like the ones presented in [7,19,23]. Fowler defined in [6] a set of 22 design flaws which are considered to hamper the maintenance of object-oriented software systems. Most of the time it is desirable to get rid off the flawed entities and in order to do this the first step is to find the existing flawed entities within the systems.

Finding manually flawed entities is time-consuming and this was the main reason automatic detection techniques of design flaws appeared. Probably the most used automatic approach for finding entities affected by various design flaws is the metrics-based technique. Currently there are many design flaws that can be detected automatically (see [12,16]) and different tools like *inFusion*[1] accompany the extraction of design flaws. Usually these tools parse the source code in order to extract the necessary information.

There are many recent empirical investigations, like the ones from [4,12,16], which show that design flaws have a strong negative influence on external quality factors like number of changes and/or defects. However, as already mentioned, we are not aware of any studies that investigate the impact of design flaws on the computational resources (memory, CPU) used by an application.

2.3   Cloud Computing Energy Efficiency

In the context of cloud computing, energy efficiency offers important research challenges and issues [25,27]. Different approaches for a *"Green Cloud"* exist, like the Green Cloud simulator[2] [14], supported by the University of Luxemburg, or the Green Cloud Project[3] [8], from the CLOUDS Laboratory of the University of Melbourne. An overview of power and energy management in data centers and cloud computing was offered by Beloglazov et al. [3], showing that *"Cloud computing naturally leads to power efficiency"* by providing a series of energy-oriented characteristics, including scaling up and down of resources, an approach that was considered in the context of our research.

Different researches directions also exists, including Virtual Machine (VM) placement and selection, together with appropriate selection policies [2,8,13] by employing power-aware scheduling mechanisms, provisioning and management of resources.

3   Case-Study Setup

The different approaches for an energy-aware cloud computing that currently exist are rather investigating optimization of cloud resource usage, by exploiting the energy-oriented characteristics of cloud computing [3]. Even if there is a clear

---

[1]   http://www.intooitus.com/products/infusion
[2]   http://greencloud.gforge.uni.lu/
[3]   http://www.cloudbus.org/greencloud/

relationship between power consumption and CPU utilization [5], there are few investigations on the impact of design flaws on the computational resources (*e.g.*, memory, CPU time) used by an application.

In order to address this intriguing research direction we arranged and performed two experimental studies, which are described in this Section.

3.1   A Small Case Study: The Data Class Design Flaw

The goal of this study is the measurement of the influence of the *Data Class* [23] design flaw on the used resources. *Data Classes* are mainly data containers which expose data instead of providing significant functionality. We choose to start our investigation with the influence of the *Data Class* flaw as previous studies have shown that this flaw has a very large lifespan in software projects [21].

As shown in Fig. 1, our experiment starts with an Employee class which contains four data members, as well as the full set of accessor methods (getters and setters) for the data members. In the first scenario (see left side of Fig. 1), we also defined a simple service for the Employee class that returns its string representation, by concatenating the representation of its four data members.

In the second scenario, we created the EmployeeUser class which just aggregates an Employee object. However, the key element of the second scenario is the transformation of Employee in a pure *Data Class* by moving its sole service to the EmployeeUser class. Table 1 summarizes the size of the generated .class files, for all the classes involved in the two experimentation scenarios. The results indicate that the storage space is significantly larger in the second scenario.

Table 1. Dimensions of the involved .class files.

Case study	File(.class)	Size(bytes)
No Data Class	Employee	1096
	Main	824
Data Class	Employee	833
	EmployeeUser	667
	Main	953

In order to run the experiment for the two scenarios we defined for each a *driver class* (*i.e.*, Main1 and Main2). Each of the two *drivers* is doing a very simple job: creates a large number of objects and calls the service. Thus, in *Scenario 1* we create Employee objects and call the toString() method, while in *Scenario 2* we create EmployeeUser objects, and call the print() service. For each scenario, we executed 40 iterations on a MacBook Pro with an Intel Core i5 2.53 GHz processor and 4 GB of RAM. In the first iteration we instantiate 100 000 objects, and in the following iteration we increase the number of instantiated objects by another 100 000.

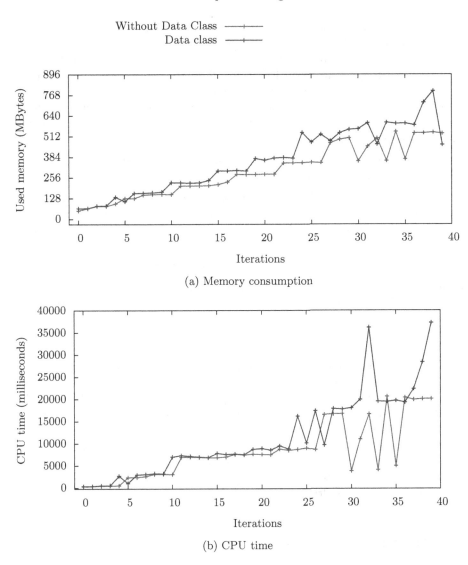

(a) Memory consumption

(b) CPU time

Fig. 2. Resource usages for the first experiment.

At each iteration we measured the *resident memory* and the *CPU time* used by the two versions of the target program, by using the *Hyperic Sigar*[4] tool. The results are summarized in Fig. 2, showing that, in most cases that are running in *Scenario 2* (*i.e.*, the one that contains a *Data Class*) the usage of *memory* and *CPU time* is larger.

Next, based on the obtained data, we will answer the following research question: *Do the runs of Scenario 1 tend to use fewer resources than the runs*

---

[4] http://www.hyperic.com/products/sigar

of Scenario 2? We consider that a run tends to exhibit a particular property if the chances of fulfilling that property are greater than 50 %. We answer this research question by employing the proportion test and running it in R [22].

According to the data from Fig. 2, for 37 of the 40 runs the used memory of the program from *Scenario 1* is less than the used memory of the program from *Scenario 2* and for 36 of the 40 runs the CPU time of the program from *Scenario 1* is smaller than the CPU time of the program from *Scenario 2*. We firstly employed the following statistical test:

```
prop.test(37, 40, 0.5, alternative="greater")
```

where the first parameter denotes the number of the runs of *Scenario 1* where the used memory was lower than the corresponding run of *Scenario 2*, the second parameter denotes the total number of runs and 0.5 denotes the true probability for a run of *Scenario 1* to use less memory than a run of *Scenario 2*. Regarding the CPU time, we run:

```
prop.test(36, 40, 0.5, alternative="greater")
```

because in 36 of the cases the CPU time of the program from *Scenario 1* is lower than the CPU time of the program from *Scenario 2*. Since in both of the cases p-value is lower than 0.05 (9.055e-08 and respectively 4.755e-07) we can conclude that running *Scenario 1* tends to use less resources than *Scenario 2*.

Since we decided to instantiate a very large number of objects, at first sight it may seem that the situation described with this first experiment setup is rather rare. In this context we want to emphasize that the investigated situation may occur quite frequently in the case of an application which was deployed in the cloud, as the number of objects gets multiplied once the application is scaling up due to a larger number of users that simultaneously access it. For example, instead of instantiating for each user the first version of the Employee class, we allow the instantiation of the second version of the Employee class (*i.e.*, the one exhibiting the *Data Class* design flaw) as well as the EmployeeUser class, then this situation will by multiplied by the number of the users that simultaneously access the application.

3.2   The JHotDraw Case Study

In the first experiment we used a rather naive example merely to investigate the impact of having a large number of instances of classes where data and functionality are separated, versus the more desirable case of working with instances of a single class that encapsulates data and provides a service based on those data. However, we are aware that an increase of the needed resources may also be encountered in the case of other design flaws. Therefore, we designed and executed a second experiment in order to investigate the relation between entities affected by design flaws and resource usages against a *real application*.

For this second experiment we used *JHotDraw* 5.4 as a subject system. *JHotDraw* is a Java GUI framework for technical and structured graphics. Our choice for this system was based on the fact that it is the subject of various empirical analyses like the one found in [1].

The Experiment. In order to setup the experiment, we needed a system with a reasonable history in order to increase the chances to spot design flaws, as it is known that the number of the design flaws is growing together as the system gets older [21]. Additionally, we decided to chose a version that is the last before a major change as this increases the chances of working on a stable release.

The experiment was performed as follows:

1. We executed all the available tests for the *JHotDraw* system, while measuring memory consumption and CPU time using the *Hyperic Sigar* tool;
2. We used *inFusion* 1.6 to detect design problems in *JHotDraw*;
3. Based on *inFusion*'s findings we performed an extensive manual refactoring process, with the goal of removing all design flaw instances detected by *inFusion*;
4. After all the modifications targeting the removal of a particular type of flaw were performed upon the source code we run the available tests and performed a new set of measurements.

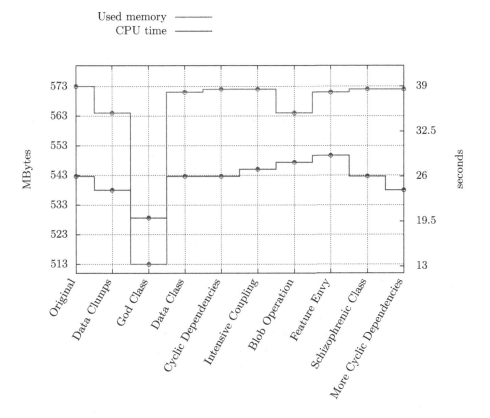

Fig. 3. Resource usage for JHotDraw.

The initial version of the system as well as all the performed refactorings are freely available for download[5]. Figure 3 summarizes the results of our measurements, by depicting the maximum values for the two measured variables (memory usage and CPU time) after each refactoring step, which involved the removal of design flaw instances of a given type.

The Findings. Next we describe the findings of this incremental refactoring process. The performed measurements from Fig. 3 show that:

- removing design flaws from a system has an impact towards the used computational resources.
- the necessarily amount of memory in all of the refactored versions is less when compared to the initial version of the system.
- the CPU time for running the tests is sometimes smaller when compared to the initial version of the system.

Next, based on the obtained data, we will answer the following research question: *Do the runs of the refactored source code tend to use fewer resources than the run of the initial version of the source code?*

According to the data from Fig. 3, for 9 out of the 9 runs of the refactored source code the used memory is less than the used memory of the initial version of the system. We run the next statistical test:

```
prop.test(9, 9, 0.5, alternative="greater")
```

and since p-value is less than 0.05 (0.00383) we can conclude that the runs of the refactored source code where some design flaws have been removed tend to use less memory than the initial version of the system. Regarding the CPU Time, only 3 out of the 9 runs reveal lowered values; since the p-value of the statistical test

```
prop.test(3, 9, 0.5, alternative="greater")
```

is greater than 0.05 (0.7475) we cannot conclude that the refactored version tend to complete in less time than the initial version of the source code.

The Flaws. According to *inFusion*, the most frequent design flaw is *Data Clumps* [6]. This flaw consists of having the same sequence of parameters passed to different methods for many times. *inFusion* detected 38 methods with *Data Clumps*, but at a closer inspection we noticed that there are only three sequences of different parameter "clumps". Consequently, the removal consisted of creating three new classes and passing as parameter instances of those classes when appropriate.

The second refactoring addressed the removal of the single *God Class* detected in *JHotDraw*. *God Classes* tend to group unrelated pieces of functionality and to access directly non-encapsulated data members from other classes [23]. In order

---

[5] http://cs.upt.ro/~cristina/jhotdraw-refactorings.zip

to remove design flaw we split the `Geom` class into two classes, having in each class only cohesive functionality.

The next refactoring targeted the removal of *Data Classes*. In the refactoring process we increased the data-behavior locality and reduced the visibility of some public data members. However, due to the excessive complexity of the refactoring, we kept one *Data Class* as we found it very difficult to solve its dependencies to the many external classes that access it.

Next, the *Cyclic Dependencies* [18] were removed by relocating some classes among packages. We also addressed the single *Intensive Coupling* [23] case, exhibited by the method `getCursor()` from the `LocatorHandle` class. This method contained a large number of methods calls from the `RelativeLocator` class, as part of a complex branching structure. We refactored the method by extracting the method fragment with the many external method calls, and moving it to the class named `RelativeLocator`.

The system does also exhibit two *Blob Operations* (*i.e.*, large and complex methods [6]). We refactored the first case (`TextAreaFigure.drawText()`) by splitting the method into some smaller methods inside the same class. In the second case (`ShortestDistanceConnector.findPoint()`) we decreased the number of the calls performed inside the refactored method by storing the values returned by the called methods into a local array whose values are interrogated.

We did also correct the *Feature Envy* flaws, which refer to methods that use heavily data from other classes instead of the data members from their definition classes [23]. The refactoring involved moving some functionalities in the classes that provide the data these functionalities rely on. Eventually, we refactored the *Schizophrenic Classes* (*i.e.*, classes capturing more than an abstraction [23]) mainly by splitting the classes. Last, but not least, we had to remove some additional *Cyclic Dependencies* which were involuntarily added while performing the *Feature Envy* refactoring.

4 Threats to Validity

In this section we present the threats to validity associated to our empirical study, following the guidelines from [26].

4.1 Construct Validity

This type of threats are connected to the extent the operational measures for the concepts being studies were established correctly [26]. Within the case study presented in this paper these threats are mainly related to the errors performed during data extraction. The possible errors are due to the extraction of (i) design entities from the source code, and (ii) measures regarding the resource usages. We consider that these threats are mitigated to a large extent as we employed a set of well-known and reliable tools.

4.2   Internal Validity

This aspect of validity is related to the causal relations that are inferred. During our study we did not modify the functionalities of the analyzed systems and this is reflected either by presenting the altered source code (for the first case study) or by passing the available suite of tests, in the case of *JHotDraw*. Since knowing that the functional behaviour of the system was not altered strongly depends on the quality of the existing tests, our confidence is based on the good test coverage of *JHotDraw*.

4.3   External Validity

This threat concerns the possibility to generalise the provided results. The reported results are obtained by analyzing mainly a single software system. We do not suggest generalizing our research results to other systems unless further case studies are performed. We intend to replicate this study against other systems in order to see if the results obtained in this study can be generalized.

4.4   Reliability Validity

This aspect concerns the fact that a later investigator that conducts the same case study like the one presented here should obtain the same results and, consequently, reach the same conclusions. We have provided all the needed information about the conducted study, and therefore we consider that the study is perfectly replicable. The source code of *JHotDraw* is freely available, as well as the refactorings we performed for removing design flaws. Also, the software tools used for extracted the presented data are properly introduced in this paper.

5   Conclusions and Future Work

In this paper we present an empirical study performed upon two case studies (a simple one, as well as a well-known software system) providing evidence about the impact of various design flaws on the used resources of the investigated systems. We showed that design flaws increase the used amount of memory and influence the CPU time.

Our approach involved an important number of design flaws – as defined in [6,18,23] – including *Cyclic Dependencies* [18], *Data Clumps*, *Blob Operations* [6], *Data Classes*, *God Class*, *Intensive Coupling*, *Feature Envy*, *Schizophrenic Classes*, and *Cyclic Dependencies* [23] in the two case studies considered.

We consider our approach as being dependent on the available tests and, consequently, a further step should be the inspection of an application actively accessing a cloud environment. In order to achieve this step, we intend to deploy an application in a real cloud environment and monitor its performance in terms of the same computing resources as considered in this work. This task could be accomplished, for example, by freely deploying the application in CloudBees[6] and perform the measurements using NewRelic[7]. Additional measurements will be performed by deploying the applications in the experimental cloud setup at the HPC center from West University of Timişoara[8].

Acknowledgments. This work was partially supported by the grant of the European Commission FP7-REGPOT-CT-2011-284595 (HOST). The views expressed in this paper do not necessarily reflect those of the corresponding project consortium members.

References

1. Bavota, G., Dit, B., Oliveto, R., Di Penta, M., Poshyvanyk, D., De Lucia, A.: An empirical study on the developers perception of software coupling. In: Proceedings of the 2013 International Conference on Software Engineering, ICSE '13, pp. 692–701. IEEE Press, Piscataway (2013)
2. Beloglazov, A., Abawajy, J.H., Buyya, R.: Energy-aware resource allocation heuristics for efficient management of data centers for cloud computing. Future Gener. Comp. Syst. **28**(5), 755–768 (2012)
3. Beloglazov, A., Buyya, R., Choon Lee, Y., Zomaya, A.Y.: A taxonomy and survey of energy-efficient data centers and cloud computing systems. CoRR, abs/1007.0066 (2010)
4. Deligiannis, I., Shepperd, M., Roumeliotis, M., Stamelos, I.: A controlled experiment investigation of an object-oriented design heuristic for maintainability. J. Syst. Softw. **65**, 127–139 (2003)
5. Fan, X., Weber, W.-D., Barroso, L.A.: Power provisioning for a warehouse-sized computer. In: The 34th ACM International Symposium on Computer Architecture (2007)
6. Fowler, M., Beck, K., Brant, J., Opdyke, W., Roberts, D.: Refactoring: Improving the Design of Existing Code. Addison-Wesley, Reading (1999)
7. Gamma, E., Helm, R., Johnson, R., Vlissides, J.: Design Patterns: Elements of Reusable Object-Oriented Software. Addison-Wesley, Reading (1995)
8. Garg, S.K., Yeo, C.S., Buyya, R.: Green cloud framework for improving carbon efficiency of clouds. In: Jeannot, E., Namyst, R., Roman, J. (eds.) Euro-Par 2011, Part I. LNCS, vol. 6852, pp. 491–502. Springer, Heidelberg (2011)
9. Grosskop, K., Visser, J.: Identification of application-level energy-optimizations. In: Proceeding of ICT for Sustainability (ICT4S), pp. 101–107 (2013)
10. Hindlem, A.: Green mining: investigating power consumption across versions. In: Glinz, M., Murphy, G.C., Pezzè, M. (eds.) ICSE, pp. 1301–1304. IEEE (2012)
11. ISO/IEC. ISO/IEC 9126. Software engineering - Product quality. ISO/IEC (2001)
12. Khomh, F., Di Penta, M., Guéhéneuc, Y.-G.: An exploratory study of the impact of code smells on software change-proneness. In: 16th Working Conference on Reverse Engineering (2009)

---

[6] http://www.cloudbees.com
[7] http://newrelic.com
[8] http://hpc.uvt.ro

13. Kliazovich, D., Arzo, S.T., Granelli, F., Bouvry, P., Khan, S.U.: e-STAB: energy-efficient scheduling for cloud computing applications with traffic load balancing. In: 2013 IEEE International Conference on Green Computing and Communications (GreenCom), and IEEE Internet of Things (iThings/CPSCom), and IEEE Cyber, Physical and Social Computing, pp. 7–13 (2013)

14. Kliazovich, D., Bouvry, P., Audzevich, Y., Ullah Khan, S.: GreenCloud: a packet-level simulator of energy-aware cloud computing data centers. In: GLOBECOM, pp. 1–5. IEEE (2010)

15. Lee, Y., Zomaya, A.Y.: Energy efficient utilization of resources in cloud computing systems. J. Supercomput. **60**, 268–280 (2012)

16. Li, W., Shatnawi, R.: An empirical study of the bad smells and class error probability in the post-release object-oriented system evolution. J. Syst. Softw. **80**, 1120–1128 (2007)

17. Marinescu, R., Raţiu, D.: Quantifying the quality of object-oriented design: the factor-strategy model. In: Proceedings of 11th Working Conference on Reverse Engineering (WCRE'04), pp. 192–201. IEEE, Los Alamitos (2004)

18. Martin, R.C.: Agile Software Development, Principles, Patterns, and Practices. Prentice Hall, Upper Saddle River (2002)

19. Martin, R.C.: Clean Code: A Handbook of Agile Software Craftsmanship. Prentice Hall, Upper Saddle River (2008)

20. Olbrich, S.M., Cruzes, D.S., Sjøberg, D.I.K.: Are all code smells harmful? a study of God Classes and Brain Classes in the evolution of three open source systems. In: IEEE International Conference on Software Maintenance (2010)

21. Peters, R., Zaidman, A.: Evaluating the lifespan of code smells using software repository mining. In: Proceedings of 16th European Conference on Software Maintenance and Reengineering (CSMR). IEEE Computer Society (2012)

22. R Development Core Team. R: A Language and Environment for Statistical Computing. R Foundation for Statistical Computing. http://www.R-project.org (2010). ISBN:3-900051-07-0

23. Riel, A.J.: Object-Oriented Design Heuristics. Addison-Wesley, Reading (1996)

24. Song, S., Ge, R., Feng, X., Cameron, K.W.: Energy profiling and analysis of the HPC challenge benchmarks. IJHPCA **23**(3), 265–276 (2009)

25. Vouk, M.A.: Cloud computing - issues, research and implementations. CIT **16**(4), 235–246 (2008)

26. Yin, R.K.: Case Study Research: Design and Methods, 3rd edn. SAGE Publications, Thousand Oaks (2002)

27. Zhang, Q., Cheng, L., Boutaba, R.: Cloud computing: state-of-the-art and research challenges. J. Internet Serv. Appl. **1**(1), 7–18 (2010)

Policy-Based Cloud Management Through Resource Usage Prediction

Cătălin Leordeanu$^{(\boxtimes)}$, Silviu Grigore, Octavian Moraru, and Valentin Cristea

Faculty of Automatic Control and Computers,
University Politehnica of Bucharest, Bucharest, Romania
{catalin.leordeanu,valentin.cristea}@cs.pub.ro,
{silviu.grigore,octavian.moraru}@cti.pub.ro

Abstract. Cloud computing services are becoming increasingly more widespread, mainly because they offer a convenient way of using remote computational resources at any time. Constantly satisfying client needs is a difficult task due to the limited nature of the physical resources. Careful handling of computing capabilities is critical. Cloud systems offer resource elasticity, which is essential for respecting Service Level Agreements (SLAs) or other types of contracts. This paper proposes a novel solution which offers an efficient resource management mechanism for Clouds. The solution is based on monitoring hosts belonging to the Cloud in order to obtain load data. A policy-based system uses the monitoring information to make decisions about deployment of new virtual machines and migration of already running machines from overloaded hosts. The policy-based solution is enhanced by prediction algorithms to optimize the resource usage and to make sure that the available hosts are capable of handling the increased load before it happens. This leads to more efficient resource usage and can help fulfill the SLA requirements even under heavy loads.

Keywords: Cloud computing · Resource management · Policy management · SLA · Prediction

1 Introduction

Cloud computing is an emerging paradigm that provides remote access to computational resources and storage to end-users. In the last few years, Cloud systems have become increasingly popular. The expansion of Cloud technologies is caused both by small to medium businesses that prefer renting computing capabilities over buying them, and by end-users accessing services located in Clouds. The current trend for companies is to shift their service systems into the Cloud, unburdening themselves from the cost of purchasing and maintaining equipment. Also, third party service providers prefer offering their services using Cloud systems, accessible over the Internet, through desktop or mobile apps.

Computing resources offered by a Cloud can range from application software or services to virtual machines, servers, data storage or even entire networks.

© Springer International Publishing Switzerland 2014
F. Pop and M. Potop-Butucaru (Eds.): ARMS-CC 2014, LNCS 8907, pp. 193–205, 2014.
DOI: 10.1007/978-3-319-13464-2_14

The usual approach in Cloud systems is to divide the provision of services into three layers of abstraction: Infrastructure as a Service (IaaS), Platform as a Service (PaaS) and Software as a Service (SaaS). In the IaaS model, Clouds provide direct access to physical resources, usually through virtual machines [1]. As opposed to this, the PaaS and SaaS models only allow access through certain APIs or applications.

Cloud systems can be divided into two categories: public and private. In public Clouds, resources are made available in a pay-per-use manner. The consumer and the Cloud service provider must agree upon the terms on which the quality and reliability of the services must be assured. After a negotiation process, a contract called Service Level Agreement (SLA) [6] is usually signed. The SLA contains different quality of service attributes such as average/maximum application response time or hourly cost that must be enforced in order to fulfill the contract. Private Clouds usually refer to organization data-centers, where resources are not made available to the public, but are destined rather to internal usage. There are also hybrid Clouds which may have components of a public Cloud, as well as private data-centers.

Resource management is a very important and complex process for both business oriented and technical fields. In order to achieve responsiveness, a Cloud system must be provided with an efficient resource management mechanism. If we refer to the IaaS level of abstraction, virtual machines must be deployed on the right hosts, at the right moment of time.

A fundamental approach in Cloud systems is reusability. Cloud consumers rent computing capabilities that must always be delivered. Not all rented resources are used at all time. Unused resources must not go to waste, hence an adequate resource manager must figure out what are the unused resources, and reuse them in order to fulfill every SLA at any given time. OpenNebula [2] is an open source cloud computing framework that aims to easily build and manage private cloud infrastructures. It offers multiple layered APIs allowing the user or developer to choose the degree of complexity of the cloud functions he/she wishes to use.

This paper presents an efficient, adaptable and easily extensible mechanism for managing virtual machines in an OpenNebula environment. The framework uses a policy-based system to make decisions regarding deployment of new virtual machines or migration of already running VMs. The policies refer to different parameters of the hosts that describe the amount of resource utilization, enhanced using prediction algorithms. This way, uniform utilization of the resources in the Cloud is guaranteed and frequent overloading of the hosts is prevented.

The rest of this paper is organized as follows. Section 2 describes other research related to the subject of this paper. In Sect. 3 we present the cloud monitoring and policy enforcement mechanisms and also contains details about the resource usage prediction which enhances the policy-based Cloud management solution. In Sect. 4 we describe our testbed and show various experiment which validate the proposed solutions. Finally, Sect. 5 draws conclusions and proposes directions for research beyond the contents of this paper.

2   Related Work

Efficient management of computational resources is a subject which has been the focus of many research projects in the past [7,8].

Many projects tackle the problem of dynamically overlaying virtual resources on top of physical resources by using virtualization technologies, and do so with different resource models. The most widespread Cloud infrastructure is the Amazon Elastic Compute Cloud (EC2) [11], which is a central part of Amazon's cloud computing platform. EC2 allows users to rent virtual computers on which to run their own computer applications. EC2 allows scalable deployment of applications by providing a web service through which a user can boot an Amazon Machine Image to create a virtual machine, containing any software desired. A user can create, launch, and terminate server instances as needed, paying by the hour for active servers, hence the term "elastic".

The purpose of Cloud resource managers is to obtain the maximum of performance with existing resources. The resource scheduler needs to maintain an optimum balance and make sure that there are no overloaded resources or that systems are kept idle, which would lead to a waste of energy. To maintain this balance, the resource manager needs to have access to real time monitoring data, as well as an estimation of future requirements, in order to take the best decisions. Other projects use prediction algorithms to further optimize resource allocation. The Network Weather Service [9] is such a solution which monitors and predicts the performance of computational resources and computer networks. The predictions are based on collected monitoring data. It is a modular system containing a name server, sensors, predictors and persistent memory, all communicating with each other through TCP sockets.

Another approach related to this paper is the Network Bandwidth Predictor [10]. It estimates the bandwidth of a path between two nodes in a network by sending a small packet and measuring the round trip time. This data is then collected and used to train a neural network-based prediction module. The neural network is a simple backpropagation model and is able to accurately predict the available network bandwidth for certain network paths.

3   Cloud Resource Management Architecture

The purpose of the proposed solution is to deliver an efficient, adaptable and easily extensible framework for managing virtual machines in an OpenNebula environment. The framework uses a policy-based system to make decisions regarding deployment of new virtual machines or migration of already running VMs. The policies refer to different parameters of the hosts that describe their usage in the last period of time. This way, uniform utilization of the resources in the Cloud is guaranteed and frequent overloading of the hosts is prevented.

The proposed architecture is shown in Fig. 1. The framework itself consists of three interlinked modules. The Cloud is an inherently dynamic environment, so careful and continuous monitoring of host load parameters is a must.

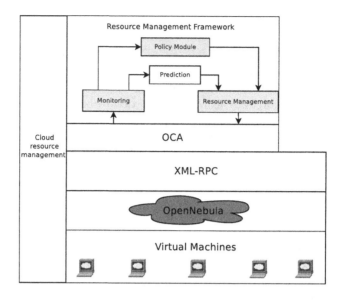

Fig. 1. Resource management architecture

The *Monitoring module* covers this aspect. Secondly, a policy-based system must be provided to help cloud administrators enforce different host loads requirements. The system periodically checks if any general or host-specific policies become active. It also makes decisions in two types of situations: when a request for deployment is made, it chooses the right physical machine that should host the new VM. If one or more policies are triggered (i.e. a host is overloaded), it picks a virtual machine running on that host and an available destination host for it. This job is done by the *Policy module*. Finally, the *Resource Management module* interacts with the OpenNebula daemon, implementing the decisions made by the Policy module.

In addition, the data extracted from the Monitoring module is fed to a Prediction module, that guesses future loads of the machines. The purpose of this component is to make the system react to possible host overloads immediately, or even before they actually happen. The framework is built on top of the Java OpenNebula Cloud API (OCA) [14], which is used to access the needed OpenNebula core functions. OCA is merely a convenient wrapper for the XML-RPC methods exposed by OpenNebula.

3.1 Performance Monitoring

The Monitoring module gathers information about hosts and virtual machines. The monitored parameters are cpu/memory/disk usage and network traffic. We obtain this information through the Java OCA API, by polling the OpenNebula daemon, at a certain time interval. By configuring OpenNebula to get the information from the hypervisors at a similar interval, we can obtain relevant data useful to the Policy module and to the prediction algorithms. OpenNebula deploys a number of scripts to the physical machines, used to obtain load data, which are remotely executed at each monitoring interval. In our testbed, we installed the KVM virtual machine monitor [4] on all hosts.

At this point, the OpenNebula core contains the desired monitoring information. We can extract this data programmatically by interrogating the ON daemon via the OpenNebula Cloud API. Extracted data must be stored in order to maintain a complete history of the loads. This is necessary in the interest of having a well functioning Policy module. Moreover, the Prediction module relies on an extensive history of host and virtual machine loads. Monitored data is stored in a PostgreSQL [5] database. We created tables for hosts, virtual machines and templates which contain mainly static information, inserted only once per monitoring session. Additionally, Host_Monitor and VM_Monitor tables contain the actual monitoring information, inserted each time the OpenNebula daemon is polled.

3.2 Policy-Based Resource Management

Cloud administrators can supply policies in order to specify the systems behavior in certain situations. Policies can be applied in two cases: when a virtual machine deployment request is issued, the suitable host on which the VM will run is chosen in respect of the defined policies; these are the deployment policies. For example, when a host becomes increasingly overloaded, one or more guest VMs are migrated to other hosts. The overload threshold is defined by the migration policies. The Policy module periodically checks if any general or host-specific migration policies are triggered.

Policy Structure. A policy is composed of three parts: the target, the policy type and the condition. The target specifies the name of the host that the policy applies to. The name must be the unique OpenNebula identifiable host alias, that can be obtained using the *onehost list* command. If we wish to apply the policy to all the hosts in the Cloud, we can specify the *all* keyword as a target.

The policy type can be one of the two keywords *deploy* and *migrate*. If we specify both a general (i.e. using the *all* keyword) and a host-specific policy (i.e. using the hosts name) for the same type of policy, only the host-specific one is considered for that host. A condition must specify a parameter, an operator and a value. Parameters may be any of the monitored parameters described in the previous section: used cpu, used memory, used disk space or network traffic. The keywords are: cpu, mem, disk and net. Operators may be any type of comparison operators and they work as expected. The value acts like a threshold for the corresponding parameter and must be given as a percentage for the first three parameter types and as an absolute value for the network traffic parameter (bits per second). Conditions may be chained using the OR operator ($\|$), the AND operator ($\&\&$) and round parentheses.

It is necessary to have separate types of policies for deployment and migration actions. If we were to consider only deployment policies, we could not avoid unpredicted host overloads. For example, if guest virtual machines would become cpu-intensive, there would be no way of unburdening the host and responsiveness would suffer. On the other hand, if only migration policies were to be considered, new virtual machines could be deployed on already overloaded hosts. The VM would then be migrated because a migration policy would activate, but an unnecessary transfer would have been made. In addition, there would be no guarantee that the new host would be suitable for the VM.

As mentioned before, conditions can be chained into more elaborate policies. For example, a complex migration policy can take the following form: $(cpu > 80\&\&mem > 70)\|net >= 10000000$. Here, a virtual machine should be migrated if both its host cpu and memory become highly loaded or if the host generates constant high network traffic (more than $10\,MB/s$).

The policies are specified in a configuration file and can be reloaded at any time when the Policy module is running. A complete configuration file is described below:

```
1  all    deploy  mem < 60
2  all    migrate cpu >= 80
3  on2    deploy  cpu < 80 && mem < 60
4  on3    migrate cpu >= 90
5  on3    deploy  mem < 90
```

The first line specifies a deployment policy for all hosts in the Cloud. New virtual machines should be deployed on hosts having less than 60 % of their available memory used. All hosts must comply to this policy, except on2 and on3. on2 defines an even stricter deployment policy, requiring also at least 20 % of free cpu to accept other virtual machines. On the other hand, on3 relaxes the global policy. This could happen in the case of hosts having more physical memory than the others. The global migration policy (defined on line 2) specifies that virtual machines should be migrated if the cpu load exceeds the 80 % threshold. The on2 host keeps this policy, as there is no specific migration policy defined for it. on3 relaxes the global policy. This indicates that on3 may have a better processor or hyperthreading enabled.

Policy Matching. The Policy module maintains a list of deployment and migration policies for each available host. When a new virtual machine request is issued, we must identify the hosts that support the deployment of that VM. In other words, we must call an evaluate() method for the hosts deployment policy. The values of the parameters that must be passed to the evaluate() method should be the sum between the hosts monitored parameters and the virtual machines statically determined parameters. The cpu, mem and disk values for a host are computed as the mean of the database entries of the last period of time. Experimentally, we decided that this period should be the last $2\,min$. In order to compute the net value, we need to find all the differences between two consecutive entries, divide each of them by the monitoring interval and then compute the mean of these values. Because the virtual machine is uninstantiated, we have no information about its cpu usage and network traffic. The mem and the disk parameters are static. Memory for a virtual machine is allocated at instantiation time, based on the description of the VM template. Disk usage is the amount of space the virtual machine image takes from the hosts total disk capability. The policy condition values are given in percentages, but the database entries store absolute values, so the cpu, mem and disk parameters must be expressed as ratios of the hosts maximum available cpu, memory and disk. The full algorithm for computing the values and checking if a host can sustain a new virtual machine deployment is shown below.

```
1  forall param in hostParameters:
2          data := obtain param values from DB
3          mean := 0
4          if param == ''net'' then
5                  for i := 1 to data.size step 1 do
6                          mean := mean+(data[i]−data[i−1])
7                          mean := mean/monitorInterval
8                  mean := mean / (data.size − 1)
9          else if param == ''disk'' then
10                 mean = data[0] * 100 / hostMaxDisk
11         else
12                 for i := 0 to data.size step 1 do
13                         mean := mean + data[i]
14                 mean := mean / data.size
15                 if param == ''cpu'' then
16                         mean := mean*100/hostMaxCPU
17                 else
18                         mean := mean*100/hostMaxMemory
19         means[param] := mean
20  vmMemory := obtain from db (vm template)
21         vmDisk := obtain from db
22         vmMemory := vmMemory * 100 / hostMaxMemory
23         vmDisk := vmDisk * 100 / hostMaxDisk
24         means[''mem''] := mean[''mem''] + vmMemory
25         means[''disk''] := mean[''disk''] + vmDisk
26         return deployPolicy.evaluate(means)
```

At each step the Policy module checks if migration policies for each host match. Computing the host parameter means is done in the same way. The only difference from the supportsVM() algorithm is that there is no new virtual machine involved. After line 19, a migratePolicy.evaluate(means) call can be issued and the resulting boolean can be returned. If a policy matches for a host, we need to migrate a guest virtual machine in order to unload the system.

Policy Enforcement. When a new virtual machine needs to be deployed, we check which hosts comply to their deployment policies. If more than one host is available, the host with fewer running guest virtual machines is preferred. After deciding which host is suitable for running the new VM, the Resource Management module comes into action. Using the Java OCA, it creates a new virtual machine and it deploys it on the designated host.

Once we decide that a migration policy was activated, we must decide which guest virtual machine should be migrated from the host and which is the destination host for the migrated VM. First, we create a list of virtual machine candidates that are suitable for migration. To do this, we subtract the VM loads from the total host loads and check if the migration policy still applies. If the resulting loads are beneath the thresholds imposed by the policy, the VM is a valid candidate. Then, we must choose one virtual machine from the resulting list. Virtual machines that were never migrated are preferred. If all VMs were previously migrated, the preferred VM is the one migrated first. Also, a virtual machine migrated less than an hour ago, will not be migrated. This is required so that virtual machines will not be continuously transferred from host to host in a short period of time. If none of the VMs were previously migrated, the VM having the highest number of load parameters greater than the others is preferred.

If the VM candidates list is empty (i.e. no virtual machine, if migrated, will reduce the hosts load to a point where the migration policy will not activate anymore), then the same sorting described in the previous paragraph is applied to the whole list of guest virtual machines. This means that we do not resolve the overloading problem in one iteration, but we rather wait for the migration process to finish, and then choose another virtual machine to migrate, sometime in the near future.

4   Resource Usage Prediction

The monitoring data collected using the modules we described in the previous sections are stored as time series. For a series of values for a parameter $x_1, x_2, x_3, \ldots, x_N$ we can use prediction algorithms [12] to estimate the values of $x_N + 1, x_N + 2, \ldots, x_N + h$, where h is the prediction horizon.

For the implementation we chose the Burg algorithm [13]. The algorithm has the goal of minimizing the sum of the square of the errors between the measured data and the forward linear prediction E_p, as well as the sum of the error between the measured data and the previous linear prediction, which is named H_p. Those two sums can be expressed as:

$$E_p = \sum_{n=p}^{N} \left(x_n - \left(-\sum_{i=1}^{p} a_i x_{n-i} \right) \right)^2$$

$$H_p = \sum_{n=0}^{N-p} \left(x_n - \left(-\sum_{i=1}^{p} a_i x_{n+i} \right) \right)^2$$

The sum of E_{p+1} and H_{p+1} needs to be as small as possible, therefore:

$$\frac{\partial(E_{p+1} + H_{p+1})}{\partial k} = 0$$

From this, the rest of the model and algorithm can be found in [13].

5   Experimental Results

We installed an OpenNebula Cloud infrastructure on four physical machines. One of them (on1) acts like the head node and the other three (on2, on3 and on4) are available hosts that can support virtual machine deployment.

In order to test the resource management system we need an automated mechanism to generate host loads. Loads should consist of CPU, memory and disk usage as well as network traffic. WikiBench is a web hosting benchmark that can be used to stress-test systems [3]. It uses the MediaWiki web application to expose a Wikipedia database. Any host that has MediaWiki and a Wikipedia database dump installed acts like a Wikipedia server. We also need a Wikipedia request trace (i.e. a history of web requested Wikipedia resources). Given all these elements we can use the Wikibench application to replay the workload onto the Wikipedia installation.

In Fig. 2 we show how the system reacts to a virtual machine deployment request. The policy configuration file for this scenario is the following:

```
all deploy mem < 55
on4 deploy mem < 90
```

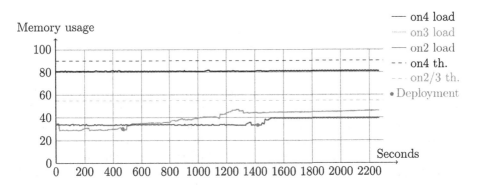

Fig. 2. Deployment of new VMs (Color figure online)

When the simulation started, one WikiBench virtual machine was running on the on3 host. Because 1 GB of RAM from the host's total 4 GB was reserved for the VM, the host's total memory usage was somewhere around 30 %. On the on2

host, two virtual machines were running: one WikiBench and one ttylinux. This
is why on2's memory usage was a little higher. The on4 host was severely loaded
because it was running multiple WikiBench machines. When about 10 min passed
from the simulation start point, we issued a WikiBench virtual machine deployment request (first yellow bullet). In this situation, the system could clearly not
pick on4 to be the destination of the new VM, as hosting another WikiBench
would send its memory usage well beyond the threshold. The system picked on3
because at that point it hosted fewer virtual machines than on2. After deployment, on3's memory usage slowly grows as the new virtual machine becomes
increasingly utilized. When a second WikiBench request was issued (second yellow bullet), on3's memory usage was somewhere around 45 %. on3 is not a valid
host candidate anymore, because another virtual machine (+25 %) would make
its memory load cross the policy imposed threshold. The new VM is correctly
deployed to on2.

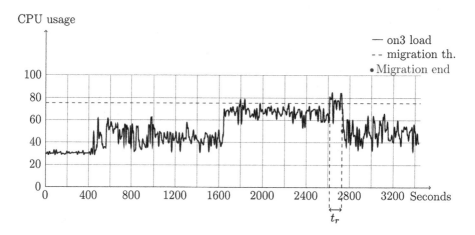

Fig. 3. Migration of a VM when reaching a threshold (Color figure online)

In Fig. 3 we show that the system reacts correctly when a migration policy
becomes active. The only policy used in this scenario was on3 migrate cpu >= 75.
The simulation starts with three running virtual machines on the on3 host:
two ttylinux instantiated images and one WikiBench machine. We can see that
because the WikiBench simulation was running, the host's cpu load resembles
real-life usage. When the cpu usage crosses for the first time the 75 % threshold
(around 1800 s), no action is taken because the mean cpu usage of the last
2 min is considered when checking the policy. This shows that the system is not
fooled by load spikes. When the cpu usage starts to constantly exceed the policy
imposed limit, the system reacts and migrates a virtual machine. The end of the
migration (i.e. the moment when the migrated virtual machine is available on
another host) is marked with a yellow bullet. We define the *response time (tr)*
as the time passed from the moment when a parameter load starts to constantly

CPU load

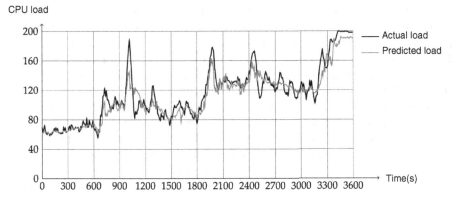

Fig. 4. Prediction of CPU load for 5 min in the future

exceed the threshold to the moment when the load is brought back under the threshold. In this case, because migration happens in just a few seconds, *tr* is approximately 2 min.

In Fig. 4 we used the values predicted by the Burg algorithm for the CPU load of a host for a moment in time 5 min in the future from the measured values. The input values are obtained through the monitoring of a host on which we launched 4 virtual machines. Each load value is collected using intervals of 5 s. For each monitoring data we received, we used the Burg prediction algorithm to determine the CPU load value 5 min in the future, based on the data collected for the last 10 min. The data obtained in this experiment is close to the actual measured information, with an average error of 18.23 %.

6   Conclusions and Future Work

Efficient resource management is critical in Cloud systems. Our solution offers an efficient way to minimize resource usage. The pool of physical capabilities is limited, therefore we take advantage of reserved resources that are not used at their full capacity.

The resource management mechanism described in this paper can be integrated into an OpenNebula infrastructure. The OpenNebula scheduler offers a minimalistic policy instrument that is used to choose the appropriate host on which a new virtual machine should run. However, it lacks the possibility of auto migrating VMs off overloaded hosts. We solve this problem. The implementation is based on monitoring load data on the hosts in the Cloud and on the virtual machines deployed on them. Current host states help us decide where to send new virtual machine requests or when and what virtual machines to migrate from overloaded hosts. Both actions are taken using a policy-based system. Cloud administrators can supply deployment and migration policies in order to fulfill custom host and virtual machine load requirements.

We tested the solution with the help of the WikiBench application which provides real load for the virtual machines using Wikipedia logs. The proposed scenarios show that the framework reacts as expected when choosing a proper host for satisfying deployment requests and when making migration decisions. The results show that the use of deployment and migration policies improves resource distribution and usage in the Cloud.

This solution can be extended in two ways. Different types of policies can easily be added to reflect application response times. This parameter can be measured in the same way as the currently monitored host parameters, but its semantics is application-dependent. When policies become active, decisions can be made regarding not only migration, but deployment of new client virtual machines that could help decrease response times. Secondly, these policies can be used to enforce actual contracts in the case of a commercial-like Cloud. The framework can be perceived as a low-level tool that can help the administration of SLAs.

Acknowledgements. The work has been funded by the *"Sectoral Operational Programme Human Resources Development 2007–2013 of the Ministry of European Funds"* through the Financial Agreement POSDRU/159/1.5/S/ 134398.

This research is also supported by the following projects: *"SideSTEP - Scheduling Methods for Dynamic Distributed Systems: a self-* approach"*, (PN-II-CT-RO-FR-2012-1-0084); *"CyberWater"* grant of the Romanian National Authority for Scientific Research, CNDI-UEFISCDI, project number 47/2012.

References

1. Fox, A., Griffith, R., Joseph, A., Katz, R., Konwinski, A., Lee, G., Patterson, D., Rabkin, A., Stoica, I.: Above the clouds: a Berkeley view of cloud computing. Report UCB/EECS 28:13 Department of Electrical Engineering and Computer Sciences, University of California, Berkeley (2009)
2. Sotomayor, B., Montero, R.S., Llorente, I.M., Foster, I.: Capacity leasing in cloud systems using the opennebula engine. In: Workshop on Cloud Computing and its Applications, vol. 3 (2008)
3. van Baaren, E.-J.: Wikibench: a distributed, wikipedia based web application benchmark. Master's thesis, VU University Amsterdam (2009)
4. Kivity, A., Kamay, Y., Laor, D., Lublin, U., Liguori, A.: kvm: the Linux virtual machine monitor. In: Proceedings of the Linux Symposium, vol. 1, pp. 225–230 (2007)
5. Momjian, B.: PostgreSQL: Introduction and Concepts, vol. 192. Addison-Wesley, New York (2001)
6. Dillon, T., Wu, C., Chang, E.: Cloud computing: issues and challenges. In: 2010 24th IEEE International Conference on Advanced Information Networking and Applications (AINA), pp. 27–33. IEEE (2010)
7. Buyya, R., Abramson, D., Giddy, J., Stockinger, H.: Economic models for resource management and scheduling in grid computing. Concurrency Comput. Pract. Experience 14(1315), 1507–1542 (2002)

8. Schwanengel, A., Kaefer, G., Linnhoff-Popien, C.: Proactive Automated dependable resource management in cloud environments. In: ADVCOMP 2013, The Seventh International Conference on Advanced Engineering Computing and Applications in Sciences, pp. 67–72 (2013)
9. Wolski, R., Spring, N.T., Hayes, J.: The network weather service: a distributed resource performance forecasting service for metacomputing. Future Gener. Comput. Syst. **15**(5), 757–768 (1999)
10. Eswaradass, A., Sun, X.-H., Wu, M.: Network bandwidth predictor (nbp): a system for online network performance forecasting. In: Sixth IEEE International Symposium on Cluster Computing and the Grid, 2006, CCGRID 06, vol. 1, p. 4. IEEE (2006)
11. Ou, Z., Zhuang, H., Nurminen, J.K., Ylä-Jääski, A., Hui, P.: Exploiting hardware heterogeneity within the same instance type of Amazon EC2. In: 4th USENIX Workshop on Hot Topics in Cloud Computing (HotCloud) (2012)
12. Castro, J.R., Castillo, O., Melin, P., Mendoza, O., Rodrguez-Daz, A.: An interval type-2 fuzzy neural network for chaotic time series prediction with cross-validation and akaike test. In: Castillo, O., Kacprzyk, J., Pedrycz, W. (eds.) Soft Computing for Intelligent Control and Mobile Robotics, pp. 269–285. Springer, Heidelberg (2011)
13. Burg, J.P.: A new analysis technique for time series data. In: NATO Advanced Study Institute on Signal Processing with Emphasis on Underwater Acoustics, vol. 1 (1968)
14. Metsch, T., Edmonds, A., Bayon, V.: Using cloud standards for interoperability of cloud frameworks. SLA@ SOI, Technical report (2010)

An Inter-Cloud Architecture for Future Internet Infrastructures

Stelios Sotiriadis[1](✉), Nik Bessis[2], and Euripides G.M. Petrakis[1]

[1] Technical University of Crete, University Campus Kounoupidiana,
73100 Chania, Greece
{s.sotiriadis,petrakis}@intelligence.tuc.gr
[2] University of Derby, Kedleston Road, Derby DE212UR, UK
n.bessis@derby.ac.uk

Abstract. In latest years, the concept of interconnecting clouds to allow common service coordination has gained significant attention mainly because of the increasing utilization of cloud resources from Internet users. An efficient common management between different clouds is essential benefit, like boundless elasticity and scalability. Yet, issues related with different standards led to interoperability problems. For this reason, the definition of the open cloud-computing interface defines a set of open community-lead specifications along with a flexible API to build cloud systems. Today, there are cloud systems like OpenStack, OpenNebula, Amazon Web Services and VMWare VCloud that expose APIs for inter-cloud communication. In this work we aim to explore an inter-cloud model by creating a new cloud platform service to act as a mediator among OpenStack, FI-WARE datacenter resource management and Amazon Web Service cloud architectures, therefore to orchestrate communication of various cloud environments. The model is based on the FI-WARE and will be offered as a reusable enabler with an open specification to allow interoperable service coordination.

Keywords: Cloud · Inter-cloud · Future internet cloud infrastructures · OpenStack · Cloud interoperability

1 Introduction

Cloud systems expose interfaces to communicate with other clouds or services by forming an inter-cloud. In this setting, users describe their requirements in service level agreements (SLA) that are usually related with infrastructure resources as well as with the relevant services (software) offered from providers. Inter-clouds involve public clouds forming a collaborative environment for distribution and common management of cloud services. This represents the communication glue between the different providers and the different provision layers including Infrastructure, Platform, Network and Software as Services (IaaS, PaaS, NaaS and SaaS). This work vision is on connectivity between resource providers that develop clouds exposing interfaces e.g. following the Open Cloud Computing Interface (OCCI) standard [4].

Today, the area of inter-clouds has gained particularly interest in academia and industry. Various works like [11] demonstrate solutions and mechanisms to achieve

© Springer International Publishing Switzerland 2014
F. Pop and M. Potop-Butucaru (Eds.): ARMS-CC 2014, LNCS 8907, pp. 206–216, 2014.
DOI: 10.1007/978-3-319-13464-2_15

inter-cloud service distribution by exploring various components. In our case the focus is on inter-clouds that emerge from the innovative area of Future Internet (FI) application development of FI-WARE [2] that offers services, called Generic Enablers (GEs). GEs provide essential functionalities, interfaces and APIs for various kinds of functionalities (e.g. authentication, Internet of Things device management, storage, cloud resource management, monitoring etc.). FI-WARE offers a cloud datacentre resource management service (DCRM) in order to control and manage IaaS cloud resources that is based on OpenStack. The inter-cloud service approach will serve as a GE that links various clouds that share characteristics derived from OpenStack API [3], FI-WARE Datacenter Resource Management GE (DCRM GE) Amazon Web Services (AWS) [16], OpenNebula [18] and VM Ware cloud (VCloud) [17]. The service will be designed as easily deployable and configurable to serve as a service for Future Internet (FI) application development based on modular cloud services [7].

OpenStack is a platform architecture that provides a framework and APIs for cloud systems. It is an open source solution that is based on open standards of OCCI. Lately, it is used widely (e.g. by FI-WARE, IBM etc.) to allow development of private or public clouds; it is simple to integrate and can be upgraded easily by providing an IaaS for managing datacentre resources [1]. The architecture defines an Inter-cloud as a Service (IC Service) that facilitates development of new IaaS based on the APIs of OpenStack, DCRM GE, AWS, OpenNebula and VCloud. This includes creation of an authentication mechanism to act as intermediate for all clouds. Based on this discussion, Sect. 2 presents the related works and motivation of this study. The rest of the paper is organized as following, in Sect. 3 we present the proposed model by defining a range of services and the projected operations, in Sect. 4 we present the experimental prototype infrastructure that demonstrates the draft inter-cloud collaboration for clouds based on OpenStack, FI-WARE DCRM GE and AWS. Finally, Sect. 5 concludes with the future research steps.

2   Motivation and Related Work

Inter-cloud has been characterized as the logical evolution of the Internet in terms of advanced service provision [6]. Today, various cloud vendors aimed to an interoperable cloud effort by jointly establishing federations of clouds. However, these vendor-oriented solutions do not base on future standards and open interfaces but in specific cloud architecture as in [12]. In [11] a discussion is presented to demonstrate a broker that acts as an SLA resource allocator by combining components to achieve the agreed benchmark among users and providers. This is a generic view of brokers that generate challenges on how to manage the most effective resource allocation and scheduling. In previous studies [19], we focused on clouds from the perspective of scheduling, and the issues arising from inter-cloud communication. Especially, when the number of clouds increases, it becomes more complex to control the various cloud resources in an inter-cloud system. In this study we aim to overcome the problem of vendor specific inter-clouds by focusing on the OCCI standard [4]. This means that cloud systems developers using such standard (FI-WARE, OpenStack, OpenNebula etc. [4]) will be able to utilize their interfaces to develop an inter-cloud service.

Lately, various FI-PPP programmes [13] (up to 16 EU funded projects) have been promoted to accelerate the development and adoption of Future Internet technologies in Europe, advance the European market for smart infrastructures, and increase the effectiveness of business processes through the Internet. All, base their developments in the FI-WARE cloud platform. Based on this, we have develop an inter-cloud service that is deployed in the intellicloud [14] infrastructure of the Technical University of Crete (TUC) and could be offered as a GE service. Intellicloud is an experimental cloud infrastructure for designing cloud-based Internet applications.

3   The Inter-Cloud Model

This section demonstrates the model to connect inter-cloud IaaS environments that are geographically dispersed based on the OpenStack architecture of Sect. 3. By using a common agreed standard in communication it solves issues regarding interoperability among such systems. Figure 1 shows the inter-cloud services along with their key operations.

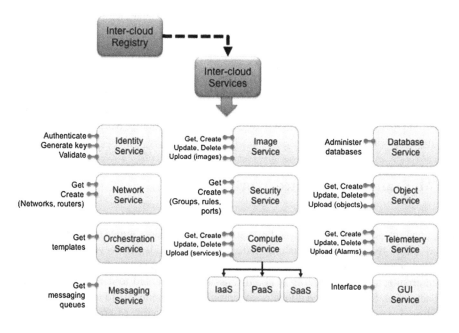

Fig. 1. The inter-cloud service and available sub-services with key operations that follow the OpenStack architecture

The inter-cloud registry keeps a list of OpenStack architecture URLs that are used by the inter-cloud services. Also, OpenStack RESTFul APIs and schemes along with the advanced messaging queuing models (AMQ [15]) define explicitly a modular set of components and standard rules for connecting OpenStack infrastructure. The REST architecture allows seamless interactions among distributed cloud services [9]. This happens in a highly secure environment where access and resource utilization is controlled in many levels (users, roles, and projects) [5].

The model of the aforementioned topology provides services to facilitate inter-cloud communication in a common platform. The inter-cloud service could list all available services, instances, offer network capabilities, security and deployment of IaaS services. The model includes the following key operations. Firstly, the inter-cloud performs authentication for the specific tenant that uses it (at this stage the users require to have credentials to all clouds of the collaboration), this is the source of certification and serves as a RESTFul deployed service. Secondly, the model proposes a new platform service as a RESTFul Inter-Cloud as a Service (ICaaS) to interfacing to other clouds. The initial plan is to integrate OpenStack, DCRM GE and AWS clouds, yet the model will be expandable to OpenNebula and VClouds. The proposed ICaaS is a platform service that offers the following capabilities:

(i) Offers a registry that contains the configuration (e.g. URL addresses of other OpenStack, AWS and FI-WARE DCRM infrastructures and ports).

(ii) The proposed ICaaS offers a SaaS that uses the OpenStack API [3] and AWS API [16] to offer the next operations:

(a) ICaaS identity service: It is responsible to Authenticate, Generate, and Validate. OpenStack tenants use it to revoke a token for access.

(b) ICaaS image service: To get, create, update, delete, and upload an image of a cloud. The service returns a list of instances, while the post action allows information from the inter-cloud to be forwarded to each respectively (e.g. in case that a user wants to update an image description).

(c) ICaaS database service: Offers an administrator service to Create a user (with credentials defined in the ICaaS) as well as to create flavors (variation of possible SLAs) to other clouds. This will be the mean to achieve new user creation in all clouds from the inter-cloud platform.

(d) ICaaS network service: Offers the option to get, create networks and routers. Usually, in case of a new user generation in the inter-cloud platform the administrators generate the networks, yet this could happen by them using the inter-cloud platform service.

(e) ICaaS security service: To get, create security groups, rules, ports, release floating IPs, associate floating IPs to linkes clouds. These are essential in order to offer the IaaS with all available options.

(f) ICaaS object service: To get, create, update, show, and delete account metadata and objects using the OpenStack service.

(g) ICaaS orchestration service: Offer a template-driven engine that allows application developers to describe and automate the deployment of infrastructure.

(h) ICaaS compute service: To get, create, update, show, and delete services (offered as IaaS VMs) in other clouds, this includes three kinds of services:

- The IaaS VM provisioning that relates with IaaS services. E.g. the ICaaS platform creates a VM instance in an inter-cloud using the available data (flavours, security, networks etc.).
- The PaaS provisioning that relates with PaaS services hosted in a cloud and listed in the inter-cloud. E.g. the platform create a VM instance (blueprint or snapshot of already deployed operational environment) ready to be utilized by other. In this case developers could configure a platform (e.g. Eclipse) to work directly on the platform.
- The SaaS provisioning that relates with already deployed instances that are listed in the platform,. These are deployed locally and are available to the platform users as VM instances e.g. accessible by their IPs.

(i) ICaaS messaging service: Operates with AMQP servers [15] of clouds in order to manage and optimize messaging queues. We use RabbitMQ that is a robust messaging mechanism for OpenStack services that is offered as open source. For inter-clouds will enable connectivity (asynchronous and decoupled) as it offers a common platform to send and receive messages.

(j) ICaaS telemetery service: Offers capabilities to list, create, gets details for, update, and delete alarms and meters.

(iii) The ICaaS integrates a messaging model to optimize the interactions of the RESTFul components and their calls. This is a usually problem when scaling OpenStack with many servers, the systems tend to decrease performance as many calls are forwarded to the database from many callers thus leading to bottleneck.

(iv) The ICaaS integrates a performance metering service, the service collects internal cloud performance measures and allows inter-cloud platform administrators to define thresholds and performance parameters for monitoring purposes.

(v) ICaaS graphical user interface service: Offers the user friendly environment that combines aforementioned services in a web based interface to manage access and provision of services. The inter-cloud will use the horizon service will provide a portal for the inter-cloud in order to allow management of the VMs, floating IPs, security groups and public keys.

The modularity of the system is high, this means that the ICaaS services will be developed based on OpenStack API, will be hosted and deployed separately and will be available as open source instances of the intellicloud infrastructure of TUC [14]. Eventually, the services will be integrated into a platform that will offer the user-friendly interfaces.

4   Experimental Prototype of Inter-Cloud

The experimental prototype is integrated using RESTFul API and implements the "Identity Service" of the Inter-Cloud Services. It uses cURL [10] and OpenStack API [8] and allows the inter-cloud to transmit and receive HTTP requests and responses. The prototype offers a direct interaction with the various components provided by the

OpenStack API, DCRM GE API and AWS API. The experiment is based on a single type of request (Identity Service of Sect. 4), that is executed on real-time, the so-called "authentication, to get token from each cloud" to be used for further authentication of services among the following clouds.

- Intellicloud, architecture (OpenStack) of TUC (Crete, Greece).
- FI-LAB, architecture DCRM GE of FI-WARE (Sevilla, Spain).
- CloudLab: Experimental Cloud OpenStack of TUC (Crete, Greece).
- Amazon AWS Cloud (Oregon US).
- VMWare VCloud (UK).

Figure 2 demonstrates the prototype inter-cloud as a Service solution and the associated cloud environments. It should be mentioned that due to size limits the VCloud is not included in the analysis.

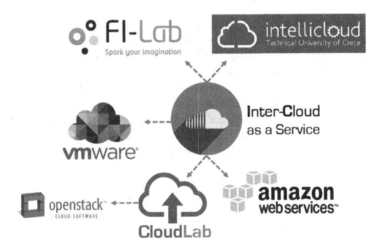

Fig. 2. The OpenStack model of an inter-cloud with available services and their key operations

The ICaaS exposes interfaces to internal procedures for further communication. It uses real time metrics to provide results. Especially, the "real" metric is the wall clock time (the time needed from start to finish of the call), the "user" is the amount of CPU time spent in user-mode code (outside the kernel) within the process, the "sys" is the amount of CPU time spent (inside the kernel within the process) and the "factor" is the actual performance of the metric to the compared value (division of worst by best performance value). To demonstrate effectiveness we present the next 4 experimental studies (where for each we execute 10 requests namely as Req1 to Req10) as follows:

- Demonstrates metric values of the ICaaS when is executed within the cloud (the benchmark).
- Demonstrates metric values of the ICaaS when is executed for two cloud systems.
- Demonstrates metric values of the ICaaS when is executed for three cloud systems.
- Demonstrates metric values of the ICaaS when is executed for four cloud systems.

4.1   1st Experiment: Internal Calls

This demonstrates calls made from the ICaaS to the CloudLab system and FI-LAB infrastructures to collect measures of real, user and sys metrics that could be used as benchmarks. The results are provided in order to characterize: (a) the real-time responses of a cloud for calls that made internally (within the system, the calls are made from and to the CloudLab services) and (b) the real-time responses of a cloud for calls that made externally (outside the system). The calls are made from CloudLab to the FI-LAB DCRM GE. Based on the comparison we extrapolate a factor as generalized metrics. The factor for calls made within and outside is 54 % (int/ext%). This means that case (b) achieves 54 % performance of the case (a). The results demonstrate realistic high performance (average 0.39 s with highest 0.435) with regards to the real-time calls.

4.2   2nd Experiment: External Call to CloudLab and FI-LAB Cloud

This demonstrates the ICaaS calls that made from the service to CloudLab and FI-LAB infrastructures (the point of calls) for authentication at both endpoints. In this case, we compare the responses for the case of FI-LAB authentication (the benchmark of 1st experiment) in contradiction of the ICaaS. The new factor is 42 %, yet the actual performance remains at realistic high levels as most of the calls (9 out of 10) have been completed in less than 1 s. This could be considered as a fast response by taking into consideration the physical locations of datacenters (Greece and Spain) and the real-time execution of the requests. Figure 3 demonstrates the trendlines where ICaaS shows a decreasing tendency for the real time metric as more requests for authentication are executed.

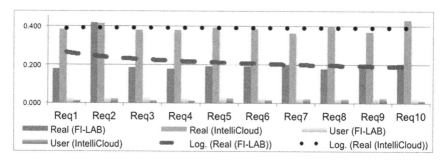

Fig. 3. Comparison of calls among IC and FI-LAB external

4.3   3rd Experiment: External Call to FI-LAB to CloudLab, FI-LAB and Intellicloud

We present an inter-cloud mechanism to compare performance of the same calls between:

– CloudLab and FI-LAB (as executed in Experiment 2) and
– CloudLab, FI-LAB and Intellicloud (three clouds request).

Figure 4 shows that the fluctuation of the ICaaS for 2 and 3 clouds is at a value of 0.256 s. Also the real time increases slightly over the 1.2 s. Similarly to previous experiments, the point of the calls is the FI-LAB.

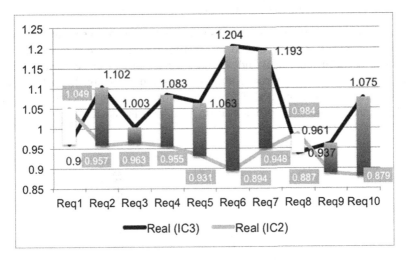

Fig. 4. Fluctuation of the IC service for 2 and 3 clouds

In this case the real time increases slightly, over the 1 s. Similarly to previous experiment, this could be considered as acceptable performance measure for real-time responses. Compared to experiment 2, the factors in such case are in very high levels, as it achieves the 89 % of the performance of the real time metric.

4.4   4th Experiment: External Call to CloudLab, FI-LAB, Intellicloud and AWS

The final experiment demonstrates an ICaaS for connection with four clouds. The inter-cloud sequence of calls include authentication in Intellicloud, CloudLab, FI-LAB, and Amazon AWS, for datacenters located in Greece, Spain and US. The factors for comparison of the four clouds are demonstrated bellow. The calls are made form an ICaaS service executed in FI-LAB. In particular, when comparing the factors we conclude to the following:

(a) Factors of four (CloudLab, FI-LAB, AWS and Intellicloud), to three clouds (CloudLab, FI-LAB, Intellicloud) are 53 % for real metric and 83 % for user. This affection in performance mainly related to the distance of the remote AWS datacenter.

(b) Factors of four (CloudLab, FI-LAB, AWS and Intellicloud), to two clouds (CloudLab, FI-LAB) are 47 % for real metric and 75 % for user. This compared to the previous case shows a slightly increase of 6 %.

(c) Factors of four (CloudLab, FI-LAB, AWS and Intellicloud), to one cloud (CloudLab as benchmark) are 20 % for real metric and 57 % for user. This means that the four clouds performance achieve 20 % of the benchmark performance (same requests executed within the cloud). Yet, realistically, ICaaS is executed in less than 2 s, a result that is considered as acceptable.

In experiment 4, calls take less than 2 s to be completed, this means that we have an increase of averagely 0.8 s compared to experiment 3. This is due to the communication time between the ICaaS and the different regions of datacenters around the world. Figure 5 shows that the real time has been almost doubled; yet this remains slightly averagely under the 2 s. To our view this is a highly acceptable value by considering that the numbers of interactions have been increased.

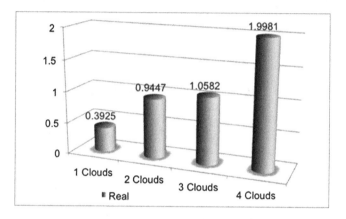

Fig. 5. Real times for combination of clouds (1–4 clouds)

5 Conclusions and Further Work

This work presented inter-cloud service architecture by utilizing OpenStack, FI-WARE DCRM GE and AWS APIs. The current version is a work on progress and supports basic functionalities in order to integrate an inter-cloud GE that is deployed into a cloud. The proposed model integrates services to facilitate inter-cloud communication in a common platform in order to list all available services, instances, offer network capabilities, security and deployment of IaaS services. The experimental prototype demonstrates the basic configurations in order to develop an inter-cloud service. The analysis shows that the ICaaS performs efficient and real times remaining in highly acceptable levels by being executed in less than 2 s for four clouds interconnections.

In future, we focus on the development of the proposed model in order to include all services and components, and to develop a graphical user interface to provide a common management platform that will be offered as a service instance. In addition, extra effort will be made to the characterization of performance metrics (e.g. by collecting the performance metrics of the servers) in order to provide optimization algorithms. This includes RESTFul APIs and schemes along with messaging algorithms for optimizing message exchanging among the inter-cloud services as in [20]. Finally, we will explore OpenNebula, AWS and VCloud along with CloudStack RESTFul interfaces and APIs in order to expand the inter-cloud services.

Acknowledgement. This work is part of the Future Internet – Social Technological Alignment Research (FI-STAR) project, which is a Future Internet Private Public Partnership (FI-PPP) run by the European Commission. FI- STAR will conduct early clinical and non-clinical digital-health use-case trials in European countries.

References

1. OpenStack Cloud Software. http://docs.openstack.org/api/openstack-image-service/2.0/content/upload-binary-image-data.html
2. FI-WARE. http://www.fi-ware.org
3. OpenStack API. http://docs.openstack.org/api/openstack-image-service/2.0/content/image-api-v2.0.html
4. Open Cloud Computing Interface. http://occi-wg.org
5. Jackson, K., Cody Bunch, C.: Openstack Cloud Computing Cookbook, 2nd edn. Packt Publishing, Birmingham (2013)
6. Sotiriadis, S., Bessis, N. Kuonen, P., Antonopoulos, N.: The Inter-cloud meta-scheduling (ICMS) framework. In: Proceedings of the 2013 IEEE 27th International Conference on Advanced Information Networking and Applications (AINA '13), pp. 64–73. IEEE Computer Society, Washington, DC (2013)
7. Sotiriadis, S., Petrakis, G.M.E., Covaci, S., Zampognaro, P., Georga, E., Thuemmler, C.: An architecture for designing future internet (FI) applications in sensitive domains: expressing the software to data paradigm by utilizing hybrid cloud technology. In: 13th IEEE International Conference on BioInformatics and BioEngineering (BIBE 2013), Chania, Greece, 10–13 Nov 2013
8. Service API Examples Using Curl. http://docs.openstack.org/developer/keystone/api_curl_examples.html
9. Richardson, L., Ruby, S.: Restful Web Services, 1st edn. O'Reilly, Sebastopol (2007)
10. Ward, S., Hostetter, M.: Curl: a language for web content. Int. J. Web Eng. Technol. **1**(1), 41–62 (2003)
11. Petcu, D.: Multi-cloud: expectations and current approaches. In: Proceedings of the 2013 International Workshop on Multi-cloud Applications and Federated Clouds (MultiCloud '13), pp. 1–6. ACM, New York (2013)
12. Buyya, R., Ranjan, R., Calheiros, R.N.: InterCloud: utility-oriented federation of cloud computing environments for scaling of application services. In: Hsu, C.-H., Yang, L.T., Park, J.H., Yeo, S.-S. (eds.) ICA3PP 2010, Part I. LNCS, vol. 6081, pp. 13–31. Springer, Heidelberg (2010)
13. Future Internet Public-Private Partnership (FI-PPP). https://www.fi-ppp.eu
14. Intellicloud. Intelligence Systems Laboratory, Technical University of Crete, Greece. http://www.intelligence.tuc.gr
15. Advanced Message Queuing Protocol. http://www.amqp.org
16. Amazon Web Services (AWS) API. http://aws.amazon.com/documentation/
17. VMWare VCloud API. http://pubs.vmware.com
18. OpenNebula API. http://docs.opennebula.org/4.6/

19. Sotiriadis, S.: The inter-cloud meta-scheduling. Ph.D. thesis, University of Derby (2013). http://hdl.handle.net/10545/299501
20. Bessis, N., Sotiriadis, S., Pop, F., Cristea, V.: Using a novel Message-Exchanging Optimization (MEO) model to reduce energy consumption in distributed systems. Simul. Model. Pract. Theory **39**, 104–120 (2013). ISSN: 1569-190X, Elsevier

Author Index

Abdelwahed, Sherif 52
Abella, Francesc 26
Antonescu, Alexandru-Florian 91
Antoniu, Gabriel 147
Apostol, Elena 113
Arjona Aroca, Jordi 71
Azadbakht, Keyvan 103

Băluță, Iulia 113
Banerjee, Ansuman 36
Banicescu, Ioana 52
Bessis, Nik 206
Bougé, Luc 147
Braun, Torsten 91

Carpen-Amarie, Alexandra 147
Chihoub, Houssem-Eddine 147
Costa, Fabio 128
Cristea, Valentin 113, 193

Datta, Pubali 36
de Boer, Frank 103
Dey, Swarnava 36

Endo, Patricia 165

Fernandez Anta, Antonio 71
Fortiş, Teodor-Florin 180

Gomes, Raphael 128
Gonçalves, Glauco 165
Gorgoi, Alexandru 113
Grandinetti, Lucio 9
Grigore, Silviu 193
Guerriero, Francesca 9

Ibrahim, Shadi 147

Kelner, Judith 165
Kielmann, Thilo 3

Leordeanu, Cătălin 193

Marinescu, Cristina 180
Mateo, Jordi 26
Mehrotra, Rajat 52
Moise, Diana 147
Moraru, Octavian 193
Morozan, Ion 3
Mosteiro, Miguel A. 71
Mukherjee, Arijit 36

Nagarajagowda, Chetan 103
Nobakht, Behrooz 103

Paul, Himadri Sekhar 36
Petrakis, Euripides G.M. 206

Rius, Josep 26
Rocha, Ricardo 128
Rodrigues, Moisés 165

Sadok, Djamel F.H. 165
Sandu, Andreea 3
Santos, Marcelo 165
Sefidcon, Azimeh 165
Serbanescu, Vlad 103
Sheikhalishahi, Mehdi 9
Solsona, Francesc 26
Sotiriadis, Stelios 206
Srivastava, Srishti 52
Stoenescu, Şerban 180

Teixidó, Ivan 26
Thraves, Christopher 71

Uta, Alexandru 3

Vazquez-Poletti, Jose Luis 9
Vilaplana, Jordi 26
Vitalino, Jônatas 165

Wallace, Richard M. 9
Wang, Lin 71

Printed in the United States
By Bookmasters